The History of
CAVALRY

Z. Grbašić
V. Vukšić

The History of CAVALRY

Facts On File
New York • Oxford

Endpapers: In the battle between Alexander the Great and the Persians under King Darius III near Gaugamela in 331 B.C., *the Greek cavalry saved the endangered infantry.* Battle of the Issus, *painting (detail) by Albrecht Altdorfer, 1529.*

Title page: Equestrian statue of Italian condottiere Bartolomeo Colleoni by Verrocchio (1436 – 1488), Venice, Campo San Zanipolo.

Below: Battle of Raclawice, during the Polish rebellion, April 3, 1794.
Painting by Woicech Kossak.

Library of Congress Cataloging-in-Publication Data
Grbašić, Z.
   The history of cavalry.
   Translation of: Die Geschichte der Kavallerie.
   Includes index.
   1. Cavalry-History. I. Vukšić, V.
   II. Title.
UE15.G7313 1989   357'.09   89-11710
ISBN 0-8160-2187-2

British CIP data available on request

General direction:
Bessa Publishing Company, Belgrade
Editor-in-chief: Nevenka Micunović

© 1989 by Motovun (Switzerland) Copublishing Company Ltd., Lucerne and Bessa (Switzerland) Publishing Company Ltd., Lucerne

© 1989 for the English language edition by Facts On File Publications, New York

Facts On File, Inc.
460 Park Avenue South
New York NY 10016
USA
or
Facts On File Limited
Collins Street
Oxford OX4 1XJ
United Kingdom

Printed 1989 in Italy

Contents

Introduction

In the early 17th century, the decline of feudalism, together with economic development, the forming of powerful centralist states and the advent of firearms, led to a diminishing role for the established form of the knights' armored cavalry in many countries of Western Europe, and to the forming of professional mercenary armies that would reach their peak during the Thirty Years War (1618 – 1648). The first standing armies that had all the characteristics of modern armed forces came into existence toward the middle of the 17th century. Military administration was set up, the standardization of uniforms began, and barracks for the troops were built. Instead of depending on local sources, the army now got its supplies from warehouses. It was also at this period that the foundations of the medical corps and the military judicial system were laid, and the first decorations and medals handed out. The officer corps was recruited from the ranks of the nobility and the aristocracy. Due to the growth in manpower and the division into various arms, the organizational structure of the armies improved. Permanent military formations such as the troop, company, squadron, battalion and regiment appeared.

The new system of replacement and the greater effectiveness of firearms had an influence on the ratio of cavalry to infantry in the armies. Infantry troops, armed with muskets and bayonets, became the most important and largest arm of the military. Artillery also became a separate branch of the military, with formations of its own. However, cavalry remained the principal maneuvering force, especially in the period of rigid infantry line tactics. It was still divided into heavy cavalry for battle, light cavalry for reconnaissance, protection and pursuit, and dragoons, who were progressively losing their role of mounted infantry and turning into combat cavalry.

The need of European armies for horses increased commensurately with their growth. To ensure fast and adequate replacement of mounts, special stables were founded from the 17th century on, and in the middle of the 18th century the remount service was established. Selective breeding resulted in new stock, adapted to conditions of service in the military. The first standards for military horses were introduced, at the same time as the first veterinarian services. To further chivalry, riding schools were instituted.

The Thirty Years War and the English Civil War (1642 – 1649) signaled the definitive demise of the knights and gentry of the Middle Ages, the armored horsemen on their big heavy mounts, whose charge for glory and riches was an instrument of victory and usually the final phase of the battle. The battle formation of individual combatants adorned with colorful flags and decorated with plumes and coats of arms shattered when faced with the wall of fire of disciplined infantry or the equally disciplined ranks of horsemen armed with pistols. Many saddles were emptied in a none too chivalrous manner before the fighting had begun in earnest.

Opposite: The battle of Waterloo (detail), charge of the Heavy Scots Dragoons, 1815. Painting by Elizabeth Thompson (Lady Butler).

The appearance of firearms and their rapid development greatly changed the way war was waged. Muskets became more accurate and their bullets deadlier, and, perhaps most important, the length of time between two shots was shortened. Military leaders realized that speed of movement on the battlefield was becoming a crucial factor in combat. The opponent had to be given as little chance of shooting as possible, in order to "conserve the more sabres for the final showdown." Further strengthening of the horses' and riders' armor would be costly, and would also necessitate heavier and slower horses, whose breeding would also add to the cost. And even such a tank on four legs couldn't offer certain protection from the effects of firearms. The solution was to do away with superfluous armor, thus increasing the horses' speed.

It had originally taken Western Europe 500 years to breed a large and heavy horse strong enough to bear its armor and an armored rider, and withstand a collision with a similar one-ton monster. Strength and weight then were given more consideration than speed and maneuverability. But as the situation changed, rulers and generals started searching for lighter and faster horses for their mounted troops. The new age of the cavalry had begun.

In this book, which covers the period from the formation of the first modern regular armies in the second half of the 17th century to the charge of the Polish cavalry against German tanks in 1939, the five most important steps in the development of cavalry organization and tactics are followed chronologically: the first properly uniformed and equipped regiments of permanent composition were formed in the army of Louis XIV; Marlborough grouped cavalry into a mobile reserve on the battlefield, whose charge could decide the outcome of the battle; Friedrich II enabled cavalry to move faster and more effectively through reforms and improved training; Napoléon I formed great cavalry masses and grouped them into divisions and corps; and in the American Civil War cavalry moved more independently and further afield.

The most space has been devoted to the Seven Years War (1756 – 1763) and the Napoléonic Wars (1804 – 1815), as these were the periods of greatest development of cavalry.

Chapter One: All the Kings' Horsemen

1661 – 1700

T he Thirty Years War ended in 1648 with the signing of the Peace of Westphalia. This marked the final breakdown of the Hapsburg-Catholic coalition headed by Austria and Spain. The decisive battles had been fought on the soil of Germany, which was now laid waste by the forages of mercenary armies, and its population decimated. As it was divided into numerous small states that were nearly completely independent of central Imperial authority, Germany would take a long time to recover fully. Sweden, one of the victors, gained Pomerania, on the Baltic coast. The threat of a universal European Catholic empire having been dealt with, it now turned to its old rival Poland, which was shaken by the Cossack uprising in the Ukraine and the war with Russia. Brandenburg was now in control of eastern Pomerania; together with Denmark, which had lost border territories to Sweden, it got involved in the Swedish-Polish war. The Ottoman Empire renewed its attacks on weakened Austria and upper Hungary. The division of Holland into the Dutch United Provinces in the north and the Spanish Netherlands in the south was confirmed. Soon after the end of the English Civil War the monarchy was restored; England now devoted its attention to asserting its domination at sea over the enfeebled Spaniards.

France was given Alsace, thus ensuring its influence in debilitated and partitioned Germany. And it was France which emerged from the Thirty Years War as the leading European power.

The Wars of Louis XIV of France

The whole second half of the 17th century was dominated by the powerful

Louis XIV (1643 – 1715), the king of France during whose reign the French cavalry got its uniforms.

9

figure of Louis XIV, the *Roi Soleil,* the most consistent representative of absolutism. He ascended to the throne in 1643 when he was only five, and after the death of Cardinal Mazarin in 1661, he ruled over France uninterrupted for more than half a century. From the very beginning of his rule Louis XIV pursued two goals in his foreign policy — the restoration of France within its natural borders, and the conquest of what remained of the dominions of the Hapsburg-Catholic coalition Austria and Spain. This foreign policy, backed with a strong army, would lead him into a string of wars of acquisition.

Louis's minister Jean-Baptiste Colbert strengthened the economy of the country, developed industry and trade and thus created the conditions for the existence of a great military power. After the reforms of Michel Le Tellier, Undersecretary of State for War from 1645, and his son the Marquis de Louvois, who occupied the same position from 1668, this is exactly what France became. De Louvois was one of the best known military organizers of the 17th century; his far-reaching reforms were soon adopted by other countries in Europe. Instead of the mercenary forces that were then the norm he created a strong, well-organized and equipped standing army, and substituted voluntary enrollment for press-ganging. Foreigners were accepted into the service too, under the motto of "one less for the enemy, one more for France, and one Frenchman more for productive labour." De Louvois was also the first to organize a national provisioning system. Among other

things, he decreed that units on the march had to have ambulances, and that military hospitals were to be set up in combat zones. To ensure a regular supply of food for the troops, he established military storehouses. He tried to introduce order into the system of purchasing colonel's and captain's ranks, and took away the right of higher commanders to name officers. For the impoverished nobility, who could not afford to buy a company or regiment, he created the ranks of major and lieutenant-colonel, and introduced a merit-list (L'Ordre du Tableau) to systematize the promotion of officers. Although several units already wore uniforms, he gradually uniformed the whole army, adhering to the motto "Without uniforms there is no order, and without order there is no army!" The dragoons were uniformed in 1667, and the rest of the cavalry in 1690.

There were many practical reasons for wearing uniforms, especially regarding unit recognition, e.g., when a regiment had to be gathered and re-formed after a charge or battle, or deserters identified. Uniforms were made from heavy cloth, and were usually gray, red, dark blue or dark green. Confusion would ensue when two mounted regiments with coats of the same color clashed, with matters further aggravated if they were dusty or muddied (which was often the case); it was hard to tell friend from foe. This being the situation, units in the field took additional measures to ensure recognition. It is known that Austrian soldiers stuck oak twigs in their hats, while the Swedes opted for sprigs of straw. The whole point of wearing

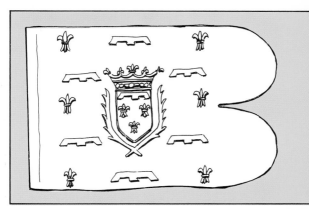

Top: Standard of the Gendarmerie de France; last third of 17th century.

Below: Guidon of the Orleans Dragoons, about 1675.

Below: Saber and long sword used to pierce the mail shirt. Weapons of the Polish hussar; end of the 17th century.

Opposite: French horseman of the Regiment de Cuirassiers du Roi, about 1680. Although other regiments in France wore a breastplate, "cuirass," this was the only one called cuirassiers.

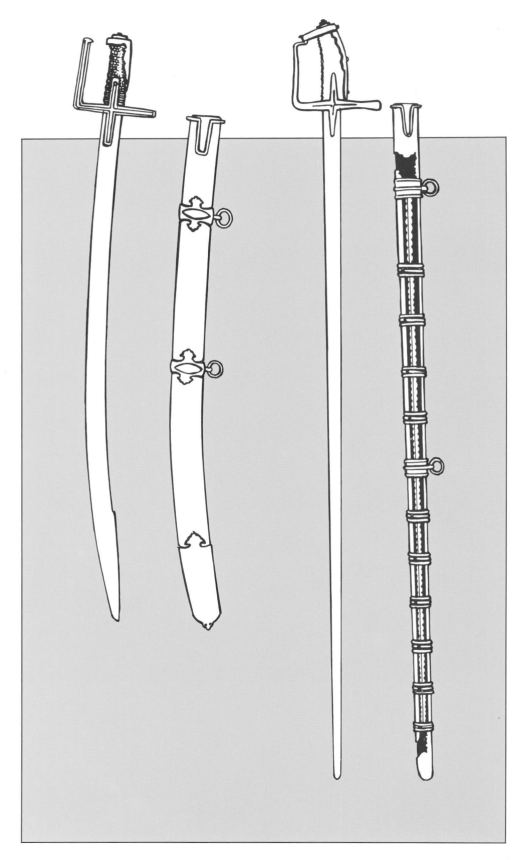

uniforms was best expressed by a Turkish sultan speaking of his Janissaries; of their clothes he said "... they should be such in color and cut as to make immediately apparent that they belong to one master."

During the Renaissance, it had been the Italian riding masters who had dominated the standards for cavalry; in the 17th and 18th centuries it was the French who set world standards of equitation that are still observed. In 1680, Louis XIV had the royal stables transferred to Versailles, where he established the famous Riding School. He brought the most renowned riding masters of the period to the school, where they practiced dressage and instructed the nobility in equestrian skills. The French High School of riding (*Haute école*) became a model accepted throughout Europe, the best-known school patterned after it being the Spanish Riding School of Vienna. The nobility, who always took great pride in appearances, made it a matter of prestige to ride well, besides having a luxurious outfit and a good horse. This would give a new boost in quality to the French cavalry, especially the guards.

On the other hand, the French army had to have a steady source of high-quality mounts from its own country's resources. For this express purpose Colbert established the State Stud Administration in 1663, an institution that was to become a model for the rest of Europe.

At the beginning of Louis XIV's rule, the French cavalry consisted of the

guards — Maison du Roi, the Gendarmerie de France — and line cavalry — de Ligne. The guards had about 1,600 horsemen in the Gardes du Corps, 250 in the Gendarmes de la Garde, 200 in the Compagnie des Chevau-légers and 300 Mousqetaires Gris, so called because of their gray horses, and made famous by Alexandre Dumas. In 1661, Louis added 300 Mousqetaires Noirs (on black horses) to the guards, and 120 Grenadiers à Cheval in 1676.

The Gendarmerie de France was formed in 1665 from 17 royal and princely companies. It was a unit of heavy cavalry, and each company numbered between 250 and 300 men.

The first French line regiments were formed in 1635, from the paramilitary Compagnies d'Ordonnance, which had been in existence since the end of the 15th century. By 1660, there were 30 line regiments. The first three were called "general staff" regiments, after similar designations of the previous period. Ranking first in seniority was the régiment colonel-général, second the mestre de camp général and third the commissaire général. The other regiments were also ranked, and the best-known among them were the Royal (fourth), the du Roi (fifth), the Royal Étranger (sixth), the Cuirassiers du Roi (seventh), and so on.

Every regiment was made up of two squadrons, each of them consisting of two companies. This gave them an overall strength of approximately 200 horsemen. Until the end of the 18th century, the basic tactical formation was the company, with 50 – 100 men. The squadron was formed on the battlefield according to need, and could consist of several companies.

Only later would it become a tactical unit. The same held true for the regiment. This first came into being as an administrative unit only, created in order to ensure uniform training and supplies for the companies it consisted of. In period accounts of battles, it was the numer of squadrons in a charge that was noted; more time was to pass before regiments, brigades or divisions went into battle under these names.

By 1668, Louis XIV had increased the number of regiments to 80; in this proliferation, dragoon regiments went from one to 14. Unlike the other types of cavalry, the number of dragoon regiments continued increasing rapidly, and reached 43 by 1688! The dragoons were placed under the control of a colonel-général and mestre de camp of dragoons.

As in other European states, the French cavalry was divided into "pure" cavalry, or so-called regiments on horse, dragoons, and, from 1692, when the first regiment was formed, hussars. Some of the regiments on horse were equipped with back- and breastplates, though they were not called cuirassiers. This partly depended on how much the owners of the regiment could afford to invest in it.

This ownership of regiments was common in Europe, and dated back to the period of mercenary armies. The rich nobility would get permission (which was often just a thinly disguised order) from their sovereign to form a regiment at their own expense. In return, they were given command over this regiment, and granted a colonel's rank. For instance, in 1673, Louis XIV gave permission to the Marquis de Listenois, the Marquis de Sauveboeuf, and the Chevalier de Fimraçon to form dragoon regiments. One of the reasons behind the later decadence of the French cavalry was that the colonels, being also the owners of the regiments, kept their horsemen out of any dangerous or heroic actions, which, as a rule, were rather expensive.

The men in the regiments on horse were armed with a straight sword, two pistols and a carbine. The dragoons, being the "mechanized infantry" of the time, had a sword of poorer quality, one pistol, and an infantry musket, for which they were later given a bayonet and an axe. The royal horse regiments and the regiments of some princes wore blue uniforms with red facings, regiments of the line had gray uniforms with red or blue facings, and the dragoons had red or blue uniforms, and a *bonnet á flamme,* a fur-trimmed cap with a hanging cloth bag. The Chevau-légers and the Gendarmes de France were dressed in red.

The French cavalry had forgotten the lesson of the Thirty Years War, in which the superior Swedish horsemen charged with drawn swords, leaving the pistols for the ensuing melee. It went back to the old tradition of the caracole,

approaching the enemy at a trot while shooting their pistols, and only drawing their swords for hand-to-hand combat. Other cavalry forces at the time attacked in similar fashion, and only at the beginning of the 18th century would Charles XII, King of Sweden, reinstate the cavalry charge with drawn sabers.

The War of Devolution (1667 – 1676)

After the death of Felipe IV, King of Spain, Louis XIV decided to annex the Spanish Netherlands, basing his claim on the right of devolution, by which children from the first marriage (in this case, Louis's wife, who was King Felipe's daughter by his first marriage) had hereditary precedence over children from later marriages. In the spring of 1667, Louis sent an army of 51,000 men under Turenne into the Netherlands. The Spanish governor, Castel Rodrigo, had only 20,000 soldiers at his disposal, and could not stand up to the French, so he abandoned the border posts and retreated to Brussels, which he had decided to defend. The French took over the Spanish Netherlands and Franche-Comté.

The next year, Louis did not continue with the war in the Netherlands, in order to avoid a conflict with Holland, which was determined to resist further conquests by the French. Under pressure from Holland, England and Sweden, the Peace of Aachen was signed. France retained the Spanish Netherlands. As the Spaniards had avoided frontal clashes, the fighting had centered mostly

Below: Saddle of the Polish light cavalry made after the light Eastern saddle; end of the 17th century.

on the fortresses. Mounted troops had been used only for reconnaissance and for guarding the flanks of the main body.

The Dutch War (1672 – 1678)

Four years later, in 1672, a French army under Turenne and Condé ventured into Holland up to the Rhine, but then the

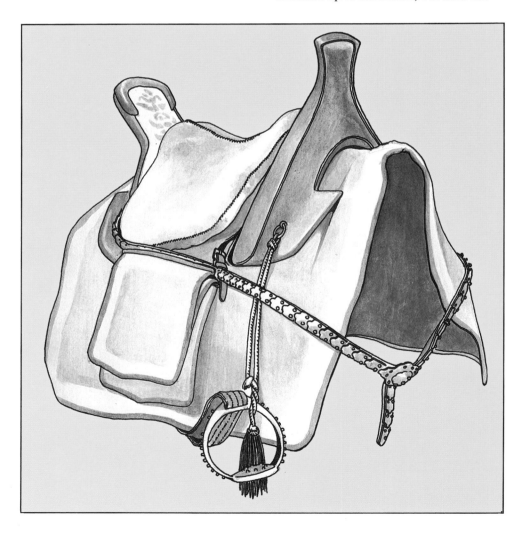

Dutch opened the dikes and stopped the French advance. Holland's only ally at the time was Spain, for Louis XIV had made pacts with Charles II, the German Emperor, and the other German rulers. In Holland, brought teetering to the edge of catastrophe by the war, Prince Willem van Orange, who accepted the English crown as King William III in 1688, became Governor General. Holland was then joined by Brandenburg, whose troops, together with those of the German Emperor, were on the Rhine. Turenne hurried to the Rhine, but no conflict occurred. Under pressure from Parliament, Charles II concluded a separate peace with Holland. The war dragged on until 1678. Condé and Willem fought to a standstill in Flanders. The French captured several large forts in the Netherlands, and clashed a few times with Imperial troops on the upper Rhine. Swedish troops intervened on Louis's side, landing in Brandenburg, but they were defeated and had to withdraw. Denmark also joined in the war against Sweden. When the war was finally over, France had managed to conquer the Franche-Comté and part of the Netherlands.

In the second half of the 17th century, two countries were dominant on the battlefields of Europe: France, with an impressive army that, at the time of the War of the League of Augsburg (1688 – 1697), numbered 400,000 men; and Poland, with a traditionally cavalry-orientated army that fought in the violent but chivalrous spirit of the Middle Ages.

Polish hussars bringing the captured Turkish flag to Jan Sobieski. Siege of Vienna 1683. Painting by Julius Kossak.

Poland

The Polish Commonwealth included Lithuania, Livonia, Pomerania, the Ukraine and part of Silesia — an expanse where the cultures, religions and military skills of North, East and West had been clashing for centuries. In this period Poland waged several large-scale wars against Sweden and Brandenburg over Pomerania and the Baltic areas; against Moscovite Russia over the Ukraine; and, for nearly a whole century, against Turkey. Frequent incursions by the Tartars and Cossack uprisings disturbed the few years when the country was not at war. The opponents facing it reflected on the appearance and quality of the Polish cavalry. The Poles knew how to assimilate the best that their enemies had to offer. From the warriors of the steppes and the light horsemen of the East they learned the value of speed, ambushes, sudden attacks and the constant wearing down of the opponent.

From the West they learned discipline (even if they could never rival Sweden in

this respect) and the violent force of the attacks of the Teutonic Knights.

Because of the cavalry, the tactics of the Polish army were decidedly offensive in character. Any complicated maneuvers were avoided; the aim was to break the enemy with a frontal attack. Battle was begun by the light horsemen who disturbed the opponent and drew his attention, thus forcing him to discover his disposition and deploy prematurely, while protecting the deployment of their own troops at the same time. After that, the heavy cavalry charged, in blocks of several hundred horsemen, reminiscent of the advance of chess pieces on the board. First came the winged hussars and the armored horsemen, and then the dragoons and the others.

Cavalry was often the decisive element in a battle. Successive charges were undertaken until the opponent was completely routed. Enemy superiority was not taken to be a matter for consideration — a Polish saying went: "*Najpierw pobijemy a potem policzemy*" — "First we beat the enemy, then we count him." The routed opponent was pursued by light horsemen for days after the battle.

The army was headed by the king, who became supreme commander in case of war, and, situation permitting, personally led his men into battle. His presence on the battlefield contributed to the élan and morale of the troops. The highest position in the military was occupied by the Great Hetman, who was responsible for the security of the country, and organization, training and discipline in the army. Lithuania, even though in a political union with Poland, had its own army and a separate command, headed by the Great Hetman of Lithuania.

Units were organized, and their manpower drawn, along territorial principles by a system of recruitment. Polish law stipulated that not a single important position in civilian state employment could be gained without and individual having fought in a war. Therefore, by and large, the middle nobility went into the army voluntarily, thus providing a constant source of very good horsemen. Mercenary units were filled out with foreigners, sometimes even completely consisting of them. There were Germans, Hungarians, Scotsmen, Dutchmen, Swedes, Wallachians, Cossacks and Tartars serving the Polish king. Members of the high nobility retained their own private armies, numbering several thousand men. Well known were the armies of Sapieha, Radziwill, Pac, Sieniawski, Lubomirski and others, which were sometimes more numerous than the other national forces put together. The

existence of these private armies was one of the causes of the later decline of Poland as a military power, for they also represented an important force in internal politics.

Cavalry was the largest and the best branch of the Polish military. It was divided into hussars, panzers, dragoons and units of light cavalry. Hussar units were the elite of the Polish army, thus the place of choice for military service of the middle and high nobility. In the second half of the 17th century, the hussar was an archaic horseman, and could still be found only in Poland.

Clash between the dragoons and the Turkish cavalry. Painting by Julius Kossak.

21

Heavy cavalry in the West had discarded the lance as a weapon, and based its might on larger horses and the protection of riders with breastplates; their main weapon was a long straight sword. This long sword was a thrusting weapon, because the battle order of horsemen riding boot to boot left no space for the sweeping movements needed for cutting. The hussars, riding on lighter horses, could only penetrate this dense mass of horsemen with heavy lances, which were about 5 meters (16 ½ feet) long, and capable of piercing the breastplates of the cuirassiers. Once the enemy formation was shattered, and the lances broken in collision, the skill of the Polish nobles in swordplay and riding would begin to tell in the newly created space. To avoid being encumbered with the heavy lance and additional equipment on the march, every hussar went to war with one or two servants.

The hussar was protected by a helmet, a breastplate invulnerable to pistol shots and a backplate to which were fastened a pair of wings, which earned them the name of "winged hussars." These wings were not merely decorative; they had the very practical function of preventing the much faster and more maneuverable Tartars or Cossacks from slipping a lasso over the rider and pulling him from his mount. In the last third of the 17th century, scale armor, to which wings were not affixed, came into use.

Besides the sword and lance, the hussar carried two pistols and an armor-piercing long sword — the *koncerz* — which hung on his saddle.

The basic tactical unit was the *choragiew* (flag), which had 100 – 150 men commanded by a lieutenant or a captain. The flag was named after its commander, and its members recognized each other on the battlefield by the pennant the hussars wore on their lances.

Panzers were cavalrymen of the middle and lower nobility, very similar to their Russian, Turkish and Hungarian counterparts. Instead of the hussars' armor, they wore a mail shirt, and were armed with a short spear, about 2.5 meters (8 ¼ feet) in length. To better protect themselves, they often carried the *kalkan,* a round shield. They were also armed with two pistols, a sword, the koncerz, a composite bow, a war hammer, and, later, a short musket. Like the hussars, they adorned their spears with pennants. The choragiew of the panzers had about 200 men.

As in other western European countries, dragoons in Poland were very similar in organization to the infantry units from which they were derived. In times of peace, their duty was to guard the borders; in war, they were assigned everything that the noblemen considered to be below them. Dragoons could fight like cavalry or like infantry, and due to this versatility they were very useful. The first royal dragoon regiment was formed in 1630, and the second in 1682. They were also the first regular unit for which a standard red and blue uniform was decreed in 1670. A great number of

Opposite: Polish pancerny *armed similary as the Turkish and Russian heavy cavalry; end of the 17th century.*

horses always perished in long campaigns, and it was always the dragoons' horses that were used to remount other units, and they would then continue the war on foot. They were armed with one or two pistols, a musket and a sword, and, unlike the other cavalry units, did not have very good horses.

The lower and poorer nobility made up the choragiew of what the Poles simply called *jazda lekka* − light cavalry. Weapons and equipment varied widely according to the wealth of the owner. The composite bow was a very desirable weapon, for it signaled the rank and status of the owner.

Poland often engaged the services of whole regiments of Cossack, Wallachian, Hungarian and Tartar light cavalry. Regiments of German cavalry were called *rajtari* (from the German word *Ritter* − "knight").

The Austro-Turkish War (1683 − 1699)

In 1667 and 1671 Jan III Sobieski turned back two large-scale incursions by Tartars into the Ukraine. This was reason enough for Turkish Sultan Mehmed IV to send 100,000 soldiers to the Polish border in 1672. The weaker Polish forces were defeated at Kamienec Podolski, and Poland lost part of the Ukraine in an unfavorable peace. This peace, however, lasted only long enough to allow Jan III to gather a new army. In 1673, the Polish cavalry completely routed the Turks at Hotin, and again at

Lvov in 1675. After still another Turkish defeat, at Žurawino, a peace treaty was concluded in 1676, but it did not last for very long, either. In 1683, Mehmed IV sent an army under Grand Vizier Kara Mustafa Basha to take Vienna. This marked the beginning of the Austro-Turkish War, which would last until 1699. The Poles, who also felt threatened by this Turkish expedition, sent an army to assist the Austrian emperor, consisting of 3,000 hussars, 8,000 panzers, 2,000 light horsemen, 3,000 dragoons, 500 rajtari and 300 Cossacks. Saxony, Bavaria and other German states also sent their contingents.

While the allies were gathering their forces, the Turkish army made its way to Vienna, and laid siege to it. The siege lasted for two months, while the allies organized. Jan III Sobieski assumed command of the army of 40,000 infantry and 26,000 cavalry and marched on Vienna in three columns with the intention of relieving the city, which was close to falling, and forcing the Turks to do battle.

The left wing and center of the allied forces appeared on the slopes above Vienna early in the morning. Five cannon shots marked the beginning of the attack. The allied force consisted of 55 Imperial, 16 Bavarian and 12 Saxon squadrons of cuirassiers and dragoons; in conjunction with the infantry columns, they managed to take Nussdorf and Heiligenstadt by noon. But then the intensity of the attack fell, and Herzog von Lothringen, Johann Georg III von Sachsen and Maximilian II,

Elector Duke of Bavaria, asked for a respite and time to regroup and re-form their units.

The situation on the battlefield was now balanced. It was time for the Turks to counterattack. Kara Mustafa gathered his Syrians, Anatolians, Kurds and Bosnians and prepared for the charge. At the same time, the Poles were having trouble approaching the positions on the right wing that they were supposed to hold according to the agreement between the allies. Since six o'clock in the morning they had been forcing their way through ravines and forest; it was not until two in the afternoon that they managed to get to the village of Dornsbach above Vienna, arriving there at the very moment when Kara Mustafa was about to launch his counterattack.

Jan III decided that his allies had sent him that way purposely, without telling him about the configuration of the ground, in order to win the battle themselves, gaining fame and vast riches. So, after coming out of the forest, the Poles struck at once. The hussars were in the front ranks, draped in bear and leopard skins, with white or black swans' wings on their backs, and the others followed behind. An eyewitness account likened the charge of the Polish cavalry to "... hosts of Biblical angels falling from the sky on the faithless enemy." The cavalry charge having thus broken through the Turkish lines and into their encampment of 25,000 tents, all resistance ceased on the left wing and in the center. Everything was over in two hours.

The Poles gained a rich booty from the captured Turkish camp, including several Arabian stallions. Descendants of these horses are still admired by many wealthy individuals who come to the occasional sales of Arabian horses in Poland.

The Austrians

By a decree of Ferdinand III, the standing Austrian army was formed in 1649; it consisted of 10,000 horsemen in nine cuirassier regiments and one dragoon regiment. In war they were joined by five or six irregular regiments of light Croatian cavalry and Hungarian hussars. In the Thirty Years War the Imperial cuirassier regiments had been 10 deep on the battlefield in order to execute the caracole-shooting from the saddle. This way of doing battle was also retained later, but with the regiments only three deep. Even though with 1,000 horsemen this meant a front line three times as wide as before, the division into six squadrons gave greater possibilities of control and command. The cuirassiers would wear a helmet, breastplate and buff coat until the end of the 18th century, while the dragoons would start waring dark blue coats with red facings in 1680. Only in 1688 would the Imperial army get its first regular hussar regiment. Emperor Leopold I ordered General Czobor to form an Imperial hussar regiment, "... from men 24 to 35 years in age, on horses 14 to 15 hand tall [one hand being slightly over four inches], and 5 to 7 years old" consisting of "10 companies, with 100 men each."

Opposite: Turkish light cavalryman, mounted and armed like most of the cavalry in the Ottoman army at the end of the 17th century.

Niels Bielke, commander of the Swedish King's Life Cavalry at the Battle of Lund, 1676.

The regulation weapons were a sword, two pistols and a short carbine, although the irregular hussars, who sometimes numbered up to 5,000, carried a lance, and some even a composite bow. In the beginning the "regular" referred only to the fact that the unit existed permanently, and that the men wore uniform light brown attilas, short coats modeled on Hungarian folk costume, with red cords and wooden toggles on the front. Otherwise, the hussars still remained wild and undisciplined, just like the Tartars and the Cossacks, but were very useful in reconnaissance, surprise attacks and border skirmishes.

The Turks

However, in Turkey, in the 17th century, erosion of the state and military administration had begun even before the defeats on the battlefield. The grand viziers clung fast to the battle tactics that had gained them the Balkans and areas surrounding the Danube a long time ago. Turkish commanders in the field witnessed something they had never seen before: a "devilishly" adaptable kind of warfare, with successive coordinated charges of infantry and cavalry, with deliberate and measured support by artillery. The Ottoman Empire would fight the battles of Szentgotthárd in 1664 and Vienna in 1683 with the same tactics as the battle of Nicopolis in 1396. All that their spontaneous massed cavalry charges could achieve was chaos. They tried to win battles in hand-to-hand combat, as if the Damascus saber were an eternal instrument of victory. For a long time, Turkish soldiers refused to arm themselves with pistols. But, at the beginning of the 17th century, the situation forced them to accept this weapon, even though the traditional spear and composite bow would remain a part of their armament for still some time.

The *sipahis,* grouped into territorial units of about 100 sabers, were the military aristocracy and only regular horsemen of the Turkish Sultan. They would continue wearing their 15th-century-type mail shirts, helmets and shields right into the 19th century. The sipahis, who were landowners, had to go to war either alone or with a certain number of equipped horsemen, depending on the

Guidon of the Swedish dragoons, about 1660.

size of their *timar* ("estate"). As central authority weakened, fewer and fewer sipahis answered the sultan's call to arms, so the standing army had to be increased. The standing army of Turkey would number as many as 100,000 men in the 17th century, which was a great burden on the state budget.

In the areas bordering Austria and Hungary mercenary units were formed whose manpower was drawn from the local populace. They were called *dzema'at,* (Arabic for "gathering"), and consisted of 20 to 50 *faris* — "horse-men." A captain was in charge of several dzema'at, and led them to war when the sultan called. Every faris had his own horse, and kept it himself. In war, the captains, with several hundred faris, would make incursions into enemy territory, robbing the populace, ambushing opponents' units and gathering military information along the way. The similarly organized Imperial territorial units repaid them in kind. Of these light horsemen from the border areas, the Austrians formed irregular Croatian and hussar units that would become the nuclei of the regular hussar regiments.

Sweden

Sweden spent the whole second half of the 17th century at war with Poland, Denmark, Brandenburg, Russia and, at one time, Austria, fighting over control of the Baltic. At this time, Sweden had barely one million inhabitants, while Poland had ten, and Russia 15 million. Therefore, it was impossible for Sweden to have sizable armed forces that would be nationally homogenous. It had to rely

on large numbers of Germans, Scotsmen and Finns, which lowered the quality of its army. The country was divided into administrative regions, where persons subject to conscription were given land to work on. In case of war, every region formed its own units, consisting of peasants and burghers who more or less all knew each other. This national and territorial principle of unit forming ensured excellent morale and a high quality of training. It was considered a great disgrace if the people back home found out that someone had shown himself to be a coward on the battle-field. But a significant drawback of this system was that the destruction of such a unit meant the loss of a great number of men from one area. The units were named after the part of the country where they were formed, e. g., the well-known Viborg, Nyslot and Kalmar cavalry regiments.

Sweden had always had good iron ore, and excellent technology for metal processing. The Arboga, Jäder, Söderhem, Roslagen and Norrtälje works produced high-quality weapons and armor, and their cannons were the best in the world. A cavalryman's breastplate had to withstand a test shot from a musket at a range of 20 paces in order to be accepted by the military weapons comission. Sword blades were bent in two directions and the flat struck hard against a pinewood plank. Only if it passed the test was the blade stamped. After the death of Gustavus II Adol-phus, the Swedish cavalry lost the élan and forcefulness for which it had been known during the Thirty Years War. At Fehrbellin, near Berlin, Swedish forces under Wrangel, which had intervened on Louis's side in the French-Dutch-Spanish war (1672 to 1678), were defeated by the Brandenburg cavalry of Friedrich Wilhelm, the Great Elector. Although the battle itself altered nothing in the balance of power, the myth of Swedish invincibility was undone. Brandenburg forces numbering 6,500 horsemen vanquished 4,200 Swedes in several charges, in a battle in which infantry hardly took part at all. A year later, in 1676, the Swedes were victorious over the Danes in the Battle of Lund, in Scania. But it may have well been the bloodiest victory they won. Their forces numbered 7,000 men, while the Danes had 11,000, but in cavalry they were equal 4,500 men on either side. At the end of the day, nearly half the men of both armies lay dead. The battle was decided by the charge of the King's Life Cavalry. Later, to reward this great victory, Charles XI gave their commander Nils Bielke a sword only recently given to him by Louis XIV.

Swedish mounted forces consisted of the National Cavalry, similar to the cuirassiers of the period, ordinary cavalry and dragoons. The men of the National Cavalry wore breast- and backplates on buff coats. They were armed with two pistols, a long sword and a carbine. Sweden, along with England, would be the first country where the dragoons became real cavalry as a result of rational and progressive military thought, but they kept their name as a reminder that they were descended from mounted infantry. In the second half of the 18th century, Sweden had three dragoon regiments —

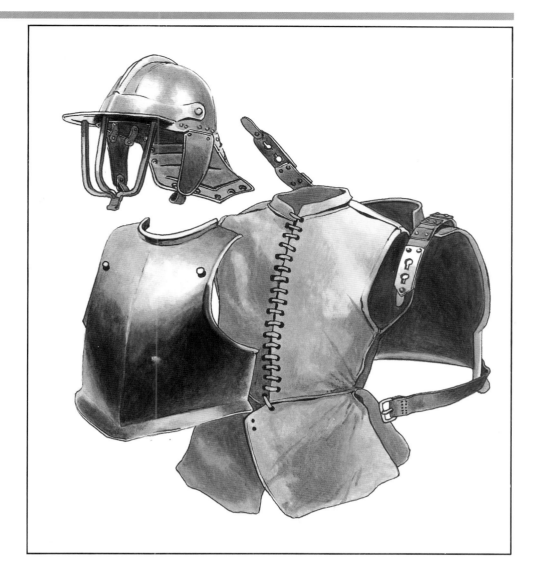

Skåwe-Bohus, Karelska and Savolaks, and an independent dragoon squadron — Åboläns Dragowskvadrow.

Lobster helmet, front and backplate armor, and buff coat of the English cavalry, about 1660.

Brandenburg

After the death of Friedrich Wilhelm in 1688, his successor, Friedrich III von Brandenburg, inherited a standing army of 30,000 men — the second largest in Germany, after Austria's — and holdings in Pomerania taken from Sweden in the war of 1674 – 1679. In 1685, Louis XIV had abolished freedom of worship for the Huguenots, which resulted in the exodus of 15,000 people to Brandenburg. This influx had a marked positive effect on the economy, arts and science in the country, as well as on the development of military organization. Together with other political opponents of Louis XIV, a

large number of Huguenots served in the regiments of Brandenburg.

Towards the end of the 18th century, the mounted forces of Brandenburg consisted of the guards — Trabantengarde cavalry of the line — and dragoons. In 1682 the Regiment Guarde zu Pferd was formed; it had dark blue uniforms with silver and gold facings. Contemporary historians noted the fact that Friedrich III was accompanied to his coronation by three squadrons, one mounted on gray horses, one on dark brown and one on black. In 1687, the company of Grands-Mousquetaires was formed from French noblemen opposed to Louis's rule, and in 1688 the Regiment Gendarmes was created, composed of German nobles.

The oldest unit of line cavalry was the Regiment Anhalt zu Pferde, founded in 1666. The others were the Regiment Kurprinz zu Pferde (founded in 1672), the Regiment Briquemalt, composed of French exiles (founded in 1683), which assumed the name of Markgraf Philipp Wilhelm after his death in 1694, the Regiment Sachsen zu Pferde, formed of Saxon exiles in 1686, the Regiment du Hamel zu Pferde (founded in 1688) and the Regiment Markgraf von Bayreuth zu Pferde, established in 1690.

In 1674, one of the units of the guard was the Leibregiment Dragoner, who acquitted themselves very well in combat against the Swedes at Fehrbellin. Other units were formed in the following sequence: in 1688, the Anhalt-Dragoner, in 1691 the Regiment Ansbach-Dragoner, in 1692 the Schwadron Prebandt-Dragoner squadron, in 1695 the Regiment Derfflinger-Dragoner and in 1700 the Lottum-Dragoner.

In 1701, Friedrich III, Elector of Brandenburg, crowned himself King of Prussia, as Friedrich I, with the consent of the German Emperor. Brandenburg remained part of the German Empire. In time, Friedrich united his far-flung possessions into a kingdom. This marked the emergence of Prussia as a European superpower.

The English

When the English civil war ended, England turned to the contest for supremacy on the high seas, and to its internal affairs. Its army would not appear on the European mainland until the end of the 17th century. In 1660, the monarchy was restored, and the new king, Charles II, disbanded the existing army and formed a new one. Of the 600 gentlemen who had followed him into exile, he formed three troops of Life Guards, heavy cavalry similar to cuirassiers. They had buff coats with back- and breastplate and a helmet, just like Oliver Cromwell's Roundheads. A year later, in 1661, the troops were named: the first one was called "His Majesty's Own Troop of Guards"; the second "His Highness Royal Duke of York his Troop of Guards," after James, Charles's brother, who would later become James II; and the third one "His Grace the Duke of Albemarle his Troop of Guards," in honor of General Monck, the former governor of Scotland, who took London with his

Opposite: A horseman of the Royal Regiment of Scots Dragoons, about 1681. Even though called dragoons they wore breastplates for some time.

troops and made Charles's return possible. After Monck's death in 1670, the third troop would be renamed "Queen's Troop." Also in 1661, the men of Colonel Crook, who had served under the Earl of Oxford, formed the basis for a regiment named the Royal Horse Guards, and a regiment known as Tangier Horse or The Tangier Cuirassiers was formed for service in the colony of Morocco. In 1678, every troop of Life Guards was given a division of mounted grenadiers called Horse Grenadiers. Only one more regiment was formed during the reign of Charles II: The Royal Regiment of Scots Dragoons, in 1681. When the English withdrew from Morocco in 1683, the Tangier Horse were renamed "King's Own Royal Regiment of Dragoons."

James Duke of York, Charles's brother, had served in France for a period of time under Turenne, and witnessed the reforms of de Louvois. He would later introduce some of them to England, during his short reign as James II (from 1684 until the "bloodless revolution" in 1688). In this period the English cavalry were given uniforms: the Guards were dressed in crimson, except for the Royal Horse Guards, who wore blue of the same shade as the livery of the Earl of Oxford. The dragoons, as well as the newly formed regiments "of Horse" were dressed in red. Scottish dragoons wore gray coats until 1687.

During the reign of James II, two dragoon regiments and four regiments of "pure" cavalry (called Regiments of Horse) were formed. Counting the Life Guards, this made for a total of nine cavalry regiments. A regiment of Horse had 300 men in two squadrons with three troops each, while the dragoons were somewhat more numerous, having 480 men in a regiment. Breastplates, inherited from an earlier period, were rarely worn, and mostly gathered dust in regimental depots, for the English cavalry did not take part in any war or major battle of this time.

Nevertheless, during the reign of James II the cavalry was raised to very high standards, and it was said that it was the best paid, best equipped and best regarded branch of the military.

In the countries of the West, riding was for the rich and privileged. Only after the first standing armies were formed did cities or rich noblemen buy horses for their soldiers in addition to their equipment. Elite cavalry units consisted of well-off citizens and the nobility, who came into the army as trained horsemen. The regular regiments of the line and dragoon were comprised of recruits who had to be taught how to stay in the saddle, and how to work with a horse.

Eastern and Western Cavalry Developments (beginning of 18th century)

As long as fighting in line was the main tactic, training and discipline were of the utmost importance, which often meant that soldiers were treated harshly, and punished severely for any mistake. In Brandenburg this went so far that soldiers had more reason to be afraid of

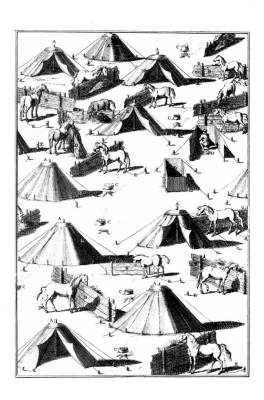

Turkish cavalry camp where each horse was with its master contrary to the Western kind of camp where all horses were kept together. Contemporary etching.

their officers than of the enemy. On the exercise fields, soldiers were first trained individually, then in pairs, in foursomes, and so on up to the level of troop or squadron, and in various forms of maneuvers. The troop was the basic tactical unit, and it numbered from 40 to 80 men. It formed and moved in one, two or three lines, or marched in columns of two, four, eight or ten abreast. The troops comprising a squadron formed behind or beside one another, and the same went for the squadrons making up a regiment. On the battlefield, the regiments that were in reserve formed with their squadrons in column, for greater ease of movement and approach to the front lines. Upon nearing the enemy, they would deploy into line and charge.

Western cavalry became a well-trained and disciplined war machine that could execute many complicated maneuvers in the field with great control. Eastern cavalry was quite a different matter. This term is used to describe the riders from the steppes — the Cossacks and Tartars of the Ukraine and Crimea, the nomads of Asia Minor, the desert riders from the Sinai and the northern part of Africa and, generally, the riders from countries under Turkish rule.

Due to the way that these Eastern mounted warriors excelled in riding skills, and could perform astonishing feats at full gallop, it was said that they were "born in the saddle." But this also referred to their way of life. Horses in the East were part of the traditional way of life, a status symbol, but also an everyday need, just like clothes. Harsh

weather and vegetation made horses from the steppes and deserts very hardy, and, in the desert, resistant to the heat of day, to cold nights and to swarms of mosquitoes and flies, and, in the steppes, to harsh winters. Such conditions also affected the appearance of these horses: they were rather small, 14 to 15 hands tall, weighing 350 to 400 kg (770 to 880 lb.), and with a lively disposition. In contrast, the cuirassier horses in Austria, Bavaria and Saxony were 15 to 16 hands tall, and weighed up to 600 kg (1,320 lb.).

In the West, the stable boys who took care of the soldiers' horses had to put a piece of red wool in the horse's mane or tail if the horse was prone to biting or kicking. This was unnecessary in the East for at least two reasons: first, the horses were treated much better, and, second, the Eastern people were great connoisseurs of horses, and could judge a horse's temperament very quickly, thus avoiding unpleasant surprises.

In the West, horsemen rode deep in the saddle, with their legs practically fully stretched out, much like the medieval knights who had to lean on their high saddle in order to better withstand the impact of the heavy lance by transmitting part of the energy to the horse. In the East, men rode with legs bent very high, similar to modern jockeys. This enabled them to stand in the saddle and shoot with their composite bows or throw their javelins. Riding during a campaign was a matter unto itself. In a meeting between Peter the Great and Charles XII, the Swedish monarch pointed out the many advantages of his army – the numerous victories, good weapons, discipline and high morale. Peter the Great answered that Russia was a great country, and that his horsemen could actually sleep in the saddle.

The mounted warriors of the East belonged to the great and sparsely populated expanse of woods, steppes, pastures and deserts. In this space they could ride for days, unencumbered by supply lines and heavy carts. In the 1950s, a group of horsemen set a stupendous record by covering 18 miles in 24 hours, riding on Don horses. The Mongols used to have two or three spare horses, and they would switch every few hours, thus covering up to 100 km (60 mi) a day; in this same time Western cavalry units generally covered only 20 to 30 km (12 to 18 mi). The Tartars and Arabs emulated the practice of the Mongols later on. The Tartars could also cross wide rivers by holding on the their horses' manes and swimming, while their equipment floated on rafts made of branches or impregnable leather bags tied to the animals' tails.

The battle tactics of the Eastern horsemen were to avoid a direct clash with the cuirassier wall, trying to envelope them instead and attack their weak flanks, or to attack at a point when it was impossible to form a solid battle order. Every charge was accompanied by a shower of arrows fired at full gallop. In the field, they were adept at concealing themselves and moving while leaving as few traces as possible. They mounted ambushed and surprise attacks in the places and at the

times when they could least be expected. Then they would suddenly vanish as quickly as they had appeared.

The Hungarians, Cossacks, Poles and Russians often clashed with Tartars or Turkish light cavalry in the border areas. In order to counter these frequent incursions, they had to organize light horsemen who fought in the same way. These horsemen were later to become regular regiments of hussars in Austria and Russia, uhlans in Poland, and Cossacks in Russia. This type of mounted soldier became common at the end of the 17th and beginning of the 18th century in all major armies except the English.

Turkish army leading away slaves. We can see the technique the light cavalry used for crossing rivers.

French Regiment, around 1680:

STAFF:

Colonel	1
Lieutenant Colonel	1
Adjutant	1
Chaplain	1
Surgeon	1
Quartermaster	1

COMPANY:

Captain	1
Lieutenant	2
Quartermaster-Sergeant	1
Corporals	3
Trumpeter	2
Troopers	50

The regiment has 10 to 12 companies.

Chapter Two: Wars for Vacant Thrones

1700 – 1735

The Grand Bourbon had behind him a strong state; Louvois, who had organized his armies; Vauban, who had built his forts; Tallard, Vendome, Villar and Berwick, who led his soldiers; also, nearly 40 years of uninterrupted triumphs in three great wars that had thoroughly depleted the coffers of state. When Carlos II, King of Spain, bequeathed the Spanish crown and dominions – then comprising the Netherlands, Milan, Naples, Sicily and nearly half of America – to Louis's son Philip, war became inevitable. Leopold I, the Austrian Emperor, wanted the Spanish crown for his son, and was joined by England and Holland, which were afraid that France would become too powerful. The anti-French coalition was also joined by Denmark, Portugal, Hanover, Württemberg and all the other German principalities except Cologne. The joining of France and Spain would bring Louis closer to his ideal, as a modern historian wrote, of "concentrating Europe in France, France in Paris, and Paris in himself," the same ideal to which Napoléon would aspire a hundred years later. As it turned out, this amibitious attempt would be unsuccessful, largely due to two outstanding military leaders: the Duke of Marlborough (John Churchill) and Prince Eugène of Savoy.

The French and the War of the League of Augsburg

At the time of the War of the League of Augsburg (1688 – 1697), the French cavalry was the best in Europe. Turenne and d'Enghien, who was later to become the Great Condé, were its most able commanders.

In 1690, at Fleurs, 50 squadrons of French cavalry executed a surprise attack from the rear on the positions of the Allied Spanish, Dutch, German and Swedish forces, numbering 20,000 infantry, 13,000 horsemen and 60 cannons, and commanded by General Waldeck. The Allied forces were defeated, and the remnants – 7,000 infantry, 8,000 horsemen and 11 cannons – made their way back to Brussels. The French lost fewer then 500 men. At Leuze, in 1691, 2,500 French cavalrymen defeated Waldeck's rear guard of 6,000 horsemen and five battalions of infantry.

At Steinkirk, in 1692, the Mousquetaires Gris and Mousquetaires Noirs, shouting "Vive le Roi!" launched an attack against the personal guard of the commander of the Allied forces, William III, King of England. After a pitched battle, they were driven back to their starting positions. There they re-formed, and, supported by the Champagne infantry regiment, charged again to cries of "Allez, allez!," and won the day for France. On that day, many black and gray horses returned with empty saddles.

At Neerwinden, in 1693, two attacks on William's positions were repulsed. In the third wave, the Duke of Luxembourg sent in 57 battalions and 77 squadrons, which made quite a dent in the Allied defense. A fourth wave,

Henri de Turenne (1611 – 1675) the best-known French commander of the second half of the 17th century. Contemporary drawing.

Opposite: French dragoon equipped to fight mounted and on foot; beginning of the 18th century.

John Churchill, Duke of Marlborough (1650 to 1722), the greatest cavalry commander in the beginning of the 18th century. Contemporary painting.

consisting of 30 squadrons, plunged into the resulting gaps, and forced the enemy to withdraw along the whole frontline.

This period was the heyday of French cavalry.

The War of the Spanish Succession

At the beginning of the War of the Spanish Succession (1701 – 1714) Louis XIV had 170,000 infantrymen and 30,000 mounted troops at his disposal. Counting the forces of his allies — Spain, Piedmont and Cologne — the total was about 300,000 men under arms, while the enemy had somewhat more, about 350,000. The French, protected by a chain of 300 fortresses along the borders, and having a good network of internal maneuvering routes, decided to attack the Austrians in Italy and on the upper Rhine, and employ defensive tactics against the Allied forces in the Netherlands and Holland.

In 1703, Bavaria joined France, thus opening for its armies a gate into the very heart of Europe. At the beginning of 1704, Louis had eight independent armies, four of them facing Austria. One was in Bavaria, spending the winter with the Elector's forces, another, under Vendome, was in Italy, preparing to break through to Salzburg through the Tyrol. The third one, under Tallard, was on the upper Rhine, ready to go to Bavaria, and the fourth, under Villeroy, in Flanders, waiting to cross the Moselle, and head for the banks of the Danube. These four armies were

supposed to converge on Vienna, and eliminate Austria from the war.

The main French and Spanish forces — about 95,000 men under Boufflers — were in the Spanish Netherlands, holding a fortified line at Antwerp. Allied forces of 60,000 men under the command of the Duke of Marlborough were at Nijmegen. Due to the extreme cautiousness of the Dutch, Marlborough was allowed to perform actions of a limited character only, and without putting his troops at unnecessary risk. But Marlborough saw that Austria could be forced to leave the coalition after a decisive defeat at the hands of the Franco-Bavarian forces, so he decided to disobey his orders. Detaching parts of his army to guard the borders, he led the main body of 18,000 men to Bavaria, in order to stop the French invasion of Austria. Marlborough, acting on his own, embarked on a 450 km (270 mi) long march that would make him England's greatest military leader of all time, but would also cost him his career.

Marlborough and Modern English Cavalry

The history of modern English cavalry begins with Marlborough. He defined and set down basic tactical procedures that would govern the conduct of the English cavalry throughout the period when it represented a force to be reckoned with. At the very beginning of the 18th century there were two schools of thought about the way to use cavalry on the battlefield, both of them based on the experiences of the first half of the

41

previous century. One, largely forgotten, was that of both the Swedish cavalry of Gustavus Adolphus and the English under Prince Rupert and Cromwell. They practiced a galloping charge with drawn swords, while the pistols were to be saved for the melee. The second was described by Montecuccoli (1609 – 1680), an Austrian field marshal, who had commanded a cuirassier regiment: "Nevertheless, if the first rank of cuirassier should wish to use its pistols, it must do so only after it has first tied them to its swords with a ribbon, or else the swords must be taken into the hands which hold the bridle. Once the pistols have been rapidly discharged, and this weapon can have no effect unless it is applied point-blank, they are tossed away or put back in the holsters — if there is time. Thereupon each reiter grasps his sword and plunges into the mêlée without attempting any caracole."

Montecuccoli was not the only one to suggest jettisoning the pistols after shooting. Fortescue notes that the

French horsemen did the same at Dettingen. The logical conclusion is that after the battle the men had to take a stroll in the field and look for their pistols. This was a serious drawback of the system, for the cavalry was supposed to give chase to the fleeing opponent, not browse through the grass searching for its weapons.

Swedish regulations at the end of the 17th century prescribed that the final 200 paces of the charge should be covered in a gallop, that the first pistol should be fired from a distance of forty paces and the second one from twenty-five. In other words, there were three seconds after the first shot to prepare for the second one, and at most four seconds after that to draw one's sword. This rather complicated the attack, making it less effective than a charge with drawn swords.

Other armies, among them the French and Austrian, adopted tactics similar to the Swedish, but with three lines of

Opposite: English trooper of the King's Dragoon Guards, the regiment that followed the Duke of Marlborough through all his campaigns; beginning of the 18th century.

Austrian cuirassier's sword from 1703.

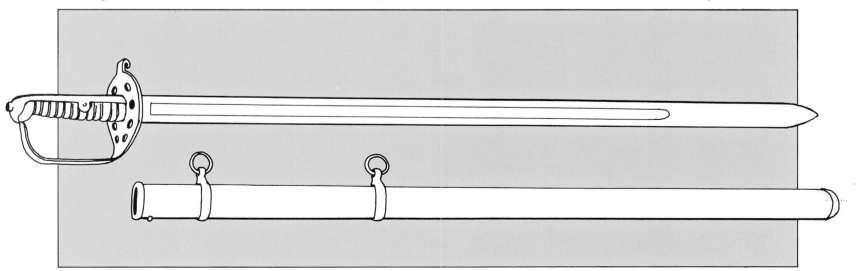

squadrons trotting forward to within pistol range and firing simultaneously, and then drawing their swords.

His activities severely restricted, and consisting practically exclusively of besieging fortresses in the Netherlands, Marlborough had ample time to train his English and Dutch squadrons for real cavalry charges with cold steel only, after the fashion of Cromwell's Roundheads half a century earlier. He would form his squadrons in two lines, boot to boot, and make them charge at a fast trot. He went so far in his effort to rid his men of dependence on firearms as to allow them only three bullets on patrol or guard duty!

In May 1704, after extensive preparations, the Duke of Marlborough, with 18,000 English, Dutch and Danish troops headed for Bavaria, in order to meet up with the forces of Prince Eugène and Ludwig von Baden. The French believed that the duke would stop at Coblentz, cross the Moselle and attack Villeroy who had 40 battalions and 39 squadrons there. When he entered Mainz, they thought that he would attack Alsace, but when he crossed the Neckar and headed for Württemberg, panic erupted in Paris. But it was too late for anyone to stop him. It became clear that the three French armies on the Danube, commanded by Tallard, Marsin and the Bavarian Elector, would be faced by three Allied armies under Marlborough, Prince Eugène and Ludwig von Baden.

On June 10th, after a 35-day march, the Allied forces met at Mondelsheim. The march was organized in three- or four-day stages, covering 60 to 80 km (36 to 48 mi) on the average, with a day's rest in between. In its time, this march was an astonishing feat, especially when the difficulties in supplying armies are considered. In the 17th century, of the five months when the weather was suitable for a campaign, six to seven weeks at the outside could be used for military operations proper; the rest of the time was needed to organize the supply lines. Marlborough was followed on his march by a supply column of 2,500 wagons, containing food for the men and horses, ammunition and camping equipment. An Austrian cuirassier regiment was followed by 50 wagons, and an infantry regiment by over 150. Every soldier carried food for four days, and the wagons for 26.

The busiest troops on the march were the dragoons. Every dragoon carried a shovel, a pick or an ax, a pointed stake for tethering the horse, spare horsehoes and food for both himself and his mount. Dragoons formed the vanguard of the column, and beside protecting the main body from any possible surprise, they also prepared its passage, removed any obstacles and improvised crossings across rivers. They were accompanied by staff officers who made maps of the route, including important details on either side, and also chose the sites for camping, watering and pasture.

In general, the organization of cavalry camps during the campaign varied, depending on use and how far the enemy was. Camps in the vanguard had to be well protected, not least from the thievery of the local populace. Patrols ranged farther, guards were doubled, and men and mounts were allowed only essential relaxation. The horses were let out to graze saddled, and tethered with a long rope. The main body's camps were much more comfortable, since there was more time to prepare them. Not more than seven or eight hours a day were spent on the march, simply because the roads would not allow it. It was not uncommon for the first units of a large army to reach their new campsite while the last ones had not yet moved from the old one. Only when communication between troops was improved did marching in parallel columns become common. These columns, or even smaller groups could assemble quickly if the need arose, and prepare for battle.

When camp was made, the horses were tied in the shade, in rows, to a strong rope stretched between two trees. If there was not enough space for this, then several rows of stakes would be driven into the ground, and a horse tied to each of them. The saddle and equipment were placed on the ground in front of every horse, and, in cuirassier regiments, the rider's armor, too. When the horses were unsaddled and securely tethered, they would be given some oats in a bag hung from their head. Meanwhile, each rider would curry and comb his horse, and apply a salve to any saddle sores, finally covering the animal with a blanket to protect it from the night cold and the dew. After the oats, the animals were given water. If there was a lake or a river near the campsite, the horses would be washed after cooling down from the march. The last

to go to sleep would be the cartwrights, smiths and saddlers, who always had something to fix. If the unit remained at a site for a longer period, the horses' front legs would be fettered, and they would be allowed to graze. In case of thunderstorms, every soldier would go to calm down his horse, and wait out the storm with it, thus getting wet too, of course. Sometimes, a horse addled by the summer heat and the bites of various insects would decide to roll in the dust, taking its rider and his equipment with it, which never failed to elicit salvos of laughter from the other soldiers.

At the end of the march, in Heidelberg, Marlborough's troops were issued new boots, saddles and equipment for the horses, all of which the commander had ordered in advance. The duke had managed to conserve his men, horses and equipment through a long march,

It is not known exactly when the first war flags were used, but since 3000 B.C. flags of the widely different sizes, shapes and colors flew over the battlefields, from the streamers attached to the carved wooden standards that fluttered over the heads of the Egyptian warriors, through the Roman vexillum, the raven flag of the Vikings, the flags of the Islamic conquerors, to medieval and Renaissance heraldic pennons, banners, streamers, standards and guidons.

Toward the end of the 16th century, with the advent of the first standing armies of western Europe, two basic shapes of cavalry flags took hold: the swallow-tailed pennon, preferred by light cavalry and dragoon regiments, and the rectangular-shaped standard, with its long, tapering fly, preferred by guard and heavy cavalry regiments.

In the first half of the 17th century cavalry flags were still elaborately decorated and complicated, as troopers were recruited from the ranks of the nobility. When uniforms came into use, flags became uniform, too, bearing the symbol of the state. Because colonels were responsible for the manufacture of the regimental flags, however, there were many variations within the same army.

Two types of cavalry flags, square-shaped (standard) for the line regiments and swallow-tailed for the dragoons (guidon).

Top: Royal Regiment of Horse, Great Britain, 1688.

Below: Cavalry guidon, U.S. Cavalry, 1865.

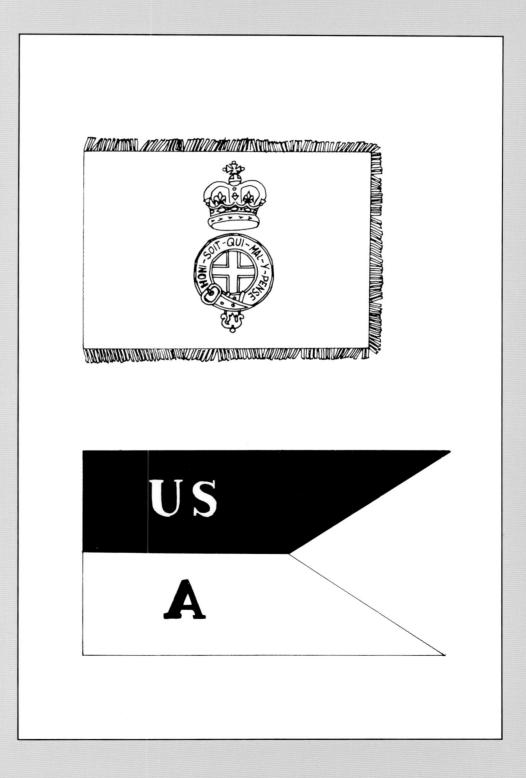

Austrian cavalry carbine with a bayonette, 1705.

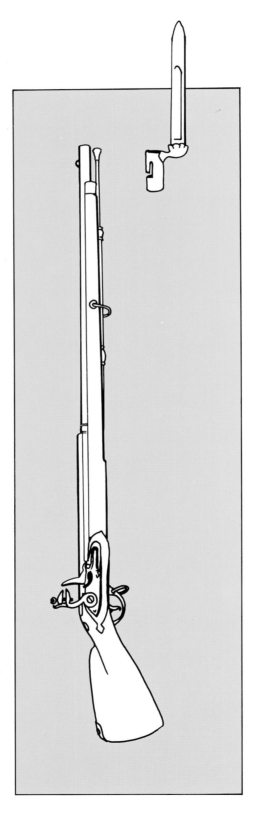

while preserving a high degree of combat readiness and morale.

The Battle of Blenheim

On the other side, when Marlborough's intentions became clear, Tallard headed with his army to Bavaria. On the march from Strasbourg to the Danube he lost a third of his 26,000 men to sickness and desertion. In August 1704 Marshal Tallard's army joined with the forces of the Bavarian Elector and Marsin. Their total strength was 39,000 infantrymen in 76 battalions, 17,000 horsemen in 151 squadrons, and 90 cannons. Adhering to the strategy of wearing out the opponent, Tallard, the commander in chief, hesitated to attack the Allied forces. He contented himself with taking and fortifying positions at Blenheim, from which he could threaten the Allied lines of communication and supply, banking on the possibility that Marlborough's removal from his base would tell in the end. Also, the previous successes and reputation of the French armed forces led him to underestimate the enemy, and he was firm in the belief that he would not be attacked. Thus, he must have been very surprised indeed when the Allied forces, formed in nine columns, emerged from the morning fog on August 13th before his positions at Blenheim. Marlborough had at his disposal 32,000 infantrymen in 64 battalions, 20,000 mounted troops in 164 squadrons and 52 cannons.

The French forces were disposed between the Schellenberg Woods and the Danube, along a 6.4 km (4 mi) front,

French Dragoon Uniform,

At the beginning of the 18th century, dragoon uniforms were very similar in all European armies. They consisted of a coat with turned-back wide sleeves, leather or woven waistcoat, knee-length trousers, woolen stockings, leather gloves, leather leggings, buckled or laced down the sides, and a tricorn hat. In grenadier units, three kinds of caps were in use: leather skull caps with a brass plate, from the Russian Empire; stiffened conical cloth caps with tassels at the top and front and rear small turnbacks, of English and Prussian pattern; and tall pointed fur caps, with a hanging cloth bag, tassels at the back and a metal plate on the front, favored by armies in the Catholic countries.

Horse troopers, cuirassiers and guards wore similar uniforms, but with heavy cavalry boots instead of the leggings. French cavalrymen used to ride in their waistcoats when marching, with the coats rolled up and tied to the saddle.

with three fortified emplacements; near the Blenheim River on the right wing, at Ober-Glaubheim in the center, and at the edge of the Lutzingen Woods on the left wing. The opposing forces were separated by a creek, the Nebel, which flowed in front of the French positions. Tallard, with 36 battalions and 68 squadrons, was on the right wing. In Blenheim, fortified with palisades, he placed 18 battalions — 16,000 of his best troops — with a reserve of nine battalions, 12 dismounted dragoon squadrons and 12 cavalry squadrons, eight of which were Gendarmerie de France. He positioned two lines of cavalry between Blenheim and Ober-Glaubheim, 23 squadrons in the first line, 21 in the second, supported by nine battalions of infantry in the rear. The left wing and center were occupied by the Bavarian Elector and Marsin, with 40 battalions and 83 squadrons. There were 14 battalions at Ober-Glaubheim, with 32 squadrons on the right, formed in two lines next to Tallard's cavalry. On the left, there were 17 battalions formed in two lines. The space to Lutzingen was taken by 51 squadrons, in the same formation, while Lutzingen itself was defended by nine battalions. Tallard decided to wait.

On the other side, Marlborough was in command of the left wing of the Allied forces, with 46 battalions and 86 squadrons, and Prince Eugène led the right wing, with 18 battalions and 78 squadrons. It was not until noon that an aide-de-camp arrived to inform Marlborough that Eugène was ready for action. The duke decided to attack Blenheim and Ober-Glaubheim while

Bavarian dragoon of 1704. Etching by A. Hoffman.

Carabinier of the Bavarian Prince Philip Regiment in 1704–1710. Etching by A. Hoffman.

Eugène tied up the Bavarians on his wing. Eugène attacked Lutzingen four times on August 13th and was repulsed with losses. At one point, a counterattack by the Bavarian cavalry was stopped only by the dogged defense of the Prussian infantry.

Meanwhile, Marlborough had launched 17 battalions of infantry formed in two lines, and supported by General Cutts's 15 squadrons, into an attack on Blenheim. The fortified French forces stopped the first line's attack. The retreating English and Hessian infantrymen were suddenly set upon by 20 squadrons of French cavalry emerging from the smoke, who would have surely cut them down had they not been stopped by the concentrated fire of the second line. In a counterattack by Cutts's squadrons, led by the Lumley's King's Dragoon Guards the French were thrown back in confusion.

At Ober-Glaubheim the situation was more serious. An Irish counterattack had pushed back the 11 Hanover battalions that Marlborough had sent forward. For a moment, the center of the Allied formation was broken. Eugène, at the duke's request, sent 21 of his reserve squadrons to plug the gap. The Irish were thrown back, and saved from utter destruction only by a timely intervention of several French and Bavarian squadrons. The situation was balanced again, due to the excellent cooperation between Prince Eugène and the Duke of Marlborough.

Without Tallard's knowledge, local commanders strengthened the defense of Blenheim with an additional nine battalions, but at the cost of weakening French lines toward Ober-Glaubheim. Seeing this, Marlborough ordered the attacks on Blenheim and Ober-Glaubheim to proceed, while Eugène continued to tie up Bavarian forces twice the strength of his own. Between Blenheim and Ober-Glaubheim Tallard had 60 squadrons and only nine battalions. The duke resolved to strike there, with a force of 23 battalions and 80 squadrons. The crossing of the muddy banks of the Nebel began. Here Tallard let slip by the opportunity to attack the disorganized Allied forces. He hesitated, and ordered the attack only when most of the cavalry and part of the infantry had already crossed the Nebel. Sixty Franco-Bavarian squadrons — nearly 7,000 men — came at a trot towards the enemy. The charge was repulsed only thanks to the good cooperation of the Allied cavalry and infantry, which decimated the first ranks of Louis's proud chevaliers with their volleys.

Marlborough then regrouped his cavalry. Eighty squadrons in four lines were ready to administer the coup de grace. A century later, Joachim Murat would arrange his forces likewise for the final and decisive blow at Eggmühl and Wagram.

Tallard disposed his 60 squadrons in two lines, with the nine battalions between them formed in infantry squares, with the cannons in front of them.

Eight thousand steel blades were drawn, and, at the sound of the trumpet, the Allied cavalry moved forward, gradually accelerating. At thirty paces, French salvos mowed down the first line. For an instant, everything stopped. It was the right moment for a counterattack. Tallard ordered his cavalry to charge, but the tired and disheartened horsemen did not move. The last chance to turn the tide had gone by. Marlborough's horsemen swooped down, and the battle was soon over. Tallard's mounted troops were in flight, and the nine infantry battalions were cut down where they stood. Tallard withdrew to Blenheim, where he was captured together with 10,000 troops, while Marsin and the Bavarian Elector retreated to Hochstädt. The French and Bavarians had 28,000 dead and wounded. Men drowned trying to swim the Danube accounted for part of the casualties. The Allies suffered losses of 12,584 men.

The Battle of Blenheim was the most important clash of the War of the Spanish Succession, radically changing the situation in Germany. The Austrians occupied Bavaria, and the French were driven back to the Rhine.

Blenheim was an example of a frontal clash with hardly any possibilities of maneuvering or flanking. In such cases, the first army to be left with no reserves lost the battle. Marlborough managed to tie up superior enemy forces in places of little relevance to the outcome, deployed his cavalry reserve at the crucial moment in order to achieve an advantage, and won.

For operations in the Netherlands, Louis XIV tended to choose Marshal

Following double-spread: French grenadier of the Guard in a skimrish with horse in hand so that he can mount quickly; beginning of the 18th century.

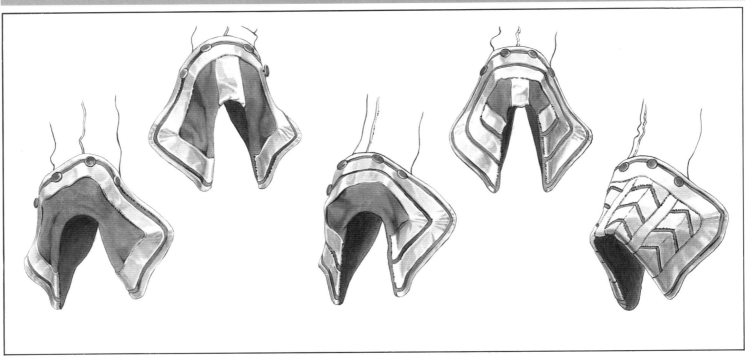

Rank insignia of the French grenadiers of the Guard; beginning of the 17th century.

Villeroy to command his troops when France had to face the British infantry – the English and Scottish regiments, well-known for their discipline, training, fighting spirit and bravery. Villeroy organized his positions with more depth, and with immediate support from cavalry and artillery in order to withstand the British onslaught. Once the pressure on his positions was relieved, and the enemy in retreat, the reserve cavalry went into action, and that was when the French came into their own.

At Blenheim, the fear of Allied infantry was present, too. Although the fortified places were defended by numerically superior troops, they were bolstered by battalions from the reserve at the first sign of anything remotely resembling a serious attack. For Tallard it was convenient that the enemy wear himself out in attacks against the earth fortifications and wooden palisades defended by a double line of French infantry, so that he could seek decisive action on terrain where he could put his mounted troops to effective use. Therefore, he left the defense of inhabited places to the local commanders, who would needlessly deplete his reserve, while he took personal command of the cavalry. At

the beginning of the battle, he lined up 76 squadrons, with 12 more in reserve, on the 3,000 m (2 mi) long front between Blenheim and Ober-Glaubheim, which gave him a strength of 10,000 sabers in a place where the configuration of the ground was suitable for a cavalry charge. Tallard had mounted troops to which hardly anyone could measure up. They were masters of the open ground, much like the German tank units at the beginning of World War II.

Marlborough could count on his unbreachable wall of infantry, behind which his cavalry could shelter and regroup in moments of crisis. He was evidently banking on this when he sent English infantry and squadrons of Dragoon Guards across the Nebel. As it turned out, he was right to do so. His infantry and cavalry cooperated well, and the French charge was repulsed, which was the decisive moment of the battle. In the key charge after that, Marlborough could pit 80 fresh squadrons against the demoralized and tired French and Bavarian forces of 60 squadrons. Tallard wondered why his chevaliers did not charge at the order, and saw that as the reason for his defeat. He noticed, for instance, that eight of his Gendarmerie squadrons fled before five squadrons of Palmes's Dragoon

Guards, and accused them of giving the victory to the Allies.

Marlborough sent 8,000 horsemen into the attack, more then half of them Dutch. The multinational composition of his forces made commanding and communications difficult, which adds to the greatness of his achievement. Denmark, Hanover, Württemberg and Hesse had also sent their units. There were relatively few English troops — only 19 battalions of infantry and 15 squadrons of cavalry. On the opposing side, Eugène also had a nationally varied army, with Italians, Hungarians, Croatians and Bohemians fighting alongside Austrians and units from other German dutchies.

At Blenheim, Louis XIV lost 171 standards (cavalry flags) and 129 colors (infantry flags), and, which probably hurt him more, the reputation of France

as the leading world power. The chance to regain it came in 1706, at Ramillies, 20 miles from Brussels, but it only cost him an additional 80 standards and colors.

The defeat of Villeroy and the Bavarian Elector at the Battle of Ramillies heading the combined French, Bavarian and Spanish forces, at the hands of the Duke of Marlborough followed a similar scenario. The front, 3,000 m (2 mi) long, was between Taviers and Ramillies. Villeroy did not underestimate his opponent, and was much more cautious than Tallard. Facing his 68 squadrons, among them the elite Maison du Roi, Marlborough had 48 Dutch and 21 Danish squadrons. The 15,000 horsemen clashed violently along the whole front. The red and dark blue uniforms of the Maison du Roi, the dark blue of the Royal Cavalerie, the gray of the French line cavalry, the

Below: French cavalry sword with Walloon hilt; first half of the 18th century.

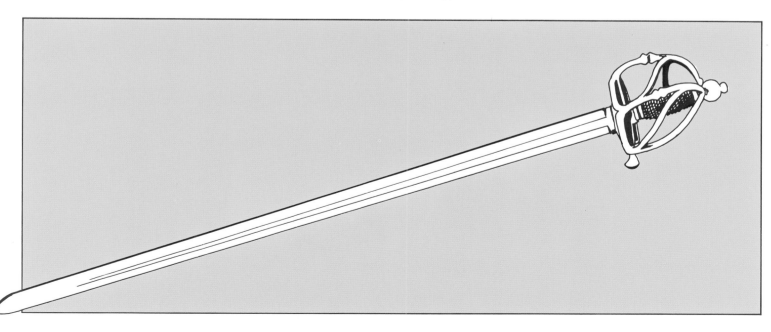

Opposite: Piedmont-dragoon, beginning of 18th century. Cavalry regiments of Piedmont and Savoy fought under the command of Prince Eugène of Savoy for the Austrian throne.

green uniforms of the Spanish dragoons, the blue ones of the Bavarians mixed with the gray and red uniforms of the Dutch and Danish forces. Even though they were initially in an unfavorable position, and under attack from two sides, the Maison du Roi troops fought valiantly and with great discipline. With firepower and cold steel they broke the Dutch right wing, which threatened the whole Allied formation. Aware of the crisis, the duke urgently demanded that Orkney send over his 39 squadrons, even at the risk of weakening his right wing, which had tied up half of Villeroy's forces, and personally rushed off to rally the Dutch troops, putting his life at stake. The squadrons, led by the white-uniformed Hanoverians, soon arrived and joined the fray, followed by the Dutch.

Allied superiority was beginning to tell, and the Franco-Bavarian line began to give way and bend toward Ramillies. Tardily, Villeroy noticed that the enemy wing was no longer a threat to him, and that there were only 15 English squadrons there, while the remaining 108 Allied squadrons were engaging his 68! When he gave the order to move his 50 squadrons from the flank, it was too late.

The front was soon breached, and Villeroy and the Elector, with their army routed, were in full flight. Marlborough sent 15 English squadrons on a 20 km (12 mi) long chase, in which they captured several thousand men and large quantities of equipment.

Pursuit of the defeated enemy after the battle was not common; Marlborough was one of the first to introduce this tactic, together with the energetic King of Sweden, Charles XII, who became well known because of it. The warehouse system of supply did not allow for long chases, and it would not be until the French revolutionary wars that the enemy was pursued for several days, or even weeks.

Characteristics and Tactics in the Early 18th Century

In the War of the League of Augsburg and the War of the Spanish Succession cavalry was usually on the flanks of the infantry in the general battle order so as not to interfere with its line of fire, and to protect its sides; alternately, it lined up behind the infantry in smaller formations, to give it local support. Cavalry started its attack at the infantry's pace. Only at 500 paces from the enemy lines was it allowed to break away and attack the opponent's mounted troops. Nevertheless, it tended to do so earlier, so as not to suffer passively under artillery fire. After a successful attack, several squadrons would chase the defeated cavalry off the battlefield, while the rest fell upon the flanks and the rear of the infantry.

At Malplaquet, in 1709, 30,000 horsemen fought a monumental cavalry battle, in which, after several changes of luck, the Anglo-Austrian forces breached the French battle order, and forced them into general retreat. The battle at Malplaquet also holds the

English standard of the Royal Regiment of Horse; beginning of the 18th century.

59

Ordre de Bataille
of the Allied Cavalry of
the Duke of Marlborough,
Flanders 1707

	I line	sq.	II line	sq.
RIGHT WING	DESTAINS		HACKEBOR	
	Stair, Scots Dragoons	2	Soenfelt	4
	Ross, Irish Dragoons	2	Anspach	4
	PALMES		Hunnerbein	4
	Lumley, Guard Dragoons	3	SPAEN	
	Cadogan, Dragoons	2	Leibrigein	3
	Schomberg, Dragoons	2	Croon Prince	3
	Palmes, Dragoons	2	Schlipenbach	3
	Wood, Dragoons	2	Heiden	2
	PENTZ		Catt	2
	Schulenburg	2	PHUDUC	
	Pentz	2	Beauvinghem	3
	Reden	2	Saint Laurent	2
	Leibrigen	2	Fréchapelle	2
	Von Bülow, Dragoons	2	Wicht	2
	CHANCLOS		Vinais	4
	Chanclos	2		38
	Glinstra	2		
	MATTA			
	Obdam	2		
	Van der Nath	4		
		37		
CENTER	**52 inf. battalions**		**42 inf. battalions**	
	BAUDITZ		DU PORTAIL	
	Guard Dragoons	5	Dopst	4
	Schippenbach	1	SCHMETTAU	
	Bauditz	4	Schmettau	4
	C. MAURICE		KRALING	
	Carabiniers	4	Frisian Guards	1
	Holland Guards	1	Prince of Orange	2
	Blue Guards	2	Oger	1
	POSAREN		Kraling	1
	Tilly	2	Hessen-Homburg	3
	Dompré	2	Athlone	2
	EEK		GROVESTEIN	
LEFT WING	Eastfrisien	2	Calock	2
	Eek	2	Prince of Auvergne	1
	BRISSELLWITZ		Govestein	2
	Rochfort	2	PAAL	
	Erbac	2	Paal	2
	Wittenhorst	1	Dreisberg	2
	WÜRTTEMBERG		Humderbein	2
	Württemberg	2	MILCKAU	
	Schmettau	2	Termager	3
	Obdam	2	Brockdorff	2
		36	Württemberg	2
			Dewitz	2
			Rantzau	2
			Württemberg Oels, Dragoons	2
				42
RESERVE			**4 inf. battalions**	
			BROCKDORFF	
			Brockdorff	4
			Schmettau	2
			Rantzau	2
			Lisbrigen	2
			Württemberg	1
			Oels, Dragoons	3
				14

Ordre de Bataille of the French-allied Cavalry of Vendôme, Flanders 1707

RIGHT WING

CENTER

LEFT WING

RESERVE

I line	sq.	II line	sq.
DE ROURE		ROSEN	
Mestre de Camp Général,		Egmont	2
Dragoons	3	Dauphin Étranger	3
VILLIERS		Rosen	2
Aquaviva, Dragoons	2	FRESIN	
St. Chaumont, Dragoons	3	La Motte	2
LE VIDAMME		Fresin	2
La Reine, Dragoons	3	Marcillac	2
Reisbourg, Dragoons	2	D'Oblestein	2
L'Éspare, Dragoons	3	Dalreau	2
BEAUVEAU		Roye	2
Maison du Roi	8	LOCATOIRE	
Gendarmerie	8	Locatoire	2
CHELODET		Coulanges	2
Du Maine	3	Bracque	2
St. Aignan	2	UFEZ	
Marteville	2	Aubusson	2
MIMEUSE		Matignon	
Fontaines	2	Royal Piémont	3
Toulouse	3		32
Colonel Général	3		
	47		
55 inf. battalions		**51 inf. battalions**	
DE NILT		BARENTIN	
Royal Étranger	3	Condé	3
Royal Roussillon	2	Barentin	2
LIVRY		Biron	2
Orléans	3	ACOSTA	
Desmartes	2	Deselainvilliers	2
Livry	2	Ligondez	2
BERINGHEN		Acosta	2
Beringhen	3	CHATELEURS	
Forsat	2	Cherizy	2
Tourot	2	La Tour	2
SANTIGNY		Paon	2
Arco Cologne	2	DU COSTA	
Poth	3	Costa	3
Cuirassiers Arco	3	Carabiniers de Montauban	3
CLOYE		MORTANY	
Carabiniers of Bavaria	6	Le Bretéche	2
Guard Carabiniers of Bavaria	1	Belleford	2
Guard Grenadiers of Bavaria	1	Royal Cravattes	2
Archers of Bavaria	2		31
Guard of Spain	2		
CHASSONVILLE			
Chassonville	2		
L'Épiray	3		
PASTEUR		**17 inf. battalions**	
Pasteur, Dragoons	2		
Vasse, Dragoons	3	PIGNATELLI	
Le Roi, Dragoons	3	Bretagne, Dragoons	3
Nautas, Dragoons	2	Pignatelli	2
	54	KRACHERBERG	
		Royal Allemand	2
		Drachot	2
		CANO	
		Belaccueil	2
		Tarente	2
		Cano	2
		Hussards	2
			17

Duke of Marlborough leading the attack of his cavalry against the French musketeers at the Battle of Ramillies in 1706. Painting by R. Caton.

Opposite: Officer of the Austrian Horse Grenadiers. Officers, like grenadier privates, were armed with muskets or carbines of better quality.

record for most squadrons engaged during the battle, with 260 French against 300 Allied, meaning nearly 60,000 horsemen in the field!

In wars at the and of the 17th and beginning of the 18th century, controlling various phases of a battle along a front several miles wide, was very complicated. A picture of the whole situation had to be pieced together from the reports arriving from the sectors and the lower commanders, and on the basis of this picture, decisions, often crucial, had to be made. Because of the cannon smoke, one could see very little, or sometimes nothing at all. Therefore, a system of fast and accurate reporting was of the utmost importance. The Duke of Marlborough had organized a service of couriers on foot and horseback, for which the best runners and riders were picked. His almost instant reaction and fast introduction of reserves at Ramillies won the day. Eugène of Savoy, on the other hand, solved this problem by often being in the front lines himself. Small wonder, then, that he was wounded by musket fire six times in his career, even though a musket's effective range was no more than a hundred paces!

Marlborough and Eugène had more in common than an obvious military talent. Both had begun their careers as commanders of regiments of horse – John Churchill in the King's Dragoon Guards, and Eugène in the Kufstein dragoons. John Churchill served for a while with the greatest military leader of his time, the French Marshal Turenne, and Prince Eugène under Ludwig von Baden, who had the reputation of the foremost expert in fortifications in the Austrian army. Both men supported the idea of cavalry attacking at a run, with drawn sabers, but Eugène could not overcome the resistance he encountered within the Austrian army, so only Marlborough carried it out. Finally, they had a common enemy, Louis XIV.

In the War of the Spanish Succession, the French army's list of cavalry regiments was by far the longest, with regiments of the line numbering over 90! Besides, Spain contributed 10 line units and three dragoon regiments, and, from 1705, the hussar regiment De la Muerte, and Bavaria a regiment of Household Cavalry, four cuirassier regiments, three dragoon regiments and a company of hussars. England (from 1707, Great Britain) increased the number of its regiments by seven, so the total was six troops of Household Cavalry, 11 regiments of Horse, and 16 dragoon regiments. Austria had 20 cuirassier, 12 dragoon and five hussar regiments, with about 30,000 horsemen. Saxony contributed four cuirassier regiments to the Austrian forces.

The term "regiment" should be treated with caution when discussing this

Fur cap characteristic of grenadiers of Catholic armies; beginning of the 18th century.

period, because, in terms of number of men, its meaning varied widely. English regiments of Horse, for example, numbered about 350 men, and dragoon regiments nearly 500. The Danish Von Labat dragoon regiment had 1,075 horsemen, while the Piedmont dragoons had only a third of that – 294 men. Thus, a Danish colonel could have under his command more men than a general in Marlborough's army.

In Flanders, the duke had seven English regiments, with a total of 15 squadrons, which was the equal of two Austrian cuirassier or dragoon regiments, which had six squadrons each. It is interesting to note that a century later the English and Austrian armies still had approximately the same number of men in regiments, with 362 and 1,000 troopers, respectively. The explanation lies in the English insistence on coordination between cavalry and infantry on the level of regiments. A smaller number of horsemen meant greater mobility, and also enabled a cavalry regiment to shelter behind an infantry battalion or regiment. An Austrian regiment was an army unto itself, operating in conjunction with the rest of the cavalry.

At the time of the War of the Spanish Succession (1707 – 1709), no unit larger than the regiment existed on a permanent basis. Generally, a certain number of squadrons or regiments would form an ad hoc unit for the purpose of a battle or campaign. Such a composite unit would be commanded by one of the colonels or a staff general. An example of this type of organization is

the *Ordre de Bataille* for the Flanders campaign of 1707 (see the chart).

Developments in the German States

At the beginning of the 18th century, the German states had mostly recovered from the ravages of the Thirty Years War. Industry and trade were growing rapidly, though economic expansion on the whole was slower than in England, France or Holland. As for the state of development of military power in the Reich in this period, there were no major changes. There still existed a large number of scattered, small, and generally ill-equipped and poorly armed forces. For all practical purposes, the defense of the divided Germany depended on the independent armies of Austria, Saxony, Bavaria, Hanover and Brandenburg — after 1701, Prussia. The ascendancy of Louis XIV, and defeat in wars against him were the main motives for reform of German military power, or *Reichskriegsheer,* the system under which ten districts were supposed to put at the emperor's disposal 12,000 horsemen, 28,000 infantrymen and 23 cannons. The dukes still sent detachments of their forces to the emperor for the military actions of the Reich, but sporadically. In order to strengthen their own absolute power, and for material gain, too, the dukes formed alliances with countries outside the Reich. In the War of the Spanish Succession, Bavaria and Cologne fought on France's side, and Hesse-Kassel hired out 8,000 soldiers to England and 3,000 to Holland in 1702. England secured its

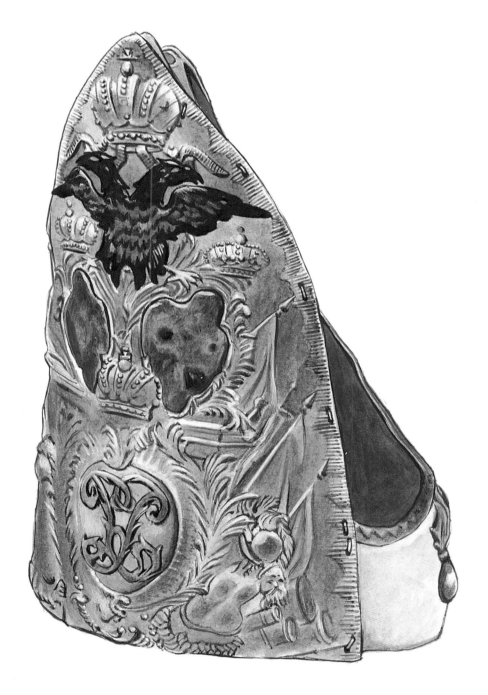

Miter cap with metal front plate characteristic of grenadiers of Protestant armies; beginning of 18th century.

65

Opposite: Swedish Trabant Garde. Of the 146 excellent horsemen that went to war with Charles XII in 1716, only 14 returned.

influence in Hanover, and later in Brunswick, with money. Its military-financial partnership with Hanover was as traditional as its enmity with France, and dated back to the battle of Neerwinden.

German Emperor Leopold I conferred the title of Elective Duke on Ernst August in 1692. Georg Ludwig, the duke's son, became King of Great Britain in 1714, ruling as George I. With his ascension to the British throne, Great Britain and Hanover entered into a personal union, which lasted until 1837. In the War of the Spanish Succession, Hanover gave Marlborough 16,000 excellent soldiers, and partly fulfilled its obligations to the Reich with a small force that fought under Ludwig von Baden.

As in other German principalities, units of the line were named after their commanders, so a regiment's history can only be followed by its number. Hanover's army list in 1707 included a cavalry regiment of Gardes de Corps, six regiments of the line — De la Croix de Fréchapelle, Pentz, Schulenburg, Saint Laurent, Voight, Reden — and four dragoon regiments — Bothmer, von Bülow, Eltz and Villars.

The best available evidence suggests that the first standing infantry troop in Germany was formed in Brunswick in 1605. From 1688, this principality also formed regular cavalry regiments. Its army list of 1700 has three white-uniformed regiments of Horse — Erbprinz August Wilhelm, De Bonac and von Fullen — and three red-

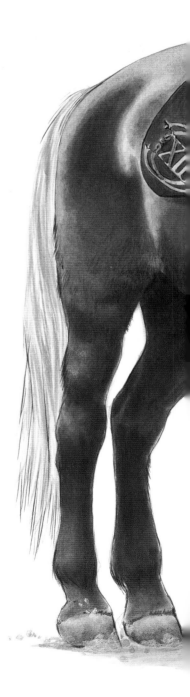

Charles XII (1682 – 1718), King of Sweden, dressed in the uniform of the Trabant Garde.

uniformed dragoon regiments – Prinz Ludwig Rudolph, von Klengel and von Schleinitz.

The Great Northern War (1700 – 1721)

Almost simultaneously with the War of the Spanish Succession, the so-called Northern War was fought from 1700 to 1721, in which Sweden faced Russia, Saxony, Denmark and Poland.

The cause of the war lay in the desire of Peter I, Emperor of Russia, to pull his country out of its medieval backward-ness by modernizing the economy and administration. The road to modernization led through the Baltic ports, held by Sweden. Denmark, on the other hand, wanted to recover territories lost in the previous war with Sweden, while August II, Duke of Saxony, and from 1697 King of Poland, wanted to force the Swedes out of Poland, and wrest Livonia from their control.

The Swedish warrior-king Charles XII was one of the great military leaders of the period, ranking with Marlborough and Prince Eugène, and perhaps the most interesting personality of them all. Compared with other monarchs of his time, he lived frugally and rationally, with the Spartans of ancient Greece as his models. His country had a long and illustrious military tradition, and he himself was a man of considerable talent in this field, which was not common among his contemporary fellow rulers.

Charles XII realized that the mixing of cavalry and infantry was not giving the expected results, and soon abolished this practice. He made cavalry into an independent arm of the military, and the main one at that. His cavalry attacked everything that could be attacked on the battlefield, from enemy infantry and cavalry to artillery emplacements, fortified positions, inhabited places and bridges, deciding the battles practically by itself. Aware of the importance of speed and impact, he reinstituted the charge with cold steel, allowing the use of firearms only in exceptional situations. He trained his squadrons of 125 horsemen, formed in two lines, to attack at a fast trot in the Carolean style — a wedge formation with men riding boot-behind-boot. The final 150 paces were crossed at a gallop.

At the beginning of the war, Charles XII had a land army of 13,000 horsemen and 32,000 infantrymen. His plan was to beat Denmark, Poland and Saxony first, and then to turn on Russia. With the help of the English fleet, he landed 15,000 men in Denmark around June 1700, and forced it into a peace agreement with a swift campaign on Copenhagen. Meanwhile, August II had besieged Riga with a Polish-Saxon army, and a Russian force of 37,000 men encircled 2,000 Swedes at Narva, a fortress near the Gulf of Finland. After

Denmark withdrew from the war, August II retreated. Charles decided to attack the Russians at Narva, with about 12,000 men.

At Narva, located on a bend of the river of the same name, the Russians had built three lines of fortifications. One faced the fort, and served a dual purpose — as starting point for attacks against the fort, and as defense against sorties by its garrison. It was backed by two lines of redoubts, palisades, trenches and earthworks that served as protection from attacks by an army trying to break the blockade. The siege artillery was between the inner and outer fortifications, as well as the camps for men and horses and the stores of food and ammunition. The Russian attacks were unsuccessful due to poor commanding, insufficient artillery support and losses from cold and disease.

After a forced march over snow, Charles's three columns reached the Russian positions. He decided to attack at once. At the center of his formation, he placed the field artillery, with eight battalions of infantry on each side. He placed six squadrons on the left, seven on the right, and four in reserve. All told, he had 2,500 horsemen. The most prominent were the Royal Yeomanry Guards in their blue uniforms with gilt facings. Charles XII wore a plain blue uniform. The king was himself colonel in chief of the corps, its captain-lieutenant had the rank of major-general of cavalry, the lieutenants equaled colonels, the corporals were the equivalent of majors and the troopers cavalry captains. This royal life guard went through many hard battles with Charles XII. Of the 147 men who went to war in 1700, only 14 came back in 1716. After the king's death, the unit was disbanded.

Charles XII gave the order to attack the Russian positions on November 20, 1700. The cavalry and infantry started forward through the thick snow that had begun to fall in the meantime. Emerging from the snowstorm, the Swedish squadrons trampled over the earthworks and artillery positions, and broke through the Russian lines. In the ensuing melee, 7,000 Imperial soldiers fell, and over 10,000 were captured. The Swedes had 2,000 casualties, including 700 dead, largely due to the tenacious resistance of two senior guard regiments, the Preobrazhenski and the Semenovski infantry.

Peter I learned several lessons from this defeat, and proceeded to reorganize his army. In 1698 he had drowned in blood the uprising of the Streltzi (sharpshooters), and disbanded their units. In their place he formed a standing force of 27 infantry and two dragoon regiments. At Narva, he found out the hard way that they were no match for the experienced and disciplined Swedes. One of the main problems facing Peter was the relative inexperience and small size of the officer corps. To improve the situation, he hired a large number of foreign officers, most of them Germans. Until 1708, when the units were given provincial names, they were called after their colonels. The first two dragoon

regiments were called Schneewanz and Goltz.

Russian dragoon regiments had ten squadrons, each with 120 men. From 1704, a grenadier squadron of 140 men was added. Because of a lack of heavy horses, Peter I organized only dragoon cavalry. In 1711, he separated the mounted grenadiers from the dragoon regiments, and formed three independent grenadier regiments. Until 1707, when Peter engaged the services of a squadron of Serbian hussars, formed of refugees from territories under Turkish occupation, the role of light cavalry was filled only by semi-regular regiments of Cossacks.

In 1709, when a Russian army organized along European principles defeated a Swedish force at Poltava, Peter's army list had 53 infantry and 32 dragoon regiments — a total of 90,000 foot soldiers and 38,000 mounted troops!

Confronted with the vast expanses of Russia, which were his theater of operations, Peter I formed flying columns, combined forces of 6 – 7,000 horsemen and 3 – 4,000 infantrymen who rode on wagons, or, in winter, on sleighs. One of these columns defeated the Swedish general Loewenhaupt at Lesna in 1708. Loewenhaupt, with reinforcements of 11,000 men (not counting drivers) and 7,000 wagons of supplies, was heading for Staroduba, where he was to join the main Swedish force — 35,000 men under Charles XII, en route to Moscow. Instead, he brought Charles 6,000 exhausted men, no supplies and no artillery. The loss of the supplies, an invitation from the

Cossack Ataman Mazeppa to the Swedes to spend the winter in the Ukraine and attack Moscow together in the spring, and a belief that he would be able to draw Turkey into the war against Russia, all influenced Charles's decision to go south.

After the defeat at Narva, the Russians avoided direct clashes with the Swedish army, limiting their activities to surprise attacks against isolated detachments. To wage this kind of war, Peter I formed two large cavalry formations, later to become a Russian specialty, one composed of 11 dragoon regiments under General Menschikov, the other of ten dragoon regiments under General Golitzin. Their task was to follow the movements of the Swedish army from afar, destroy supplies of food, to impede by their presence the deployment of the Swedish troops, which then had to move in a group, making marching, camping and life in the field generally harder, and to destroy, if the chance came, any stray unit. At the river Gorodna, Menschikov surprised two dragoon regiments and annihilated them, which made Charles even more cautious.

Mazeppa had promised Charles XII 20,000 horsemen for the march on Moscow. But an attack by Peter I on the fortified city of Baturin decimated his forces, and only 2,000 Cossacks joined the Swedes. During the Swedish army's wintering in the Ukraine, it became clear that Turkey would not join in the war. So, in the spring of 1709, Charles decided to move on to Kharkov, and thence to Moscow. His plans came to

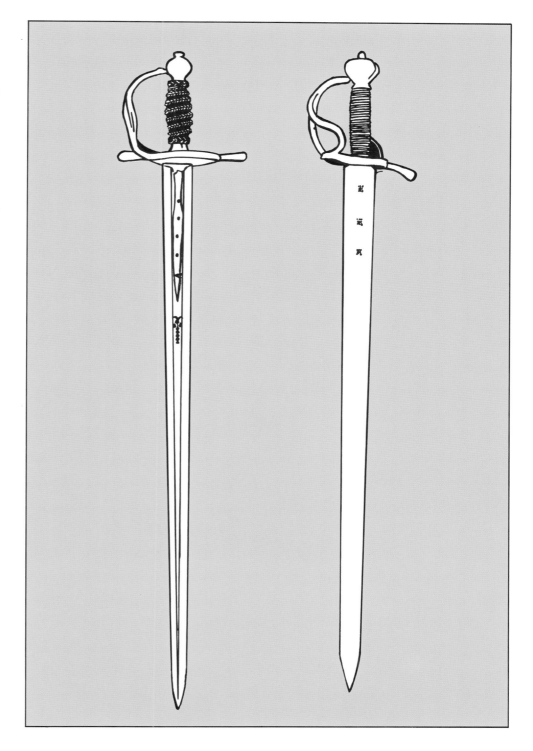

nought, for he was routed by a superior Russian army at Poltava. Charles barely managed to escape to Turkey.

Poltava was the Swedes' Blenheim — a decisive battle in which a long-standing myth of invincibility was debunked. Over 330 captured Swedish Standards, Guidons and Colors were shown at the victory parade in Moscow. After the battle of Poltava, Sweden concentrated on its own defense, and the end of the Northern War in 1721 signaled its passage into the ranks of second-rate world powers.

The Cossacks

For the Cossacks, Mazeppa's defeat at Poltava meant the end of their freedom. Peter I conquered their territory and subjugated them. From that time on, the Cossacks provided the Russian

Emperors with a large number of light horsemen for their war campaigns, and the defense of the borders against Tartars and Turks in peacetime.

Cossacks belonged to many nationalities, Slavic and non-Slavic, and were, for the most, escaped serfs, who inhabited the free steppes between the Caspian Sea and the lower Dnieper after the destruction of the state of Kiev by the Tartars. Mixing with the local populace, they settled along the great rivers Don and Dnieper. They formed military alliances in order to survive, and erected fortified settlements at suitable places on the banks of the rivers. In time, larger Cossack alliances were formed, which controlled whole swaths of territory in the border area between Russia, Poland and Turkey. Each of these alliances was, in fact, a small military state, called a *voiska,* and named after the territory it covered. In

Battle of Poltava in 1709. The most severe defeat of the Swedish cavalry under Charles XII. Contemporary etching.

Opposite: Russian dragoon. Under Peter I the line cavalry consisted only of dragoon regiments; beginning of the 18th century.

73

Russian two-headed eagle, common symbol used by cavalry regiments in tzarist Russia.

the middle of the 16th century, we have the Zaporozhian voiska on the Dnieper, and the Don voiska on the Don.

The Cossacks often fought among themselves, but when they were not occupied with that, they used their fast and light horses to attack Muscovite, Tartar and Turkish traders and despoil whole regions, while not one of the neighboring states could stop them. Moscow, Poland and Lithuania made use of various promises to lure the Cossacks into border service. They would keep their self-government, and, for a certain fee, have a military obligation to the state.

In the middle of the 17th century, Russia engaged the services of 20,000 Cossacks, for three rubles and 2,400 kg (5,280 lb.) of rye and oats a year per man. On the southern borders of Russia, the Cossacks were organized into the Akhtirsky, Sumsky, Kharkovsky, Izyumsky, Chernigovsky, Seversky and Kievsky cavalry regiments. Every regiment was an administrative and military territorial center. It was divided

into *sotni* of a hundred horsemen each. A Cossack assembly chose the atamans, who exercised civil and military authority for a year. At first, Peter only approved the choice of atamans, but after appointed them himself. At the end of the 17th century, the Cossacks were getting five rubles a year and land for their services.

In peacetime, when payments from the state were often delayed, Cossacks would raid the neighboring territories to replenish their supplies. As can be imagined, this rather complicated relations between Russia and its neighbors.

Cossacks rode small, hardy horses, about 14.5 hands tall, needing very little food, and very resistant to the harsh Russian climate. They were armed with a spear, saber and composite bow. Toward the end of the 17th century they also started using firearms. In combat they rode in the lava formation. At a sign, they would ride out as a group, and then deploy in a single wide line, using the expanses of the steppe, tending to envelop any enemy cavalry that attacked in a tight formation. Larger formations of Cossacks attacked in several lines, with two or three sotni in each. During the attack they would let out bellicose screams.

At the end of his rule, Peter I had 45,000 regular cavalry troops, and could raise about 40,000 Cossacks in case of war.

Saxony

Saxony simultaneously took part in the War of the Spanish Succession, where it

had six infantry and four cuirassier regiments at Blenheim in 1704, and four infantry and three cuirassier regiments at Malplaquet in 1709, and in the Northern War, in which it was repeatedly defeated by Charles XII between 1702 and 1706, and its ruler, August II, was forced to relinquish the crown of Poland.

These two wars, and previous conflicts with Turkey, had emptied its war chest, so a curious event was recorded in 1717. At a meeting between Prussian King Friedrich Wilhelm I and August II, the Duke of Saxony suggested a swap: he offered to exchange a collection of priceless porcelain vases and dishes for 600 Prussian dragoons and cuirassiers. Friedrich Wilhelm I accepted the offer, and his men marched off to Saxony.

After the Northern War, August II decided to reorganize his standing army, and in 1732 Saxony's army list looked like this: a squadron of Chevaliergarde, a squadron of Grand-Mousquetaires (similar to the Trabants of Charles XII, where ordinary horsemen had the rank of captains of line cavalry), a regiment of Gardes de Corps consisting of six squadrons, seven regiments of cuirassiers – Kronprinz, Prinz Friedrich, Promnitz, Nassau, Polenz, Brand and Criegern – with three squadrons each, a regiment of Grenadiere zu Pferde of two squadrons, and four dragoon regiments of three squadrons each – Arnstädt, Goldacker, Chevalier de Saxe and Katte.

The cuirassier and dragoon regiments had about 450 riders each.

Saxon cavalry standard made in 1709.

Opposite: Saxon officer of the von Polenz Cuirassier Regiment, 1733. It was one of the seven cuirassier regiments in the service of Augustus III.

Saxon Cuirassier Regiment, 1733

STAFF:

Colonel	1
Lieutenant Colonel	1
Major	1
Quartermaster	1
Adjutant	1

COMPANY:

Captain	1
2nd Captain	1
1st Lieutenant	1
2nd Lieutenant	1
Cornet	1
Sergeants	2
Standard Bearer	1
Quartermaster-Sergeant	1
Saddlemaker	1
Corporals	4
Trumpeters	2
Troopers	80

The regiment has three squadrons with two companies each.

Chapter Three: New Powers on the Stage

1735 – 1763

In their onslaught on Europe at the beginning of the 16th century, the Turks defeated Hungary, which lost its independence and broke up into three parts. One of these parts was annexed by Turkey, another by Austria, while the third one crowned its own king, and existed for a while as a sovereign state named Upper Hungary. Part of the Hungarian nobility recognized the authority of Vienna in the hope that Austria would help them in their struggle against the Turks; another faction converted to Protestantism, seized the estates of the Church, and fought openly against the Hapsburgs, who were trying to subdue them. Owing to superior military power and more ample finances, by the beginning of the 18th century Austria succeeded in making former Hungarian territory its own. Nevertheless, open rebellion and conflicts did not cease.

In the great Turkish march on Vienna in 1683, the flag of Mohammed was followed by several thousand Hungarian light horsemen, who, together with the Tartars, devastated the Austrian lands. European rulers, notably Louis XIV, supported the rebellious nobles in order to weaken Austria from within. Due to this situation, the French and Prussian courts welcomed Hungarian nobles who were opposed to the Hapsburgs.   .

For nearly three hundred years, from the mid-15th century on, Hungary and Turkey had a common border. A strong Eastern influence was therefore apparent in Hungary in the codes of

Engraving from the first half of the 18th century depicting an Austrian hussar colonel.

Hungarian hussar in the service of France; beginning of 18th century.

dress and war — especially in the cavalry. This influence ranged from the choice of equipment, manner of riding and the breeding of horses to the excessive adornment typical of the opulent Arab culture. Riding equipment, richly decorated saddles and saddle cloth, filigreed sabers and leopard and tiger skins were procured in the East, by theft or by commerce, while the West offered firearms and shiny buckles and ornaments. History records the fact that the Hungarian nobility of Augsburg gave up, in the course of only one year, several tens of thousands of heads of cattle in barter for arms and ornaments.

Hungary's Light Horsemen

Hungary is a mostly flat country, once covered for hundreds of miles on end by pastures and woods. It was country ideally suited for the breeding of horses and cattle. The constant danger of Turkish attacks forced the populace to cattle breeding, because cattle was something that you could take into the woods with you. On the other hand, the Turks on their forays stole the livestock and led the people off into slavery but never touched the vineyards, plum orchards and pigs, because their religion forbade them alcohol and pork. Hungary therefore never lacked for good horses, meat, brandy and wine.

This, then, was the society that gave birth to the light horsemen whom every European ruler wanted to have in his army. The Hungarian noble was

arrogant, stubborn and constantly opposed to authority, and took badly to any sort of discipline, while enjoying good food, wine, and frequent duels and fights. He especially appreciated good horses, skill at riding and good swordsmanship. The annual fairs held in the free royal cities were known for epic drinking and mass fights that regularly resulted in numerous deaths and woundings.

There were several ways of demonstrating mastery in handling the sword. One was to pass the blade through the flame of a candle as quickly as possible, without putting it out. If the blade was even fractionally inclined, the resulting turbulence would extinguish the flame. Another one was to cut a candle in half, but in such a way that the upper part would remain in its original position, as if the candle were still whole. All this served to demonstrate the speed and precision of stroke that could serve to sever the head or the arm of an enemy.

The Hungarian light horsemen also competed in performing various stunts and exploits on horseback. Favorite occasions for these were provided by the wedding processions and honor guards of certain high nobles and rulers. They would ride at the head of the column at full gallop, standing on the horses' croups, or throwing their caps into the air and catching them. If a cap fell, they would pick it up effortlessly, only to throw it into the air again; all this was accompanied by shouting and whistling.

Similar in character and behavior to the Hungarian light horsemen — hussars —

were the Cossacks and the Polish light horsemen. It is interesting that Europe first accepted the hussars at the beginning of the 18th century, the Polish light horsemen – the uhlans – at the end of the same century, and the Cossacks at the beginning of the 19th. At first they were naturalized foreign units serving in the armies of various countries, while later on local units modeled on them were formed.

There are several theories as to how the Hungarian horsemen came to be called hussars. Some sources date back to Byzantine times, but the one that appears to have greatest claim to the truth comes from the period of early feudalism in Hungary, when one man out of twenty had to be sent to the king in case of war; in Hungarian *husz* means twenty, so hussar is the name given to that twentieth man.

Austrian hussars played a distinguished part in the War of the League of Augsburg and the War of the Spanish Succession. In fact, they were Hungarian horsemen loyal to the Hapsburgs, serving in the regular regiments of the Austrian army or the regiments of some high nobles. Today, we could classify their way of fighting as a kind of guerrilla warfare. Their actions included ambushes, surprise attacks, reconnaissance with armed skirmishes, destruction of supply lines and magazines, capture of staff officers and couriers, stealing horses and robbing the local populace. Organized pursuit of hussars usually ended at the edge of a wood or the bank of a river.

Austrian commanders were inclined to solve their problems by sending the hussars behind enemy lines. In this way, they avoided damage on their own side, which was particularly important if they

Below: French hussar sabers manufactured on the Hungarian model; beginning of 18th century.

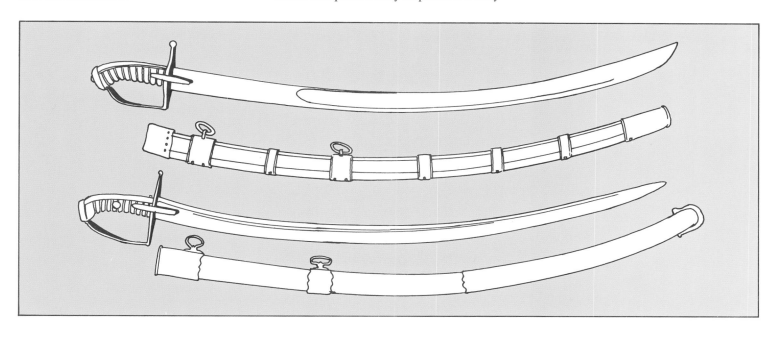

were on allied territory, and certainly inflicted it on the enemy. Clashes between the inhabitants of an area — often too "civilized" for the hussars' liking — and the men of a hussar regiment camping nearby were frequent. A chronicle reports that a hussar regiment, nearly 1,000 men strong, camped by a village on enemy territory, and that no one was killed or robbed. This seems to have been a fact well worth recording. For many of the officers of the other regular regiments, the hussars were "little better than bandits on horse."

Hungarian hussars could be found on the other side in these same two wars; they belonged mostly to the rebellious Protestants. In 1687, Louis XIV formed two squadrons of Hungarian deserters; by 1692, they had grown to a regiment consisting of six squadrons.

The fancily dressed Hungarian nobility, who were more than a match for the French in temperament, drinking and chasing after women, soon became popular in baroque Paris. Many European states accepted the hussars as a type of light cavalry, and the Hungarian folk costume as their uniform. In 1707 Baron Rattzky became commander of the first French hussar regiment, which received standardized uniforms patterned after the Hungarian model in 1720. That same year Hungarian Count Ladislaw de Berchény received royal permission to recruit riders for his regiment in Wallachia, at the time a Turkish province, but which had formerly belonged to the Hungarian crown. He came back with 100 men,

who became the core of the new regiment. Only Hungarians and some Frenchmen of German descent could serve in this regiment. The criteria for service in the regiment were gradually relaxed, so finally only the officers had to be Hungarians, while the rest of the men were from Alsace.

In the War of the Polish Succession the regiment earned such a reputation that their colonel became Marshal of France and Inspector-General of Hussars.

From 1721 a troop of Hungarian hussars was in the service of Prussia. Nevertheless, Friedrich Wilhelm I of Prussia was so impressed by the appearance, demeanor and riding skills of a group of hussars who rode out to greet him during a visit to Bayreuth that he formed his own hussars of the guard in 1731. At the time it was common to recruit hussars on the other side of the Austrian border, or from among refugee horsemen from the Turkish territories.

In 1735 Count Esterhazy formed the third hussar regiment for the French king. This took place in Strasbourg, near the Austrian border, precisely for the purpose of enabling potential recruits easier access.

In 1741, four hussar regiments were formed in Russia from refugees from Austrian and Turkish territories. They were: Slavonisch-Serbski (Serbian), Venguerski (Hungarian), Grouzinski (Georgian) and Moldavski (Moldavian). In 1751, an additional two regiments were formed from Serbian refugees — the Serbski and Novoserbski.

French hussar, about 1740. Contemporary etching.

Monogram of Augustus II of Saxony.

On its territory along the border with Turkey, Austria formed the *Militärgrenze,* a zone under military administration that was intended as protection against the incursions of the army and armed robbers from Turkey. The populace was awarded the land and freed from all taxes and contributions; their only obligation was military service. At first, this obligation was local, but later became general military duty in regular regiments. These soldiers were called Croats and Pandours, and served either as infantrymen in light regiments or as hussars. In the multinational Hapsburg monarchy they were among the most loyal and fiercest soldiers, and they gained a very bad reputation among their enemies on the battlefields of Europe. A prayer preserved in a German church testifies to this: it asks for protection "from the plague and from the Croats."

Hussar regiments were owned by the Hungarian high nobility devoted to Vienna, and consisted of Hungarians, Croats, and refugees from the territories under Turkish power – Serbians, Moldavians and Wallachians. In the War of the Spanish Succession, Austria had three hussar regiments; in the War of the Polish Succession, their number increased to six.

Bavaria and Spain each had a hussar regiment, and a troop of hussars could be occasionally found serving in one of the German states.

The hussars had a distinctive uniform, which consisted of a *dolman* with cords and embroidery on the chest, and a fur-trimmed *pelisse,* usually worn as a jacket, or else draped over the left shoulder. Hussar headgear consisted of a fur-trimmed cap, the *colpack,* and from the middle of the 17th century, a cap named the *mirliton.* Their hair was woven into three braids – one over each cheek, and one in the back. Perforated pistol balls hung on the ends of the braids; they served as weights to keep the braids snug against the head during battle, as hair offered good protection against sword cuts. A mustache was also considered a part of the uniform.

Around the waist they wore a sash, which consisted of a bundle of cords fixed together and wrapped around the waist several times. On a bandolier hussars wore their sword, and a bag called the *sabretasche,* which was descended from the woollen or leather shepherds' bags. Besides the sword, they were armed with two pistols and a carbine approximately 1.3 m (4 ¼ ft.) long.

Hussars rode smaller, lively horses, about fifteen hands tall, which had quite

Friedrich II; in background General von Zieten in a hussar uniform and General Seydlitz in a cuirassier uniform.

a lot of Eastern blood. A good part of the horses' equipment was adopted from the Turks — the wooden saddle with cushion, light leather reins and other straps with various metal ornaments.

Hussars were individual fighters who had become used to fighting in groups. They knew only a few orders and several basic maneuvers and modes of deployment. They avoided clashes with the disciplined ranks of opposing cavalry, and tended to scatter when faced with such a foe, but only to regroup later in another place.

Nevertheless, they had no match when it came to pursuit, and they could be very tenacious if offered the prospect of rich loot. Without doing them injustice, it could be said that the skill required to drain a jug of wine while sitting in the saddle of a horse that stood on a table in an inn was of some importance to their manner of fighting.

Prussia

In 1740 Friedrich II the Great and Maria Theresa mounted their respective thrones. Together with Catherine the

Great and Louis XV they were to mark the 18th century. They had two things in common: their long reigns and the many wars they led.

Although France continued to play an important role in international relations, the death of Louis XIV in 1715 marked the beginning of the decadence of the French monarchy. Prussia, on the other hand, continued its expansion in all directions, by conquest, inheritance, marriage and purchase. Spreading from the Niemen to the Rhine, a string of dominions large and small without territorial connections, it represented neither a geographical nor an ethnic unit. A strong army was the basis of the Prussian state, and its most important cohesive factor the loyalty of the numerous privileged nobility to their ruler. Seeing soldierly order and blind obedience as the pinnacle of virtue, Friedrich Wilhelm I created an army perfectly suited to the general and military conditions of its time.

The ranks of the Prussian army were filled by recruitment within and without the country; press-ganging was resorted to in extreme circumstances. Such a system could be effective only if backed by a very strict code of discipline.

In Prussia, this code reached the extremes of harshness. The power of the officer over the soldier was practically unlimited; the only restriction was that the soldier must not be disabled for service. Training and discipline created a great tactical potential, but frequent mistreatment and the hard conditions of service led to a growing number of desertions. Therefore, camping in the vicinity of woods was avoided, as well as night marches and inhabited places, while night attacks were strictly prohibited. Officers were mostly recruited from the ranks of the rural nobility. A young Junker noble entered the regiment as a noncommissioned officer, and achieved officer's status after three years' service. In exceptional cases, noncommissioned officers who were not of noble descent could become officers after twelve years of service.

Regimental commanders reported their officers' marks to the king annually. Seniority was strictly observed in promotion; counter to practice in other European monarchies, the Prussian nobility had no privileges in this respect. Recruitment, bringing up, equality and control of official and private behavior made the Prussian officer corps into a separate caste, the likes of which were nowhere to be found at the time; this contributed to the rise of Prussian militarism.

Guidon of the Prussian dragoons, about 1740.

Left: Monogram of Friedrich II.

Following double-spread: Cornet and officer of the well-known 3rd von Zieten Hussar Regiment from the Seven Year's War. The hussars in the second half of the 18th century wore a mirliton or a busby on their heads.

Prussian hussar of the 5th Regiment nick-named "Totenköpfe" after the skull they wore as their insignia; from the time of the Seven Year's War.

Toward the end of 1740, soon after taking power, Friedrich II had at his disposal 22,544 horsemen, divided into 12 cuirassier regiments with 60 squadrons, six dragoon regiments with 45 squadrons and two hussar regiments with nine squadrons. Immediately after his accession he founded a thirteenth cuirassier regiment — Gardes du Corps — and changed the names of the 10th Cuirassiers to Gendarmes and the 3rd Cuirassiers to Leib-Karabiniers. These three units became his heavy guard cavalry.

Together with infantry and artillery Friedrich had an army of 100,000 soldiers. Such vast military power upset the basic balance in divided Germany. Friedrich II decided to exploit the situation ruthlessly, and used his indisputable military talents and his very good army for numerous conquests.

After the death of Austrian Emperor Charles VI in 1740, Prussia, Bavaria, Saxony and Spain made known their inheritance claims upon the Austrian lands. Friedrich II wanted the rich province of Silesia, and he entered it with a force of 27,000 men; this signaled the beginning of the War of the Austrian Succession.

War of the Austrian Succession (1740 – 1745)

The entrance of Prussian forces into Silesia caught Austria by surprise. The new empress, Maria Theresa, had been crowned only a month earlier. The Austrian army, numbering 108,000 men, was dispersed throughout the Empire; there were only 7,000 troops in Silesia. In the spring of 1741, an Austrian army of 9,000 infantry and 8,000 cavalry under the command of Field Marshal Neipperg was defeated by the Prussians at Mollwitz. After this, a treaty between Prussia and France was signed that was later joined by Spain, Bavaria, Saxony, the Kingdom of Naples, Pfalz, Cologne and Sweden. As France was on that side, Great Britain had to be on the other one, so it backed Austria, together with Holland, Hanover, Piedmont, and, from 1747, Russia. The War of the Austrian Succession was spreading.

After defeating the Austrians once again, at Hotusice in 1742, Prussia decided that the conquest of Silesia was enough to satisfy it, and withdrew from the war. This event marked the end of the first part of the war, also known as the first Silesian War.

Saxony soon followed its example. With two opponents less to worry about, the Austrian army threw the French out of Prague, and captured Munich in 1743, after which Bavaria agreed to negotiations.

In the beginning, Great Britain helped Austria only financially and at sea, but later on also sent troops to the Continent. Under the command of King George II, the allied forces of Britain, Austria, Hanover and Hesse, 43,000 strong, defeated the French army of Marshal Noailles at Dettingen, in 1743, and pushed the French back across the Rhine.

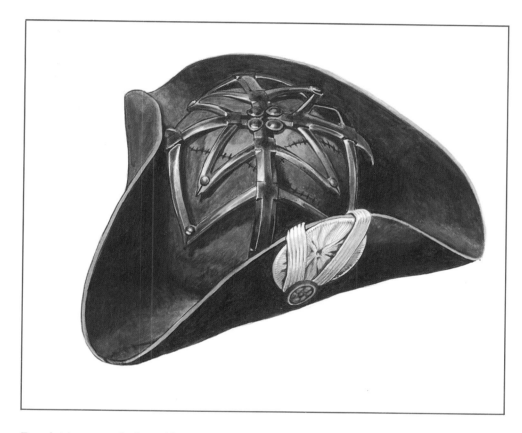

French tricorn cavalry hat with a metal safety part that was worn inside the hat; from the time of the Seven Years War.

In the spring of 1744, the French took the offensive. An army of 80,000 men under Maurice of Saxony (or de Saxe, as the French called him) started for Flanders; 30,000 men under Marshal Belle-Isle guarded the border on the Mosel, and Marshal Coigny's force of 48,000 men advanced on the Rhine, toward Austria. Prussia, concerned about the Austro-British successes, violated the peace treaty and entered Bohemia, and Saxony changed sides and allied itself with Austria. Friedrich II entered Prague with 70,000 men. By deft maneuvering the forces of Karl von Lothringen threatened the communications of the Prussians. A prominent part in this was played by the hussar units. As his supply lines were no longer safe, Friedrich II withdrew to Silesia at the end of the year. In 1745, after defeating the Austrians several more times, Prussia withdrew from the war, which marked the end of the second Silesian War. The French, under Maurice de Saxe, laid siege to one of the strongest forts in Flanders, Tournai, defended by 7,000 men. The fort fell to the French as a result of de Saxe's victory at Fontenay.

Monogram with initials of Maria Theresa.

The same year, Austrian and Piedmontese troops defeated a Franco-Spanish force at Trebia, in Italy. Soon after this setback, Spain withdrew its army from Italy and France. In 1746, de Saxe defeated the Austrians under Lothringen at Raucoux, and next year at Lauffeld the Allied forces under Cumberland. The French also captured a number of important forts in Flanders and the Netherlands. In 1748, the Russians joined the Austrians and the British on the Rhine, and soon after that the Peace of Aachen was signed, ending the war.

Prussian Improvements

In the War of the Austrian Succession, Friedrich II had noticed the weakness of his cavalry, which was slow and ineffective, and had been constantly defeated by the Austrian horsemen. Austrian hussars had systematically cut his communication lines and destroyed his supplies. Friedrich was thus faced with a paradox: even though he won battles, he was forced to withdraw from the conquered territories and to retreat nearer to his operations base, in order to shorten his lines of communication and make them more secure. As Friedrich II himself wrote, he had inherited a bad cavalry force from his father. Hardly any of the officers were competent, the men were afraid of the horses, few of them could ride well, and training was performed on foot – just like infantry. The worst of it was that Friedrich's cavalry was very slow. He decided to reorganize and improve his cavalry, and set forth his intentions in several instructions and orders.

Because of fear of the Austrian hussars, the number of hussar regiments in Prussia was increased to eight by 1745. Each of these regiments consisted of ten squadrons, and numbered over 1,000 men. Only Hungarians were recruited in the beginning, but Friedrich II concluded that one did not have to be a Hungarian in order to be a good hussar, and allowed recruitment in Prussia, with the sole condition that riders' height must not exceed 160 cm (64 in). For these units he purchased small horses in Poland, Russia and Turkey. Only the 2nd and 5th Hussar Regiments gained reputations as good units equal to the Austrians. The others were said to have horses that were too large, and to lack hussar spirit. Their strength rested on two points: their great numbers, and a good ratio of noncommissioned officers to enlisted men, which was a distinctive trait of the Prussian army.

A squadron of Bosniaks was founded in the 5th Hussar Regiment; its men were recruited from among Russian and Polish Moslems, were armed with a lance and dressed according to Turkish customs, with a turban on their heads. By 1760, their number had so increased that a separate regiment, consisting of ten squadrons, was formed. In the same period Friedrich II formed five dragoon regiments.

In 1735 the Prussian cuirassiers' leather coat was replaced by a tan-colored coat made of heavy woolen material that offered some protection against saber cuts. The black lacquered breastplate remained a part of the uniform. Only the Gardes du Corps retained unpainted

armor. The helmet used until then was supplanted by a metal cap worn under a tricorn. In 1745 Friedrich II decreed that the recruits for cuirassier regiments should be healthy and strong, and not less than 5 feet 4 inches tall. The best recruits from the regimental cantons were chosen, and mostly sons of peasants, who had some knowledge of horses. The minimum height for the horse was 15.5 hands. The most sought after horses were of the Holstein breed. Cuirassiers were armed with a carbine, two pistols and a long straight sword, the *pallasch*. A complete regiment had 840 men in five squadrons.

Dragoon regiments had five squadrons, the same as the cuirassiers. Only the 5th and 6th Dragoons had ten each. At first, about 1740, the Prussian dragoons were halfway between the English dragoons,

Maria Theresa (1717–1780), Austrian empress during whose reign the Hungarian hussars were regarded as the best light cavalry in Europe.

Opposite: French horseman of the Mousquetaires Gris, named "Gris" after the gray
horses they rode, about 1740.

*Marshal Maurice of Saxony (1696 – 1750),
who during the war against Austria renewed
the fame of the French cavalry.*

who were a real cavalry force, and their French namesakes, who underwent infantry training, and represented rather a contemporary equivalent of today's mechanized infantry than true cavalry. As a rule, the dragoons were given the worst and cheapest horses. As they evolved into true cavalry, however, the need arose to give them better mounts, and improve their equipment in general. In 1745, Friedrich II decreed that they be given a light blue uniform, and that their muskets be exchanged for carbines. Only the bayonets and mounted drummers remained of the original dragoons; in everything else, they had become cavalry of the line. Black or dark brown horses were habitual for dragoon regiments.

Friedrich's rules of engagement of 1744 stated that cavalry, lined up in three ranks, should take up position on the flanks of the infantry, or else in the general reserve. The first rank consisted of cuirassiers, ranked three deep, whose task was to defeat the enemy cavalry, or to breach the lines of the opposing infantry and artillery. The second rank consisted of dragoons, also three deep. Their squadrons were spaced farther apart, so that they could attack in echelons if necessary, one after the other, or rush into the breaks created by the cuirassiers. The third rank consisted of hussars, two or three deep, who were stationed off toward the flanks in order to protect them and the rear. They were also supposed to attack the enemy cavalry as a reserve line, to give the cuirassiers and dragoons time to reform for a new assault, or an attack on the enemy's flanks. As soon as a defeated

opponent started to retreat, the hussars would give chase, turning the retreat into flight. Prussian hussars were the only ones of their kind who were trained to fight as cavalry of the line, and also had in their everyday duties the capture of draft evaders and deserters, in addition to patrolling and reconnaissance, thus fulfilling the role of some sort of mounted military police. When the Prussian army made camp, hussars took all the important points near roads and towns, in order to control all movement and discourage potential deserters.

In 1748, Friedrich II ordered that cavalry must begin its charge from 1,000 paces, and that it must go into full gallop at 300 paces from the enemy, with sabers or swords drawn, and with as much shouting and trumpet noise as possible. Later, wishing to make cavalry the main striking and maneuvering force, and also because of the increased range and precision of artillery, Friedrich II moved back the initial position for charging to 2,500 paces (1,800 meters or 6,000 feet) from the enemy lines. This required special training at a very high level of quality.

Regimental commanders, however, tended to avoid training, because it meant an increase in the number of sick and hurt horses, and an increase in the amount of food they consumed because of additional exertion by at least 5 kg (11 lb.) a day. Additional training also meant more worn out and ruined equipment, and more work for regimental saddle-makers, smiths, tailors etc. All in all, good training was

Opposite: French Morlier Dragoon, one of the many independent light units formed during the Seven Years War.

very expensive. Friedrich II gave regimental commanders a larger number of surplus horses and more money. Training was organized systematically, from the acquisition of riding skills in the manège and the individual training of each soldier, to group exercises on difficult terrain with precisely set tasks to accomplish, constant exercises in motion and the maneuvering and evolution of great numbers of horsemen.

Such demands reflected on the choice of horses, which had to be fast, strong and above all resistant. Both men and animals had to be kept constantly in top form through strenuous exercise.

These changes, together with the ban on the use of firearms during the charge increased the speed and the

maneuverability of the Prussian cavalry. Toward the middle of the 17th century, Friedrich II certainly had the best mounted fighting force in Europe. In imposing discipline, he went so far as to punish officers who allowed the enemy to attack before they did.

French dragoon saddle with a pike, a shovel, a musket and a gun; from the time of the Seven Years War.

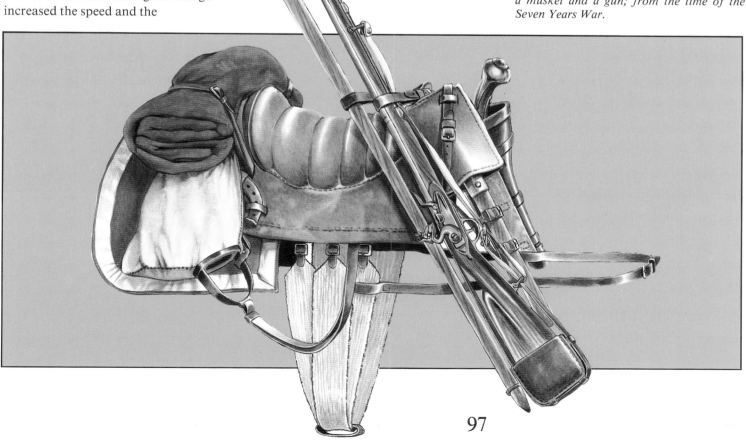

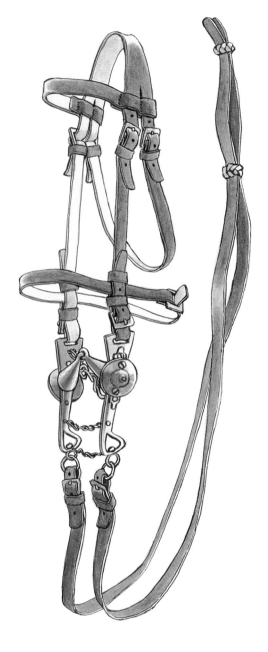

French reins used by line and dragoon units; from the time of the Seven Years War.

The Evolution of Cavalry during the War of the Austrian Succession

During the siege of the French army in Prague in 1742 in the War of the Austrian Succession, an officers' manservant named Fischer earned himself a good reputation by taking officers' horses out to graze on the island of the river Moldau; to do this, he had to pass through the Austrian lines. De Saxe heard of his feats, and took him under his own command, granting him permission toward the end of 1743 to form a free company of Chasseurs, consisting of 40 horsemen and 60 foot soldiers, and modeled on the Austrian Pandours and Croats light units. Friedrich II formed a similar unit from gamekeepers and woodsmen, and called them Jägers, which means the same thing as Chasseurs — huntsmen. These men were used to life in the wilderness, good shots and skilled at setting traps for game poachers as well as for the game. In 1744, the Prussian king had 168 Jägers in his service. The name of these light mounted troops changed to Jägers zu Pferde, and in France Chasseurs à Cheval; in both countries they were seen as the best response to Austrian light troops and hussars.

As a reward for good service, Louis XV permitted Fischer to follow him with his Chasseurs in the Battle of Lauffeld, in 1746. Fischer was soon promoted to Brigadier of Cavalry, and his Chasseurs de Fischer grew to four companies. In a similar way, other officers and nobles formed so-called free companies of light troops, with mixed complements of horsemen and foot soldiers. Among them: Arquebusiers de Grasin, with 546 horsemen, Volontaires royaux, with 480 dragoons and 100 hussars, Fusiliers de la Morlière, with 540 dragoons, Volontaires cantabres, with 300 hussars, Volontaires de Gantès, with 144 hussars and 53 dragoons, and Volontaires bretons, with 540 hussars.

On the other side, Maria Theresa did not sit idle, either. During the War of the Austrian Succession she formed three regiments of hussars and four regiments of Grenz hussars, whose complements were made up of Croats and Pandours light troops, so she had at her disposal 10,000 hussars in 13 regiments.

Besides the hussar, chasseur and Jäger light units, the beginning of the War of the Austrian Succession saw the forming of the first units of uhlans, whose men were recruited mostly from the territory of Poland and the Ukraine. In 1740 Friedrich II engaged the services of a squadron of Polish light horsemen known as the Natzmer Uhlanen; by 1741, they had already grown in size to a regiment. In 1742, they became the 4th Natzmer Hussar Regiment. The 5th Hussar Regiment had a squadron of Bosniaks. Maurice of Saxony formed his Volontaires de Saxe regiment in 1743; it consisted of six companies with 160 men each — 80 dragoons and 80 uhlans. Uhlans were noble volunteers of Polish, Tartar and Lithuanian origin. They were renowned for their bravery and fighting spirit, as well as for their drunkenness. They were armed with a lance approximately 4 m (13 ft) long,

French Cavalry Regiments of the Line, 1759:

1. Colonel Général
2. Mestre de Camp Général
3. Commissaire Général
4. Royal
5. du Roi
6. Royal Étrangers
7. Cuirassiers du Roi
8. Royal Cravattes
9. Royal Roussillon
10. Royal Piemont
11. Royal Allemand
12. Royal Pologne
13. La Reine
14. Dauphin
15. Dauphin Étranger
16. Bourgogne
17. Aquitaine
18. Berry
20. Orléans
21. Bellefonds
22. Condé
23. Bourbon
24. Clermont
25. Conti
26. Penthièvre
27. Archiac
28. Poly Saint Thiébault
29. Lusignan
30. Marcieux
31. Des Salles
32. Talleyrand
33. Noe
34. Chabrillant
35. Charost
36. Saint Aignan
37. Grammont
38. Bourbon-Busset
39. Viefville
40. Trasnegnies
41. Saint Jal
42. Fumel
43. Rochefoucauld-Langeac
44. de Vienne
45. Bussy-Lameth
46. Crussol
47. Fleury
48. Toustain-Viray
49. Dampierre
50. Heinrichemont
51. Moustiers
52. Saluces
53. Württemberg
54. Noailles-Ayen
55. d'Harcourt
56. Fitzjames
57. Descars
58. Berchény Hussards
59. Turpin Hussards
60. Schonberg
61. Raugrave
62. Nassau-Saarbrück
63. Montcalm
64. Besons
65. Royal Nassau Hussards
66. Corse
— Polleresky Hussards

which could also serve as a tent pole. Dragoons were recruited from among their servants.

Friedrich II and Maria Theresa learned the most from the War of the Austrian Succession. The Prussian king would not forget the Battle of Mollwitz, when the Austrian cavalry defeated his own, and he learned of Prussian victory when he was already in flight. In the absence of the king, Marshal Schwerin had managed to vanquish the Austrians, mainly thanks to this excellent infantry. After defeats in Bohemia and Silesia, the Austrian empress decided to reorganize her army. George II, King of England, decided to bring some order to cavalry uniforms in 1742, and passed a decree to that effect. For reasons of economy, he abolished the 3rd and 4th Troops of Horse Guards, and turned three senior regiments — The King's own Regiment of Horse, The Queen's Regiment of Horse and 4th Regiment of Horse — into the 2nd, 3rd and 4th Dragoon Guards.

The successes in the last war lulled the French army into a state ever more removed from the spirit of action of the times of Louis XIV. During the reign of Louis XV (1715 – 1774), most of the accomplishments of his predecessor were undone. The French military was saddled with an excessive number of officers — one for every fifteen men — who were recruited from the ranks of the exclusive nobility. The army had become arrogant and undisciplined, and there was a lack of cooperation among officers. During campaigns, officers took along their private servants and

cooks, their lovers and even troops of itinerant acrobats and actors. An army of 40,000 men often had as many as 10,000 baggage carts, so it is small wonder that a column like this could cover no more than seven miles a day.

The army list for 1749 tells us that Louis XV had 2,164 horsemen in the Maison du Roi, 800 in the Gendarmerie, 1,200 in the Carabiniers, 13,320 in 56 regiments of the line, 7,680 dragoons, 960 foreigners, 800 hussars and 1,320 light troops. This made for a grand total of 28,000 horsemen, less than the number Villeroy commanded at Malplaquet 40 years earlier, and nearly twice less than Louis XIV had at the peak of his power. Except for the Maison du Roi, practically all the other regiments were the property of the individual colonels who commanded them, and who paid more attention to finances than to the training and the quality of their horsemen. Horses seldom left their stables in winter. In periods of peace, horses that had been written off were not replaced with new ones, so it was not a rarity for a regiment to have twice as many men as horses.

In the War of the Austrian Succession, the French cavalry continued to advance at a walk, or a trot, while charges were executed at a moderate canter. The practice of firing from a distance of approximately 20 paces was also continued.

Louis XV, as well as the King of England, published new regulations concerning uniforms in 1750. In order to improve his cavalry's battle

Louis XV, King of France (1715 – 1774). During his reign the French cavalry decreased in quality and size.

Cross with fleur-de-lis, emblem of the Mousquetaires Gris; 18th century.

performance, he also published new tactical rules in 1755. Commanders, however, hardly paid any attention.

The Seven Years War (1756 – 1763)

The War of the Austrian Succession (1740 – 1748) did not eliminate the basic causes of contention between the leading European powers. A new war was a distinct possibility. Prussia's aggressive policies were aimed at weakening Austria and limiting Maria Theresa's power, thus opening the way to Prussian hegemony in Germany. Under the terms of the Peace of Aachen, Silesia had become a part of Prussia, but Austria was loath to give up this rich province. Friedrich II was intent on conquering Saxony, and planned to take Bohemia from the Austrians, in order to give it to the Elector of Saxony as a consolation. He also had designs on Polish Pomerania and Courland.

Looking for an ally for its war against France, Great Britain found an ideal partner in Prussia, which had only recently broken its alliance with the French. Abandoned by Prussia, France turned to its former enemy, Austria; the two countries signed a defense pact. In order to weaken the power of the Prussian king and lessen the danger of Prussian aggression, and also to facilitate the realization of its designs on East Prussia, Poland and Courland, Russia joined the Franco-Austrian agreement. The other European countries took sides according to their own interests. The northern German

states – Hanover, Hesse-Kassel and Braunschweig – backed Prussia, while the southern states – Saxony, Bavaria, Pfalz, Württemberg, Hesse-Darmstadt, and others – sided with the European coalition. Each of the members of the European coalition had its own aims regarding Prussia, and these were hard to reconcile. Austria wanted to crush Prussia entirely, while France only wanted to lessen its power; both Austria and France feared the strengthening of Russia.

On the strength of numbers, Prussia looked hopelessly outclassed: it had only five million inhabitants, the countries of the coalition ninety. On the other hand, Friedrich II had an excellent army, and substantial financial aid from Great Britain.

In the summer of 1756, Friedrich II crossed the border into Saxony, and the Seven Years War had begun. At that moment, the King of Prussia had 147,000 men under his command, while the countries of the coalition had nearly half a million soldiers. Friedrich II decided to surprise his opponents, and moved first. Inside of two months, Saxony was out of the war, its army disbanded and its regiments pressed into service under the Prussian flag.

In 1757, Friedrich decided to push the Austrians out of Bohemia. Even though he was victorious in the Battle of Prague, he did not succeed in capturing the fort of Prague and the tower. Field Marshal Daun, with a force of 35,000 infantry and 19,000 cavalry, set out to lift the siege of Prague. Friedrich, with

19,000 infantry and 14,000 cavalry, marched out to meet him. The encounter took place at Kolin. The Prussians were within a hair's breadth of winning the battle, but then lost it due to a series of coincidences.

Austria's Marshal Haddick took advantage of this situation, marching through Saxony with three hussar regiments – Haddick, Esterhazy and Batthyany – and arriving at the Prussian border under the very noses of the Prussian troops. Then he turned toward Frankfurt an der Oder. When the Prussians moved to stop him, he abruptly changed direction, marched to Berlin, and captured it practically without resistance, as there were hardly any troops in the city. Haddick held Berlin for 24 hours, and then retreated.

Three months later, at Gross Jägersdorf, in East Prussia, Marshal Apraxin and his 55,000 Russians defeated a Prussian force of 22,000 men. Apraxin, however, did not pursue his advantage, but withdrew, for which act he was relieved of his command and court-martialed.

After the retreat from Bohemia, the Prussian army waited for occasions to engage its opponents one by one. Meanwhile, the forces of the Allies were closing a circle around Prussia. The army of the southern German states, 33,000 men strong, was heading toward the province of Thüringen, by way of Nürnberg; a French army of 30,000 men, under the Prince de Soubise had started for Erfurth; another one, of 100,000 men, had defeated Cumberland

at Hastenbeck, and subsequently captured Hanover and Braunschweig. A Swedish force of 17,000 soldiers had landed at Stralsund. At the end of October Friedrich II, at the head of 22,000 men, marched to attack the Prince de Soubise, who had in the meantime been reinforced by 11,000 new troops from the South German states, commanded by Marshal Hildburghausen. At St. Micheln the French had gathered 48 battalions, 40 squadrons and 33 artillery pieces, and their allies 14 battalions, 43 squadrons and 12 artillery pieces. At Rossbach Friedrich II had 27 battalions, 45 squadrons and 25 artillery pieces.

The Battle of Rossbach

On November 6th the Prussian forces took up a position with Rossbach on the left, and the village of Bedra a mile to the right. At Rossbach, the first line consisted of the 7th Dreisen and 3rd Leib Cuirassiers, ranked three deep. The center was held by 20 battalions of infantry, and the right wing by the 8th Rochow, 10th Gendarmes and 13th Gardes du Corps Cuirassiers, also formed in three ranks. The second line consisted of the 4th Czettritz Dragoons behind the 7th and 3rd Cuirassiers, 6 battalions of infantry in the center, and the 3rd Meinicke Dragoons on the right. The 1st Czekeln (green) Hussars and 7th Malachowski (yellow) Hussars, together with one battalion of light infantry, stood in reserve.

The Allies moved in four parallel columns, and rounded Zeuchfeld in

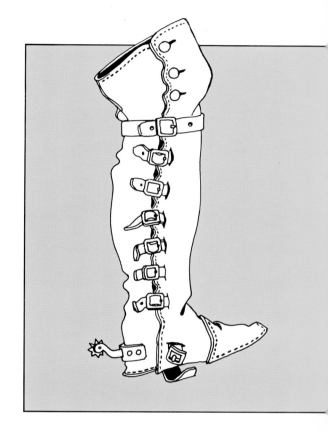

Dragoon's leather gaiters similar to the cloth gaiters of the infantry; from the time of the Seven Years War.

Opposite: Austrian cornet of the Löwenstein Dragoon Regiment. Usually trumpeters were dressed in bright colors and rode gray or white horses so that they could be easily spotted as noncombat troopers; from the time of the Seven Years War.

Saber of French grenadier of the Guard; first half of 18th century.

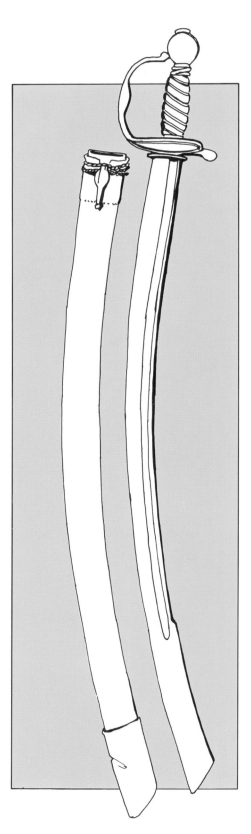

Following double-spread: Austrian hussar of the Esterhazy Regiment, owned by one of the richest Hungarian aristocrats and one of the best cavalry officers ever to fight for the Austrians; from the time of the Seven Years War.

order to outflank the Prussian forces on the left, and threaten their rear. De Soubise put practically all his cavalry in front of his columns. The cavalry itself was organized in two columns. One had 15 squadrons from the Austrian Brettlach and Imperial Prinz Friedrich and Hohenzollern Cuirassiers and Württemberg Dragoons, the other 17 squadrons from the Austrian Trautmanndorf and Imperial Brandenburg-Bayreuth Cuirassiers and Brandenburg-Anspach Dragoons, under the direct command of Marshal Hildburghausen. These columns were followed by the French cavalry, formed in brigades of six squadrons each, which were named after the senior regiment in them. The La Reine brigade comprised the 14th La Reine, 37th Bourbon-Busset and 56th Fitz-James (Irish) regiments, the Commisaire-Général brigade had the 3rd Commisaire-Général, 69th Voluntaires Liegois and 22nd Bourbon regiments, and so on. Among the other regiments were the 2nd Mestre du Camp Général and 7th Cuirassiers du Roi. De Soubise detailed Saint-Germain, with a force of eight battalions and 12 squadrons, to secure their march from the Schortauer heights, and Loudon, with three light battalions and three squadrons of Austrian hussars to take the heights of Galghen. He kept the Austrian Szecheny hussar regiment and French Nassau-Saarbrück Hussars and 13th Apchon Dragoons — a total of 12 squadrons — at the rear of the line.

Around noon, Major-General Seydlitz, commander of the Prussian cavalry, received word from his advanced reconnaissance detachments that the

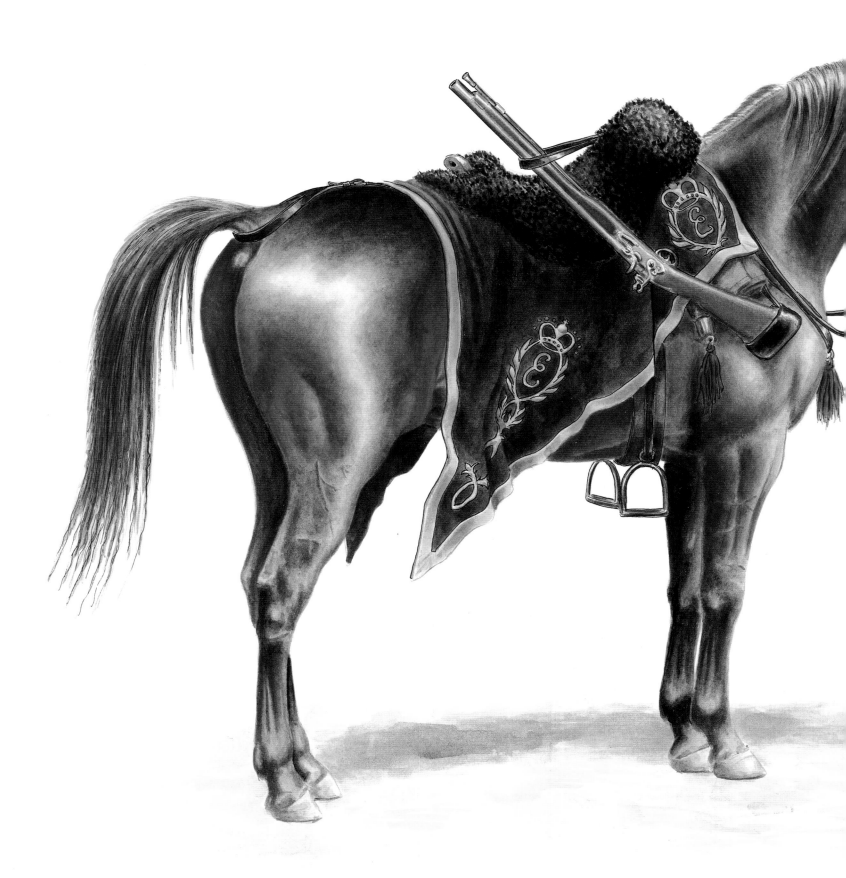

Friedrich Wilhelm von Seydlitz (1721 to 1773), commander of the Prussian heavy cavalry that became famous at the Battle of Rossbach.

Allies were preparing to move. Without informing the king, Seydlitz ordered his men into readiness; saddle straps were tightened, the officers mounted, and flags were unfurled. Friedrich II was having lunch when news came that the Allies had started a flanking movement on the Prussian left wing. At 2 P.M., Friedrich ordered Seydlitz to intercept the Allies.

Seydlitz immediately sent off the 10th Czeklen Hussars as an advance force. They were followed at a light canter, and in a *zuge* ("platoon") formation — with 16 – 20 men in a line — by the 3rd Leib cuirassiers and 4th Czettritz and 3rd Meinicke Dragoons. In the meantime, the 13th Gardes du Corps, 10th Gendarmes, 8th Rochow and 7th Dreisen Cuirassiers formed a column in the same way. Two miles away, the regiments formed into line in order of arrival. The first line was composed of the 15 squadrons of the first column, the second line of the 18 squadrons of the second one. The hussars were detached on the left wing. The whole formation was hidden from the Allies' view by the hill of Polzen. Eighteen artillery pieces arrived soon after the cavalry, and were placed on the neighboring hill of Janus.

De Soubise's column moved on, unaware that Seydlitz's cavalry was lying in wait on the far side of the Polzen heights. Seydlitz lit his pipe, which was a sign that he was about to give orders to charge. When around 3 P.M. the Allied column came within 300 yards of Polzen hill, the Prussian cannon emplaced on Janus hill opened fire. At Seydlitz's order, the 15 squadrons of the first line charged, suddenly appearing from behind the crest of the hill. The full brunt of the Prussian charge was born at first by the Austrian Brettlach and Trautmanndorf cuirassiers, then by the other regiments at the head of the column. The ensuing confusion was used by the 1st Czeklen hussars to attack from the flank. Hildburghausen tried to organize his regiments, but there was no time. Seydlitz rode out in front of the four cuirassier regiments of his second line, showed them his pipe, threw it away, and drew his sword, which was the signal to charge. The Prussian second line broke up the head of the Allied column. When he saw what was happening, de Soubise ordered his infantry to stop and form into a line, with the French cavalry protecting their movements.

While the cavalry battle was raging at the head of the column, the Prussian infantry arrived and attacked de Soubise. After defeating the Austrian and imperial cavalry, which retreated toward Storkau in disorder, Seydlitz stopped his men, and ordered them to

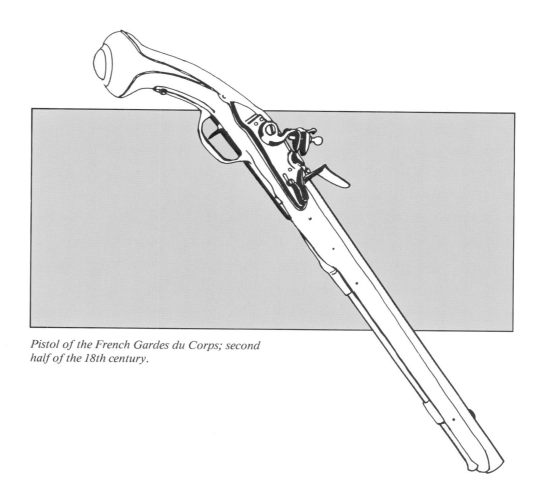

Pistol of the French Gardes du Corps; second half of the 18th century.

Austrian two-headed eagle.

Following double-spread: Horseman, equipment and uniform of the French de Fumel Regiment. French cavalrymen wore buff undercoats as shown. They were coats only for battles and parades; from the time of the Seven Years War.

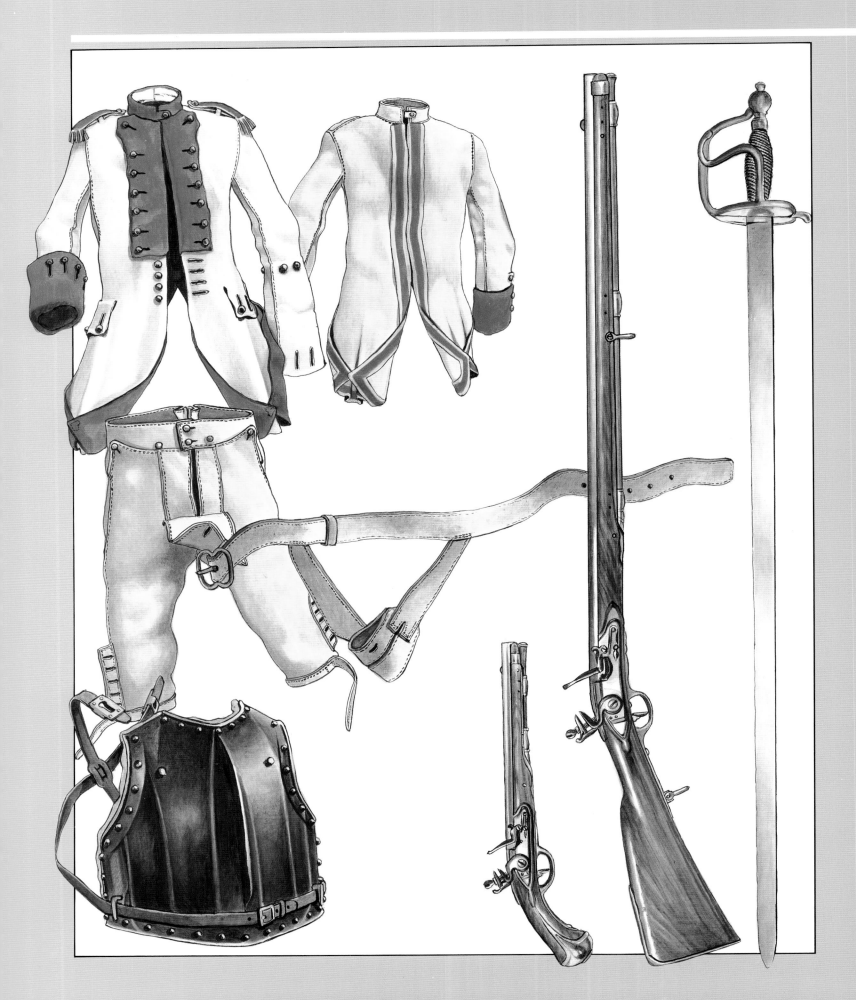

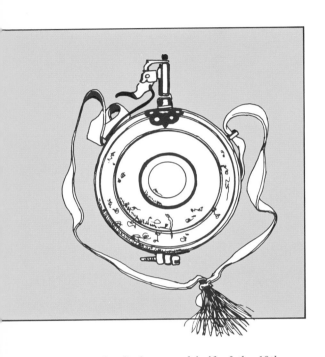

Powder flask; second half of the 18th century.

regroup on the right side of the enemy column. First the standard-bearers took their places, and then each squadron gathered and formed behind its flag at the sound of a trumpet. As in the beginning, the squadrons formed in three ranks. The Prussian artillery pounded away at the French infantry, from which several regiments had been detached in a futile attempt to attack the Prussian infantry while it was still arriving. This time around, Seydlitz threw his hat instead of his pipe into the air, and 43 Prussian squadrons charged. The La Reine and Commisaire-Général brigades of horse tried in vain to stop Seydlitz's cavalry. Under attack from two sides, the Allied front collapsed, and the troops started to flee. Saint-Germain and Loudon gathered the fleeing troops, and stopped the hussars who were giving chase. Eyewitness accounts inform us that the vanquished French troops turned into a wild mob that robbed its own supply column. In less than two hours, Seydlitz's cavalry backed by artillery and infantry, broke the Allies, who lost nearly 10,000 men and all but a few of their artillery pieces. Prussian losses came to a total of 550 men.

The Battle of Leuthen

With this victory at Rossbach Friedrich's situation was significantly improved. Only a month later, after a forced march that lasted 12 days and in which 155 miles were covered, Friedrich met up with the forces of the Duke of Braunschweig-Bevern at Parchwitz. These forces had been defeated by the Austrians at Breslau several days earlier, on Novemver 22, 1757. Although he was weaker, with a force of 48 battalions, 133 squadrons and 167 artillery pieces, Friedrich II decided to attack the Austrians. Marshal Lothringen had under his command 85 battalions, 125 squadrons and 235 artillery pieces, a total of 65,000 men, as opposed to Friedrich's approximately 35,000.

Before the attack, the Prussian cavalry forces were addressed by their king, who threatened that every cavalry regiment that failed to charge home would be dismounted, and that he would strip away their standards and guidons, swords, lace and braid, and turn them into ordinary infantrymen.

Lothringen awaited the Prussians in a position at right angles to the road for Breslau, with a line nearly 7 km (4 mi) long, anchored at the village of Leuthen. What the French and imperial forces did not accomplish at Rossbach, Friedrich II pulled off at Leuthen. Marching in front of the Austrian lines, he outflanked them, and "crossed the T" of Lothringen's forces. The whole Prussian army now faced the Austrian left wing. The cavalry elite of Prussia and Austria faced off at Leuthen. Friedrich II had six hussar, 11 cuirassier and five dragoon regiments, among them the 2nd Zieten Hussars, 13th Gardes du Corps and 10th Gendarmes Cuirassiers, and 5th Bayreuth Dragoons. Lothringen had at his disposal forces from Bavaria, Württemberg and other German states, in addition to three hussar, 12 cuirassier and seven dragoon regiments, which included the Nadasdy and Esterhazy Hussars, Stampach, Anhalt-Zerbst and O'Donnell

Below: Attack of the Prussian hussars on the Russian artillery during the Seven Years War. Painting by Julius Kossak.

Cuirassiers, and Zweibrücken, Erzherzog Joseph and Württemberg Dragoons. Friedrich had succeeded in achieving local superiority, and he now attacked. Zieten, at the head of 53 squadrons, rejected the charge of the Austrian left-wing cavalry. The Prussians took Leuthen and stopped. Lothringen turned his front, and brought reinforcements from the right wing. At that moment, the battle came into balance. Austrian General Lucchese gathered 70 squadrons of cavalry from the right wing, which had still seen no action, and started at a canter toward the Prussian left wing. But before his forces could take up a battle formation, they were charged by Seydlitz. Thirty-five cuirassier squadrons attacked the Austrian cavalry from the front, ten squadrons of Bayreuth dragoons from one side and 35 reserve squadrons from the other. This turned out to be the decisive moment of the battle. The Austrian cavalry was thrown back in disorder, and the infantry followed soon after. The Prussians lost about 6,500 men, the Allies 22,000, 12,000 of them as prisoners.

By the end of the year Friedrich II had taken advantage of the inactivity of the Russians, and broken the offensive of the French-Imperial and Austrian armies in the battles of Rossbach and Leuthen, retaking all of Silesia in the process, with the exception of the fort of Schweidnitz. The situation at the end of 1757 was, as a matter of fact, hardly any different from that at the beginning of the war.

In 1758, Great Britain had sent an expeditionary force to the Continent. It consisted of 17 battalions and 13 regiments of cavalry, with a total of 29 squadrons. The regiments were the 1st King's Dragoon Guards, 2nd, 3rd, 7th Dragoon Guards, 1st and 2nd Royal Dragoons, Royal Regiment of Horse Guards, Carabiniers, and 6th, 7th, 8th, 10th and 11th Dragoons. These British forces joined the Hanoverian army, and were placed under the command of the Herzog von Braunschweig. This united British-Hanoverian army pushed the French out of Hanover, Braunschweig, Westphalia and Hesse-Kassel.

It is interesting that England was the last of the large European states to form

Below: Prussian hussar saber tache engraved with the monogram of Friedrich II.

English guidon, 2nd Dragoon Guards; mid-18th century.

units of light cavalry known as Light Dragoons. They were incorporated into the Dragoon Guards and dragoon regiments as separate troops of 68 men. Unlike the other soldiers in the regiments, they were dressed in leather jacket, cut-down grenadier cap and light jockey boots.

In 1759, the first regiment of Light Dragoons was formed, with the number 15, and it remained a part of the standing army. Its purpose was different from that of hussar and other similar units, for it did not include guerrilla actions and "uncivilized" war practices, but only reconaissance, protection of communications and escort for staff officers and convoys.

The main Prussian forces, under Friedrich's personal command, were to face the main Russian and Austrian forces, with the main intention of preventing their quick meeting up. With this in mind, Friedrich, with 55,000 men, marched into Silesia which had been invaded by the Austrians again and captured Schweidnitz, and then, at the

Marking on General von Zieten's colpack; from the time of the Seven Years War.

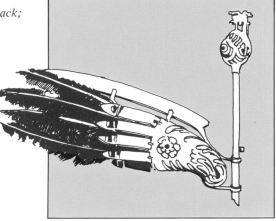

beginning of May, entered Moravia and besieged the fort of Olmütz. His plan was to draw the main Austrian forces from Bohemia into Moravia, and beat them decisively at Olmütz, after which he would turn to deal with the Russians. Austrian forces under Marshal Daun bypassed the Prussian positions, and entered Olmütz. At the same time, Loudon cut the Prussian lines of communication. Toward the end of June, at Dormstadl, he destroyed a Prussian supply column of 4,000 cars, using the Nadasdy hussars, Warasdiner Banalist Grenz hussars and dragoons from the Württemberg and Zwei-brücken regiments. Friedrich had no choice but to discontinue the siege and retreat into Bohemia.

When he heard of the victory of the British-Hanoverian army over the French at Krehfeld, and of the massing of Russian forces at Poznan, Friedrich again decided to act first. He left 51 battalions and 75 squadrons, as a strong protection against the Austrians, and at the head of 14 battalions and 38 squadrons marched off to meet the Russians. The passivity of the Austrian army allowed him to meet up with Prussian forces at Küstrin.

The Battle of Hochkirch

Now, Friedrich turned his attention back to the Austrians, who had entered Saxony again, this time with a force of 77,000 men. The King of Prussia gathered about 40,000 troops, and took up position near Hochkirch. Marshal Daun, under cover of night, sent

Loudon, reinforced with the Kaiser Franz I, Károly and Dessewffy Hussars, to round the Prussian positions and attack their camp. Loudon divided his force into two groups. One, under his own command, consisted of five battalions of light Grenz infantry and 26 squadrons of regular and Grenz hussars, the other of 20 squadrons, among them the light dragoon — or chevau-léger — Saint Ignon Regiment, and the ubiquitous Zweibrücken Dragoons. Daun attacked early on the morning of October 14th, while Loudon's first group, supported by the second, captured the Prussian camp. Daun organized his attack in three columns. By noon, the Austrians had taken several important positions. Friedrich II decided to retreat, protected by the cavalry. The Austrians were satisfied with the capture of the Prussian camp, and did not pursue him. Friedrich lost 9,100 men and 101 artillery pieces, the Austrians 7,500 men.

At the end of the year, the Russians were on the Vistula, the Austrians in Bohemia, the Swedes in Straslund, and the French on the Rhine. The concentrated attacks of the forces of the Coalition had not given much in the way of results, primarily due to lack of a joint plan of operations, and difficulties in coordination among the Allied armies.

The Minden Campaign (1759)

In 1759, the significantly weakened Prussian army began to lose the

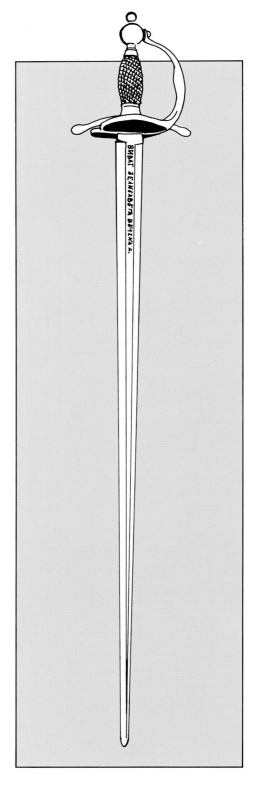

initiative. Toward the end of June, Field Marshal Daun started from Bohemia for Silesia, at the head of 75,000 men, and Field Marshal Loudon proceeded with 20,000 men toward the Oder, to meet up with the Russian General Saltikov and his force of 51,000 troops. Before joining forces with the Austrians, Saltikov had defeated on July 23rd a Prussian corps of 28,000 men, under Wedell, at Palzig. On August 1st, 1759, the Herzog von Braunschweig, with 42,500 troops, defeated 54,000 Frenchmen at Minden. At the beginning of the battle, the French cavalry charged the Allied infantry positions unsuccessfully. At one point, 63 French squadrons were engaged in the attack, among them the Gendarmerie de France, 12th Royal Carabiniers, 1st Colonel-Général, 2nd Mestre de Camp Général, 3rd Commissaire-Général, 5th Du Roi, 6th Royal Étranger, 8th Royal Cravattes and 10th Royal Piémont, but they were all thrown back. Charges succeeded one another, while the Allied cavalry stood passively at the back. The Herzog von Braunschweig several times ordered Lord George Sackville, the commander of the British cavalry, to attack, but he vacillated. When he finally made his mind up, the moment for action was past. The French retreated over the Minden. The Allies had 2,800 casualties, while the French lost 7,000 men and 43 cannons. After the defeat of Wedell at Palzig, Friedrich II set out at the head of reinforcements to assist Wedell. With 50,000 men, he crossed the Oder at Kunersdorf and attacked on August 11th the joint Austro-Russian forces. The Russians had 70 battalions, 53 squadrons, 200

Monogram of the Russian empress Elizabeth I.

cannons and about 10,000 Don and Tchougaev Cossacks, while Loudon had 17 battalions, 40 squadrons and 48 artillery pieces. The Prussians had 53 battalions, 97 squadrons and 280 pieces. Saltikov took up positions on the Mühlberg and Grosser Spitzberg hills, with the Oder at his back, thus risking turning his possible defeat into a total catastrophe.

Friedrich attacked Mühlberg from three sides, pounding away at it with nearly all his artillery. He succeeded in taking it after a charge that overcame the fortifications, and captured 42 guns in the process. After that, he turned to the Grosser Spitzberg. The Russians tried to retake Mühlberg with 12 battalions and three regiments of Grénadiers à Cheval — Kargopol, Riazan and St. Petersburg, a total of nine squadrons. This attempt failed. Friedrich II brought all his infantry, and practically all his cavalry, to the foot of the Grosser Spitzberg. His first attack was rejected, the second one got as far as the first fortifications, but was also thrown back, as well as the third one, which Seydlitz's cavalry executed on very difficult ground, and which was repulsed by concentrated artillery fire, and in which the 3rd Leib, 1st Schlabrendorff and 7th Horn Cuirassiers suffered heavy losses.

The retreating Prussian cavalry was attacked by the Cossacks. Nevertheless, Friedrich continued to send his troops into new charges. Then the Russians retook Mühlberg in a counterattack. Seydlitz's cavalry charge was beaten back once more, again with great loss of life. The Austrian and Russian cavalry counterattacked, with the Russian Thronfolger, Kiev and Novotroisk cuirassiers, followed by the Horse Grenadiers, Arkhangelsk and Tobolsk dragoons, and the Austrian Kolowrat, Württemberg and Liechtenstein dragoons.

After the wounding of Seydlitz, the Prussian cavalry broke. Friedrich organized a last stand on the banks of the Hühner stream, but the Cossacks forced him to retreat. The Prussian front fell apart, and general flight followed. At Kunersdorf the Prussians suffered the most terrible defeat in the Seven Years War. They lost 19,000 men and close to every artillery piece they had in the field. Saltikov lost 14,000 men, the Austrians slightly less than 2,500.

With this defeat, Prussia's situation became critical, but the Allies missed the opportunity to destroy its army completely, and capture Berlin.

At the beginning of 1760, both sides began to show signs of war weariness.

Operations mainly consisted of maneuvering and evading decisive clashes. Austro-Russian forces took Berlin and held it for four days, and Friedrich defeated the Austrians at Liegnitz and Torgau, but these were victories without significance, for he did not manage to dislodge them from Saxony.

In a radically different showing, at Warburg in 1760, 22 English squadrons under the command of General Granby, in a manner reminiscent of their old glory, broke through the center of the French formation, driving 32 squadrons before them into flight. Among their victims were regiments such as the 6th Royal Étranger, 10th Royal Piémont and 4th Royal Dragoons.

Next winter, Austro-Russian forces captured the strategically very important fort of Schweidnitz, and spent the winter on Prussian territory. In 1762, Empress Elizabeth of Russia died, and Russia withdrew from the war. Friedrich's position improved overnight, literally. One moment, his country was threatened by the possibility of coordinated attacks by its enemies, and forays into its very heartland; the next, forces were equal, and a Prussian offensive was feasible.

Peter III, the new Russian emperor, offered to form a coalition with Prussia, and to prove his good faith, defeated an Austrian army at Burckersdorf. Peter was soon assassinated, and his wife became Empress Catherine II, also known as Catherine the Great. Russia definitely withdrew from the war.

In 1763, the Seven Years War came to and end. Great Britain had become a first-rate colonial and naval power; Prussia had not succeeded in acquiring Saxony, which had been the cause of the war, but it had kept Silesia, and also become a power of the first rank, paving the way for its future hegemony in Germany; France had lost not only its dominating position on the seas and in the colonies, but also its role as the leading European power; Austria came out of the war significantly weakened, and Russia's role in Europe was now larger than before.

Developments of Russian Cavalry

Although Peter the Great had acquired a good military reputation by defeating the Swedes at the beginning of the 18th century, at the time of the Seven Years War Russia was an enigma for the other European countries. Friedrich underestimated the Russians, and suffered several serious defeats as a consequence. Just before the war, the Russian army had 331,000 soldiers, 170,000 of them in the standing forces. Forty thousand horsemen were organized in two guards, five cuirassier, three grenadiers on horse, 29 dragoon and eight hussar regiments.

In 1730, during the reign of the Empress Anne, the Life Guards Horse Regiment was formed. At the insistence of Field Marshal Münnich, larger and better horses were acquired in Germany, and used to form three cuirassier regiments. In his honor, the Viborg dragoons were re-formed as the Münnich cuirassiers.

In 1756, at the beginning of the Seven Years War, cavalry regiments consisted of five squadrons, each of two troops of 69 soldiers. With officers and staff, a regiment's complement was about 800 men. In addition, dragoon regiments had a sixth company of grenadiers, two guns and four mortars.

Line tactics were predominant in Russia. Armies were usually formed in three ranks, with 200 to 400 yards between them; the third one was the reserve. The cavalry's position was on the wings, and between lines, and artillery was placed in front of the formation. The battle would be opened with the bombardment of the excellent Russian artillery. When the enemy came within musket range, the infantry would open fire, and the cavalry would charge at a propitious moment. The retreating enemy was pursued by Cossacks and hussars. During the battle, small groups of cossacks roamed the battlefield in search of isolated enemy units to attack, which forced opponents to be constantly on guard, and not to let small groups wander away from the main force.

Cavalry tactics were rather varied. Regiments which were garrisoned in large towns were well trained, and taught to charge with drawn swords, as in the times of Peter the Great. Dragoon regiments, whose companies were scattered in small border hamlets, had hardly any serious training at all. They received enemy attacks with fire from the saddle, or even dismounted and fought back with bayonets. This was the reason why only three dragoon regiments marched off to Prussia at the

Russian officer's cartridge box; middle of 18th century.

beginning of the war. The mainstay of the Russian cavalry were the cuirassiers and horse grenadiers, who were quite equal to their Prussian counterparts until the end of the war.

The Russian army was characterized by its extreme slowness, which was a result of the system of command, and of the enormous baggage trains that followed the army to war. In 1736, during the war with Turkey, a force of 58,000 men marching to Crimea was followed by 40,000 carts; the 70,000 men besieging the fort of Ochakov had a field train of 28,000 carts and 2,000 camels.

The supply units of a dragoon regiment had 54 carts, with food for 30 days, and if the campaign was expected to last several months, the field train could grow to over 200 carts. In 1757, 55,000 men under Marshal Apraxin were followed by 6,000 carts, and 6,000 more were sent after them later on.

In Prussia, the king and the whole General Staff rode with the army; in Russia, field commanders had to have approval for every important decision from the Council of the Imperial Court in St. Petersburg. Correspondence of this sort was sometimes known to take months, which left Friedrich a lot of time to concentrate on the other fronts.

The harsh climate of the country had made both men and animals very resilient, and Russian armies were always renowned for this quality. Therefore, campaign losses due to sickness and exhaustion were relatively small.

Following double-spread: Persian horseman, whose equipment hardly underwent any changes since the late Middle Ages; 18th century.

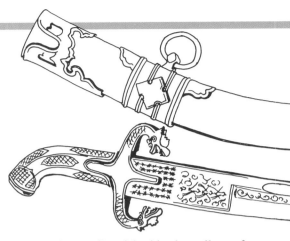

Wars and Cavalry of the East

At the time of the War of the Austrian Succession and the Seven Years War, cavalry columns several times larger than those seen in Europe cruised the expanse that is now Iraq, Iran, Afghanistan, Pakistan, the north of India and the southern republics of the USSR. These were the territories that lay within the borders of ancient Persia. In this space, which consisted of deserts and steppes in the north, and high, ice-bound mountain chains in the east, lived the descendants of the old civilizations that had once flourished in the valleys of the great rivers, and numerous nomadic tribes that were nearly completely independent of any central authority.

Tribal chiefs were rewarded for their service to the Shāh of Persia or the Sultan of Turkey with an appanage which depended on their merits. Traditionally, the backbone of the armies of this area were excellent riders and marksmen — horsemen armed with a lance, saber and composite bow. Members of the nobility, and the better-off among the soldiers, wore a helmet, breastplate and mail shirt, which were usually of very fine quality and richly adorned. Museums have on display armor and mail shirts made in the 18th century, which are very similar to those made in the 15th century.

Firearms were for the most given only to infantry units, which were poorly trained and undisciplined. Some rulers had regular units armed with muskets, trained by European instructors, but there had never been more than a few thousand of them at any one time, so their influence on the outcome of conflicts in this area was negligible. Desert and steppe riders, together with the national horsemen of Afghanistan and the highlands, ruled this part of the world.

During the reign of Husain Shāh, the Afghan tribes rebelled. Under the leadership of Mir Mahmāud, they rode down into the Esfahan valley, and brought down Persian power. In 1735, Nadir Shāh liberated Persia from the Afghans, and founded a new dynasty.

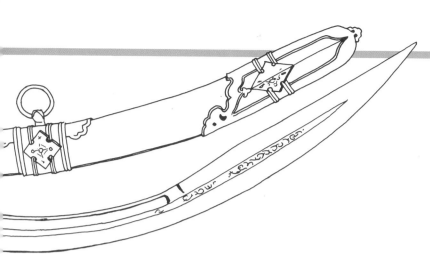

In 1736, he defeated Turkey, and forced Russia into negotiations, which left him free to deal with Afghanistan, a constant source of danger. The next year he started a series of conquering wars, in the course of which he covered 3,700 miles. He defeated the Afghans and entered Kabul, continued to India, took Delhi, captured the towns of Buhara and Hiva in the north, and pushed the Turks out of Georgia and Armenia. Nadir Shāh was assassinated in 1747, at the height of his power, and his great state was torn apart in a protracted civil war.

The same year, Ahmad Shāh Durrāni came to power in Afghanistan. He had achieved superiority over the other tribal chieftains, and founded a powerful state. It was a tribal feudal state, and the basis of its military might was its national cavalry. Ahmad Shāh made several incursions into India, and captured Kashmir and most of Punjab. In the battle of Panipat, in 1761, in which over 100,000 soldiers took part, he defeated the army of the Marāthā, the tribe that ruled India. Even though a part of the infantry was armed with muskets, the battle was fundamentally a cavalry conflict, conducted in much the same way as in the Middle Ages. The forces were formed with a center, backed by a reserve of the best troops, and a right and left wing, with the camp in the back. The battle was decided when Ahmad Shāh introduced his reserves into the fray. They consisted of 2,000 horsemen of the Royal Guard, 10,000 Afghan horsemen and 1,000 camels. The dromedaries were veritable "gun platforms," with cannon strapped to their backs.

Indian armies used strong animals like elephants and camels to carry cannon of smaller caliber and their crews. Tactics were simple — come within range, fire the gun, and return to the rear, unless the animal, panicked by the shot over its head, decided otherwise. These "self-propelled" cannon were taken up by the peoples living on the borders of India, among them the Afghans.

After the battle at Panipat, the Indian state entered into a period of decadence; soon, the colonial army of Great Britain was at its borders.

Persian saber made in Damascus; 18th century.

Prussian Hussar Regiment, 1756

STAFF:

Colonel	1
Lieutenant Colonel	1
Quartermaster	1
Surgeon	1
Smith	1
Saddlemaker	1

COMPANY:

Captain	1
1st Lieutenant	1
2nd Lieutenant	1
Junior Officer	1
Sergeants	2
Corporals	6
Trumpeter	1
Troopers	102

The regiment has 10 squadrons.

Chapter Four: Time of the Revolutions

1775 – 1815

T he situation in Europe had not changed much as a consequence of the Seven Years War, but the relations among the colonial powers had been altered. Great Britain had profited most. Making use of the large number of its colonists and the strengthening of its colonies, Britain drove Holland and France out of America. But the thirteen colonies, experiencing a period of rapid growth, wanted more independence from the mother country in matters of economy and politics. Great Britain, on the other hand, wanted them to remain only sources of raw materials and a market for its industrial products. Open conflicts between the colonists and regular English troops started in 1775, and marked the beginning of the American War of Independence.

The American Revolution (1775 – 1783)

During the Seven Years War in Europe, between drawn-out maneuverings of large armied that waited for favorable occasions to take up battle, or frittered away their time in long sieges, a whole series of smaller clashes took place, which were not conducted according to the rules of engagement valid for large-scale, orderly battles. Line tactics and constant drilling on the exercise fields were designed to eliminate a soldier's initiative, and make of him an automaton who was supposed to execute orders without thinking. Nevertheless, short, surprise clashes and skirmishes demanded speed of reaction, initiative

and a large degree of improvisation. The English military authorities realized this, and formed seven regiments of Light Dragoons, who were free from rigid line tactics and the accompanying harsh discipline. They made for excellent reconnaissance troops, like hussars, chasseurs à cheval or Jäger zu Pferde.

As the situation in America grew more serious, the 16th and 17th Light Dragoons were sent over. They became a model of cavalry accepted by George Washington's Militia, although the first cavalry unit formed after the beginning of the war was a troop of German mercenaries and veterans of the Seven Years War named the Pennsylvania Hussar Company. They were, however, disbanded after only a few weeks because they were too expensive.

Clash between the American and English light dragoons near Cowpens, South Carolina, 1781.

Opposite: American light dragoon from the unit of Colonel Henry Lee, who was the father of Robert E. Lee, Commander in Chief of the Confederate army during the American Civil War, 1861 – 1865.

Below: Broadsword of Brunswick origin used by American light dragoons.

At the end of 1776, when war between the British and Americans was gaining in intensity, Washington wrote to Congress: "From the Experience I have in this Campaign of the Utility of Horse, I am Convinced there is no carrying on the War without them, and I would therefore recommend the Establishment of one or more Corps." On the strength of this recommendation Congress allowed the equipping of 3,000 light horsemen. Four regiments of Continental Light Dragoons were formed from provincial militia detachments at the beginning of 1777. Bland's Virginia Light Horse became the 1st Regiment, the second, commanded by Col. Elisha Sheldon, became known as Sheldon's Dragoons, and the third and fourth were known, respectively, as Baylor's Dragoons and Moylan's Dragoons. Following English practice, a regiment was divided into six troops, each of which was supposed to have 280 men at full complement; in reality, they rarely had more than 150. Owing to lack of equipment and armaments, each horseman carried the weapons he had managed to procure for

himself; it was definitely not unheard of for American dragoons to be armed with Indian spears and tomahawks. The colors of coats for each regiment had been set forth in principle, and were as follows: tan with green facings for the 1st, blue with buff facings for the 2nd, white with blue facings for the 3rd and red with blue facings for the 4th.

Instead of grouping his four new cavalry regiments into a larger fighting formation, Washington split the Continental Light Dragoons up into a number of smaller units with the tasks of scouting, maintaining communications and patrolling on "no-man's land." In the following years, a series of lesser conflicts, with never more than a few hundred horsemen taking part on both sides, were recorded. One of the biggest of these happened in 1781, at a place in South Carolina, called Cowpens. American General Morgan, commanding 800 infantrymen, 80 horsemen of the 4th Continental Light Dragoons, under Col. William Washington, and 45 horsemen of McCall's Mounted Militia, defeated

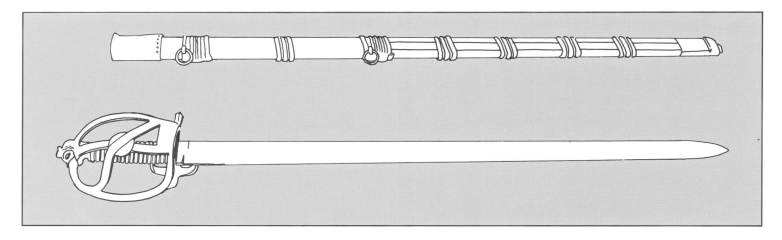

Revolutionary War general of the light cavalry about 1795. Painting by C. D'Ache.

British General Tarleton, at the head of 700 infantrymen, 200 green-uniformed dragoons of the British Legion, 50 horsemen of the 17th Light Dragoons, and a battery consisting of two artillery pieces. The battle was decided when Washington's 80 dragoons, previously hidden from the enemy, charged and broke the green dragoons, and forced the already demoralized English to lay down their arms. Tarleton succeeded in escaping with 150 of his men; all the others were killed or captured.

In 1783, America gained its independence, the army was disbanded, and the horsemen went home.

Types of Cavalry

At the end of the 18th century, cavalry consisted for four basic types, although in some armies this division was not so apparent. The heavy cavalry consisted of cuirassiers, carabiniers and some guards regiments that traditionally had other names. Like the knights of the Middle Ages, the heavy cavalry had the task of administering the coup de grace to a shaken enemy, to breach his battle formation and create on opening for the infantry, which was supposed to finish the opponent off, and the light cavalry, whose task was to pursue the remnants of his force. In principle, this was akin to German tactics of 1941, when

Wehrmacht tanks rolled through the Allied lines on the Western Front. Because of their weight, and the characteristics of the horses they rode, the cuirassiers and carabiniers could not go fast or far. Consequently, their position was usually behind the lines, in the reserve, where they waited for the signal to move toward the enemy, as slowly and inexorably as a steam roller.

Dragoons made up the medium type of cavalry. Owing to their universality, they were the most numerous of the cavalry troops. With the appearance of firearms, a mounted foot soldier became a dragoon. At the time of the greatest expansion of cavalry, he lost nearly all his original characteristics. In modern times, he would remain the only mounted soldier, and revert to his original role — a foot soldier on horseback. Dragoons were trained to fight like cuirassiers, but also to reconnoiter and patrol like light horsemen; as they were armed with carabins, musketoons and bayonets, they could play the part of infantry, too. They lacked, however, the impact of the heavy cavalry, the speed of the light cavalry, and the firepower of infantry. Also, dragoons presented the most variations among armies. Where there was no heavy cavalry, dragoons were the real battle cavalry.

Reconnaissance, patrolling, pursuit of the enemy, cutting of his communication lines, capturing and guarding inhabited places or bridges until the arrival of infantry, as well as foraging, were the tasks of the light cavalry — Hussars, Jägers zu Pferde, Chevauxlegers, Chasseurs à Cheval or Light Dragoons. Most of the other light cavalry units were cheaper alternatives to the hussars, whose richly decorated uniforms were extremely expensive. For an army, it was easiest and most economical to equip a light horseman, who did not need so much training as a cuirassier or a dragoon. At the beginning of the 19th century, a cuirassier's horse in France cost 300 francs, a dragoon's horse 200 francs, and a light cavalryman's horse only 100 francs. Horses of very high quality, for officers or guards units, could cost in excess of 500 francs (today about 800 U.S. dollars).

The fourth, and youngest, of the regular army cavalry units combined the speed of light cavalry with the force of impact of the heavy cavalry. These were the uhlans, light horsemen armed with a spear, who had been a part of the Polish and Lithuanian armies since the 16th century. Their name derives from the Turkish word *oğlan,* meaning "young man"; they were dressed in traditional Polish costume, with the characteristic *czapka* on their heads, and a double-breasted uniform coat called the *kurtka.* Countries that were frequently at war with Turkey, or else bordered on Poland, appreciated the worth of these riders, and took them into their service. Friedrich II had Bosniaks in his cavalry, and from 1793, when Prussia occupied part of Poland, Towarczys. In 1784, Austria formed its first regiment of uhlans, and in 1803, Russia changed its Odesky hussars into uhlans.

At the end of the 18th century, the cost of equipping and training a horsemen in

Austria was 2,200 crowns for a Jäger zu Pferd, 2,800 crowns for a hussar, and 3,300 crowns for a cuirassier. In comparison, a musket cost 10 crowns, a pair of shoes two, a 12-pound gun 460 and a dragoon horse 80 crowns. The cost of equipping and training a foot soldier was 200 crowns, which also given us an idea of how expensive cavalry was.

Horses were bought, or sometimes simply requisitioned in the field, with the issuing of a paper stating that the state would pay this debt at some future

Following double-spread: Uniform, weapons and equipment of a horseman from the French 7th Hussars, 1802.

Austrian dragoon from 1800. Contemporary etching by R. von Ottenfeld.

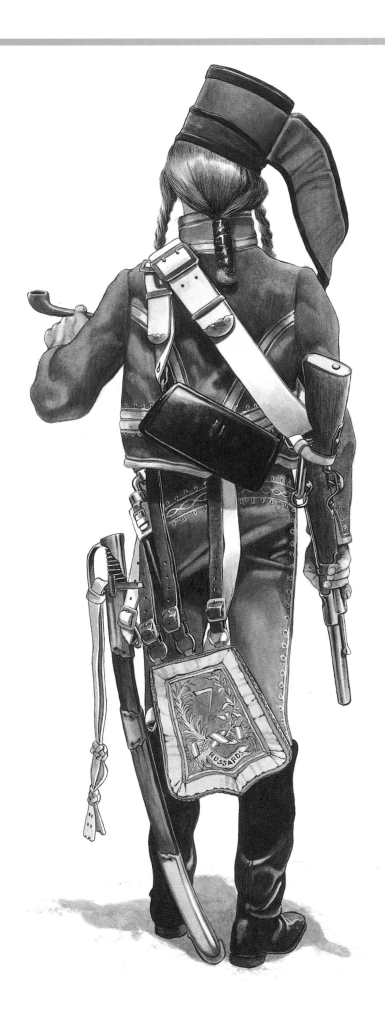

Napoléon Bonaparte (1769–1821) in the uniform of a chasseur à cheval of the Guard. Painting by J. Chabord.

Opposite: An officer of the French cuirassiers, called "The Big Brothers" because of the big horses they rode, 1805.

time. In peacetime, the criteria for the acquisition of horses were very strict, but during war, because of high losses, every horse was a good horse.

The French Revolution

The American War of Independence, and especially the Declaration of Independence, had strong repercussions in France. At this time, the throne of France was occupied by Louis XVI, who had managed during his short reign to triple the national debt, thus adding to the burdens of already depleted state coffers. Four thousand noble families in the Court and around it accounted for over one-quarter of budgetary spending. The bourgeoisie controlled most of the riches of France, but had no political rights, and no influence on government.

The development of the means of production created a gap between the bourgeoisie, who represented economic advancement, on one side, and the nobility on the other. The differences between these social strata culminated in the French Revolution of 1789.

In defending the regime, the king could not rely on the army, which was as corrupt as the administrative apparatus. High commands were usually won by bribes, or by influence at court. The lower nobility could not aspire to these positions, regardless of merit and ability, its members could rise no higher than troop commander. An unbridgeable social chasm divided the officers from the soldiers and noncommissioned officers. An edict published in 1781

Below: Mameluke trooper of the Napoléonic Guard in 1805.

eliminated the possibility of anyone not of noble birth becoming an officer. Noncommissioned officers were openly dissatisified, any many left the army in protest. The king could rely only on the foreign regiments in his service, which made up nearly a quarter of the French army's strength. As it turned out, this was not enough. Louis XVI was deposed and guillotined, and France became a republic.

War of the First Coalition

The young Republic soon had to face a coalition of Prussia, Austria, Great Britain, Russia, Spain and the lesser German and Italian states, which had been formed with the express aim of suppressing the Revolution and restoring the absolutist feudal regime. This war lasted until the end of the century. In 1793, the French army had close to a million men under arms. All supporters of the ancien régime had been purged, and there was great confidence between the enlisted men and the officers. The officers, many of them elevated from the ranks, gave an example by their self-sacrifice. Discipline was maintained by the threat of harsh punishment.

The fiery French had inherited a rich equestrian tradition, which, coupled with high revolutionary morale, became the basis for the creation of a very good cavalry force. After Louis XIV, Marlborough and Friedrich II, and his commanders Zieten and Seydlitz, it was again the turn of the French to take the next step, and introduce great attacking masses of cavalry.

In the first years of the Revolutionary Wars against the forces of the Coalition, the French cavalry was weakened by the collapse of line tactics. It also had difficulties in regenerating itself, as there were insufficient officers and few adequate horses. All mounted troops were converted into light cavalry, although the regiments kept their old names. Divided among the combined units, the cavalry was scarcely noticed on the battlefield. A decree of 1793 created 29 regiments of heavy cavalry (two of them carabiniers), 20 regiments of dragoons, 23 regiments of Chasseurs à Cheval and 11 hussar regiments. Each regiment had 4 – 6 squadrons that varied in size. Altogether, there were 440 squadrons, with 95,000 men. Cavalry regiments, or brigades consisting of two regiments, were part of infantry divisions. Nevertheless, the need for independent cavalry divisions soon arose. The first such division, albeit temporary, was formed by General Jourdan, from units drawn from the armies of the Sambre and Meuse. General Hoche acted in the same way in 1797. From that time on, French cavalry began to make its presence felt. At Marengo, in 1800, cavalry brigades commanded by General Kellermann charged the Austrian infantry, and converted an imminent defeat into victory.

Napoléon

In eight years of war against the Coalition, a young and energetic officer named Napoléon Bonaparte rose from artillery captain to first man of the French Republic. In 1800, when he assumed power, Napoléon offered to make peace with the Coalition, but in vain. The measures he subsequently took to secure the continued prosecution of the war met with widespread approval among the bourgeoisie and the masses, who had become convinced that peace could be achieved only through victory. The élan present at the beginning of the Revolution was restored. There were no difficulties in war production and the filling up of the armies. Men and war materiel were sent to the operative armies without delay. Not realizing the changes that had taken place in France after Napoléon's accession, the Austrians planned to move concentrically on Paris, starting from Italy and Germany. After defeats at Montebello, Marengo and Hohenlinden they were forced to accept a peace treaty. The other countries of the Coalition soon followed suit.

Napoléon's Plans of Conquest

After the preliminary peace with Great Britain, signed in Amiens in 1803, France's economy grew significantly stronger. Overseas trade, primarily with the colonies, increased. Together with a bumper harvest in 1802, this influenced the revitalization of other parts of the economy. Bonaparte's monetary policy was based on hard money. In order to create as much cash as possible, he opted for a mercantilist approach: spend as little as possible abroad, earn as much

French standard of the Chasseurs à Cheval de la Garde Imperiale in 1805.

Opposite: French dragoon of the 26th Regiment carrying a rolled coat over his right shoulder. This was good protection against being wounded by a saber, 1805.

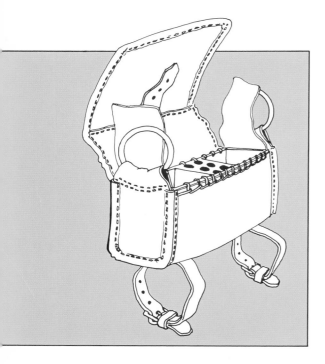

French dragoon catridge box, model AN X, 1799.

as possible by export, or, failing that, by conquest. In Europe, Bonaparte was ruthless. He considered the north of Italy his backyard, intervened in Switzerland, and forced his Constitution on the Swiss, and continued his occupation of Holland in spite of the terms of the Treaty of Amiens. British endeavors to open the French market to their products met with no success. Even though the two countries were at peace, British imports were seized in French ports. In return, Great Britain started seizing French ships on the high seas, but still without a declaration of war. Nevertheless, that was practically the beginning of the war, a war which Bonaparte evidently wanted, but not yet, not until he had had time to strengthen his naval forces.

After drawing up a plan for the invasion of Great Britain in 1801, Napoléon commissioned the construction of the Camp de Boulogne, a base where the invasion was to be prepared. After a short interruption caused by the Peace of Amiens, 1803 saw the beginning of the construction of the main center for the reorganization and training of the French army, in the vicinity of Boulogne-sur-Mer. To command the army, Napoléon created a General Staff (État-major général), and separated it from the Ministry of War, headed by General Berthier, which was in charge of the reorganization.

From 1802 to 1805, Napoléon conducted a thorough shake-up of his cavalry. Of the 25 regiments of heavy cavalry, the first 12 were changed into 10 regiments of cuirassiers (the 8th Cuirassiers du Roi wore their old armor) and 2 regiments of carabiniers, while the 13th to 18th were turned into dragoon regiments. The number of hussar regiments was decreased from 14 to 10, the 7th, 11th and 12th also being turned into dragoons, thus increasing the number of dragoon regiments to 30. Chasseurs à Cheval were given serial numbers from 1 to 26; numbers 17 and 18 on the army list were vacant, and never formed though.

Regiments of the line had three squadrons each, and numbered 550 men with a full complement.

When Napoléon proclaimed himself emperor in 1804, the Garde des Consuls became the Garde Impériale. It included a regiment of heavy cavalry − Grenadiers à Cheval − with 1,018 men, divided into four squadrons of two companies each. Attached to the Grenadiers were the Gendarmes d'Élite, with two squadrons numbering 632 troopers. The light cavalry of the guard was made up of the Chasseurs à Cheval, also organized into four squadrons. Their tasks included the constant guarding and escorting of Napoléon. The emperor was always followed by a lieutenant, a *maréchal-des-logis,* two brigadiers, a trumpeter and 22 troopers. Whenever the emperor dismounted, the Chasseurs dismounted too, armed bayonets, and surrounded the emperor with weapons at the ready. Napoléon could be approached without special permission only by the commander of cavalry, Marshal Murat, and the Minister of War, General Berthier.

The Cavalry in Napoléons Grande Armée after the Prussian Campaign of 1806

	Sqds.	Btns.	Guns	Men
GARDE IMPÉRIALE				
Inf.Bde. Lefebvre;	–	8	42	3,761
Cav.Bde. Bessierse;				
Grenadiers à Cheval, Gendarmes d'Élite,				
Chasseurs à Cheval, Mamelouks	10	–	–	1,253
1st CORPS Bernadotte;				
Inf. Div. Dupont, Rivaud, Drouet;	–	18	38	14,135
Cav.Bde. Tilly;				
2nd and 4th Hussars, 5th Chasseurs	9	–	–	1,119
3rd CORPS Davout				
Inf.Div. Morand, Friant, Gudin;	–	28	44	20,980
Cav.Bde. Marulaz;				
1st, 2nd and 12th Chasseurs	9	–	–	1,527
4th CORPS Soult				
Inf.Div. Saint-Hilaire, Leval, Legrand;	–	26	46	24,106
Cav.Bde. Guyot;				
8th Hussars, 16th and 22th Chasseurs	9	–	–	1,443
5th CORPS Lannes;				
Inf.Div. Suchet, Gazan;	–	21	24	16,522
Cav.Bde. Treillard;				
9th and 10th Hussars, 21st Chasseurs	9	–	–	1,049
6th CORPS Ney;				
Inf.Div. Marchand, Vandamme;	–	17	24	13,860
Cav.Bde. Colbert;				
3rd Hussars and 10th Chasseurs	6	–	–	706
Inf.Div. Desjardins, Heudelet;	–	17	24	12,210
Cav.Bde. Dursonel;				
7th and 20th Chasseurs	6	–	–	1,441
RESERVE DE CAVALERIE Murat				
Cav.Bde. Lasalle;				
5th and 7th Hussars	6	–	–	935
Cav.Bde. Milchaud;				
1st Hussars and 13th Chasseurs	6	–	–	774
Cav.Bde. Watier;				
11th Chasseurs and				
Chevau-légers Bavarois	6	–	–	842
1st CUIRASSIER DIVISION Nansouty;				
1st and 2nd Carabiniers,				
2nd, 3rd, 9th and 12th Cuirassiers	18	–	6	2,605
2nd CUIRASSIER DIVISION d'Hautpoul;				
1st, 5th, 10th and 11th Cuirassiers	12	–	2	1,367
1st DRAGOON DIVISION Klein;				
1st, 2nd, 4th, 20th and 26th Dragoons	18	–	3	2,181
2nd DRAGOON DIVISION Grouchy;				
3rd, 6th 10th and 11th Dragoons	12	–	3	1,771
3rd DRAGOON DIVISION Beaumont;				
5th, 8th, 9th, 12th, 16th and 21st Dragoons	18	–	3	2,487
4th DRAGOON DIVISION Sahuc;				
17th, 18th, 19th and 27th Dragoons	12	–	3	1,792
5th DRAGOON DIVISION Beker;				
13th, 15th, 22nd and 25th Dragoons	12	–	3	957
Horse Artillerymen	–	–	–	988

Total strength of the Grande Armée

Infantry	107,389/135 Btns.
Cavalry	25,569/158 Sqds.

During the campaign in North Africa, known as the Egyptian Campaign (1789 – 1801), General Kléber formed a mounted company of Turks, and brought them back to France. This company, 124 men strong, was dressed according to Turkish customs, and was called the Mamelukes. They were attached to the Chasseurs.

In honor of his empress, Napoléon formed the Regiment de Dragons de l'Impératrice in 1806; they were the medium cavalry of the guard. The regiment was divided into three squadrons, and had 60 officers. The first two squadrons had 476 troopers each, while the third one, of *vélites,* had 296 younger soldiers.

During the Revolutionary Wars, cavalry divisions became established as operative units. At the Camp de Boulogne, the corps became a permanent formation, consisting of artillery and two or three regiments of hussars or chasseurs, under the command of a brigadier general. Along with seven corps, Napoléon formed the Reserve de Cavalerie, which had two cuirassier and five dragoon divisions, with slightly more than 20,000 men. The army corps and the independent cavalry reserve became the main elements in Napoléon's maneuvers.

Even the best equipped and trained cavalry force could not be effective without good horses that would be able to withstand the hardships of a campaign. Napoléon, even though he was not the best of riders himself, always showed an interest in the

condition of the regimental horses during an inspection. One of the usual questions was how many Norman, Flemish, Breton or German horses a regiment had. Colonels were allowed to acquire horses locally to maintain their units at full strength. Captain Parquin, who joined the 20th Chasseurs à Cheval in 1803, recalls in his memoirs that the regiment was excellently mounted, with the 1st squadron having black horses, the 2nd squadron bay horses, the 3rd squadron chestnut horses, and the 4th squadron gray horses. But there were also different situations. In 1805, a whole dragoon division, 7,200 men strong, went on foot because of the lack of mounts.

France had always had good heavy horses, like the Percheron, Boulonnais

Officer of the French Dragoon Guard, 1806.

143

or Ardennais breeds. There were enough of these large horses to satisfy the needs of the cuirassier regiments, which were consequently much heavier then their counterparts in other armies. An incident narrated by the Baron de Marbot in his memoirs best describes what sort of horses these were. De Marbot had lost his horse, and borrowed another one temporarily from a cuirassier regiment. He describes it as a large and slow animal that was not capable of carrying an aide-de-camp swiftly from one part of the battlefield to the other. Marshal Lannes saw the predicament of his ADC, and interceded with the colonel of the Württemberg Light Horse, to find him a lighter and swifter mount.

In 1806, Napoléon increased the number of squadrons in a regiment to four, so that regimental strength increased to between 800 and 950 troopers.

Since 1776, the French cavalry had discontinued the practice of using pistols in charges, and attacked with cold steel, as all the other armies already did. According to regulations, the cavalry left its positions at a moderate trot, which was maintained for most of the time, in order not to tire out the horses, changed to a slow gallop at approximately 200 paces from the enemy, and started the charge at some 80 paces, after the trumpeters signaled the change to full gallop. In practice, there were deviations from the rules. Parquin tells us that at Eylau the 20th Chausseurs received the Russian charge standing in their places, and mowed down the entire enemy first line with a volley fired when they were only six paces away.

It was typical of the French that deviation from the rules was a rule unto itself. This was mostly due to an officer cadre of exceptionally high quality, who often proved that bad units with good officers were superior to opponents who had a reverse situation: good soldiers and incompetent officers.

Regiments usually formed in a line, with squadrons one beside the other, if there was enough place, or in a column, with squadrons or companies one behind the other. Heavy cavalry usually attacked in columns formed by companies, with 25 men abreast; in this way, each company was formed in two lines. Another often-used formation was the formation of squadrons into echelons, also known as the chess formation (*en échiquier*).

In battle formation, the cavalry's place was on the wings, or in the center, behind the infantry. It was usually strongest in the direction of the main thrust, which was executed in waves, and prepared and supported by artillery. They tactics of the French cavalry under Murat, Grouchy, Lasalle, Kellermann and other brave commanders were very simple: as soon as a favorable position in relation to the enemy was achieved, the attack was launched. Only in clashes with superior enemy forces was flanking attempted. The battle formation consisted of deeply echeloned masses of regiment or brigade width, which was not only a reflection of new mass tactics but of the insufficient training of the lower units. Regiments, or brigades,

Opposite: Russian cuirassier officer of the Chevaliers Garde, which sustained heavy losses at the Battle of Austerlitz in 1805.

were ranked one behind the other, with very little space in between, so an attack looked like a series of repeated charges. In attacking enemy heavy cavalry, or a firm infantry front, the first line usually consisted of cuirassiers and the second one of dragoons. Light cavalry protected the flanks. In attacking infantry, the width of the front was that of a squadron, and the attack was directed at the corners of the infantry square.

War of the Third Coalition (1805 – 1807)

Since the accession of Napoléon Bonaparte to power, Austria had watched the changes in France with increasing frustration, and it did not take much prompting from Great Britain and Russia to nudge it into a coalition in 1805. Soon, the Austrian army was on the Rhine. When Napoléon found out about the offensive of the Third Coalition, it took him only an hour to dictate to the Quartermaster-General the plans for moving the army from the Camp de Boulogne to the Rhine, with all details – the makeup of columns, the routes to be used, sites for camps – and he did not forget a single regiment. He had evidently already prepared all this in his head, as an alternative if he gave up on the invasion of Great Britain. An army consisting of 149,000 infantry and 30,000 cavalry, organized in six corps and Murat's cavalry reserve, started toward Germany, to face 284,000 Austrians and 90,000 Russians.

The Austrian army designated for operations in Germany crossed the border at the river Inn. The Bavarians, allies of the French, retreated to Bamberg, and the Austrians arrived at the river Iller, where they stopped. It was risky to expose oneself to a French strike with still unorganized forces, but General Mack, at the head of 89,000 Austrian troops, counted on the Russians' arriving before the French.

The evening of October 1st found the Grande Armée on the Stuttgart-Bamberg line, with a front 110 miles wide. On October 6th, the front on the bank of the Danube had narrowed down to 50 miles. From that line, the Grande Armée could cross the Danube, but also take up battle on the left bank, in case that Mack decided on such a course of action. Mack did not do this, but grouped his forces on his right wing, at Ulm, believing that Napoléon would attack him there. He had no inkling of Napoléon's intention of striking at him from the north, from his rear; this was because he had not detached his light cavalry for reconnaissance duties.

A day before the whole force was to cross the Danube, Napoléon sent Murat's cavalry reserve across to secure the entire operation. After the crossing was completed, Murat marched straight toward the Austrians, while the main body of the Grande Armée embarked on an outflanking of the enemy's position. When the French heavy cavalry, headed by the hussars and chasseurs, entered the Black Forest, Mack became convinced that the main strike would come from that direction. Nevertheless,

Austerlitz 1805

Time was on the Allies' side. Nevertheless, partly at the insistence of Russian Emperor Alexander I, partly lulled by Napoléon's offers of negotiations, they decided to move toward the French, overriding the objections of their commander in chief, Kutusov. The clash occurred at Austerlitz. No other large and important battle was ever lost in such a quick and imprudent way as this one.

According to the plan of Austrian General Weyrother, 33,000 men, General Kienmayer's cavalry, and three Russian divisions were sent to outflank the French left wing. Russian General Bagration, with 12 Russian battalions and 40 squadrons, was approaching the French left wing along the road to Brünn. General Kollowrath remained at the center of the Allied formation with only 27 battalions. In the rear, commanded by Grand Duke Constantine, was the reserve, consisting of the Russian Guard and 80 squadrons under the Duke of Liechtenstein. The Allied position was getting very stretched out. Liechtenstein was sent to assist Bagration, so only Kollowrath and Constantine protected the center. That was precisely where Napoléon struck. Kollowrath was forced back. An intervention of the Russian Guard stopped the French momentarily. The Russian Chevaliers Garde broke a battalion of the 4th Infantry Regiment and captured its eagle. At this, Napoléon sent in his Guard. The Grenadiers à Cheval, under General Rapp, pushed back the Russian

Left: Charge of the French 4th Dragoons, who captured the Prussian flag in 1806. Painting by E. Detaille.

the attack came from the back. Mack had no choice but to surrender, together with the forces that did not manage to extricate themselves. Forty thousand men gave themselves up, together with 60 guns and 3,000 horses.

After Ulm, Napoléon marched into Vienna, while the Allies retreated to the north, waiting for the arrival of the Russian reinforcements. A calm ensued. The French had to secure their lines of communication and supply. Napoléon entrusted this task to the dragoons. One dragoon division secured the base at Augsburg, another one guarded the Prussian border, a third one was in Vienna, protecting the road toward Brünn, and an infantry dragoon division was ouposted near Pilsen. Two cuirassier and one dragoon division remained facing the Austrians and Russians.

cuirassiers, inflicting heavy losses.

Murat's cavalry reserve, together with Lannes's corps, attacked Bagration and Liechtenstein's cavalry. In a great cavalry battle on the road to Brünn, the Allied mounted troops were chased off the field, which was practically the end of the battle. The Allies lost 27,000 men, the French 7,000. Several days later, a peace with Austria was signed, while the Russians withdrew into Poland.

The Austrian Cavalry

At the beginning of the century, the Austrian cavalry was considered to be superior to the French. It comprised 8 cuirassier, 6 dragoon, 6 chevaux-léger, 3 uhlan and 12 hussar regiments. Every regiment had 8 squadrons. In the light cavalry, a squadron at full complement had 151 men, in the heavy cavalry, 131.

Although the Austrian regiments were individually well-trained, well-equipped and well-mounted, they lacked training at the level of larger formations, with several regiments operating together. The attack of Liechtenstein's cavalry was executed in an uncoordinated and confused fashion. Some of the regiments went too far out, others did not move at all, but waited for the attack in place, even though this was strictly prohibited by regulations. The only exception was envisaged in clashes with the Turkish light cavalry, when it was deemed permissible for the regiment to dismount and defend itself with firearms.

The basic tactical formation was a division, consisting of two squadrons. Rules said that a squadron was supposed to attack in three lines; in practice, this was reduced to two, because a rider from the second line could conceivably succeed in avoiding a fallen rider from the first line, but this was practically impossible for a rider in the third line. Clearly borrowing from the French, who used the column formation for attack, thus gaining the advantage of a deep strike, the Austrians used columns only during marches, and for taking up positions.

The reason that there were no larger units in the Austrian standing army was that the role of the Austrian cavalry was to protect and support the infantry. Larger cavalry formations, like the 80 squadrons of the Duke of Liechtenstein, were formed only for individual occasions, and could not measure up to the divisions of the French cavalry reserve. The Russians went one step further. They had combined units in their standing army. For example, the 6th Division of General Sedmoratsky had 18 battalions of infantry, including heavy cavalry regiments with five squadrons each — the Ekaterinoslav cuirassiers and Kiev dragoons; light cavalry regiments with 10 squadrons each — the Alexandria hussars and Tatarsky uhlans; and five squadrons of Popov cossacks. The 6th Division also had five infantry batteries, one horse battery, one company of sappers and one company of pontooniers, with 50 pontoons. All this came to a total of 10,800 infantry, 3,500 cavalry and 72 guns. In this way, the Russians scattered

their heavy cavalry among the infantry divisions, and, like the Austrians, could not use it as a powerful mobile reserve.

Archduke Charles had urged the formation of larger units even before Austerlitz, but it was only after the battle that he was allowed to realize his plans. The Austrians had learned their lesson. The Russians had not.

Under intense pressure from Napoléon, 16 small German states from the south of Germany and the right bank of the Rhine, headed by Bavaria and Württemberg, seceded from the Reich and formed the Confederation of the Rhine. This entity assumed the obligation of providing Napoléon, its protector, with 63,000 soldiers in case of war. The news that Napoléon might cede Hanover to Great Britain under the terms of the peace treaty caused Prussia to intervene in 1806, and war broke out again.

The Jena Campaign of 1806

The Prussian army gathered in three groups behind the Thuringian Forest. General Rüchel, at the head of 20,000 men, was at Eisenach, Duke Wilhelm Ferdinand, commanding the main body of 58,000 troops, was at Erfurth, and the corps of General Hohenlohe-Ingelfingen, 48,000 men strong, was at Weimar. A strong detachment commanded by General Blücher guarded the flank at Kassel. The reserve corps of the Herzog von Württemberg, with 20,000 men, was at Magdeburg, and General

L'Estocq, with an equal force, was in East Prussia. The Prussians planned to wait for the French to attack north of the Thuringian Forest, and then to counterattack with their main forces.

Napoléon grouped 160,000 men in the general area of Bamberg. He decided to take the assembled forces along the Leipzig-Berlin axis, and attack the enemy where he found him. The French moved in three columns, in a front 50 to 60 km (30 to 36 mi) wide. These forces, formed *en échiquier,* could gather for battle in a day's march in the center, and in two days' march on the wings. The advance was covered by the light cavalry of the corps and three light brigades that Murat had detached from the cavalry reserve. Advancing down the valley of the river Saale, Napoléon received intelligence of the presence of a strong Prussian force west of Jena. He immediately decided to make for Jena and to attack the Prussians there with his main force, and sent Marshal Davout and his 3rd Corps by way of Apold, to secure a position behind the Prussians.

Davout had three infantry divisions and a brigade of light cavalry consisting of the 1st, 2nd and 12th Chasseurs à

Opposite: Prussian dragoon of the 5th Regiment. Prussian dragoons were considered the best in Europe until their defeat at Jena in 1806.

Gebhard Leberecht Blücher (1742 – 1819), one of the best-known Prussian commanders, served as a hussar in his youth.

Opposite: French Grenadier à Cheval de la Garde Imperiale who belonged to a unit that was never beaten, 1807.

French Chasseur à Cheval de la Garde Imperiale, 1808.

Cheval. All in all, he had just over 28,000 men. The corps was headed by the three regiments of light cavalry, each with a detached squadron as an advanced guard. Vialannes, commander of the light brigade, sent his Chasseurs forward to secure bridges on the river Saale and gather information. After several small clashes between his men and Blücher's hussars, Davout realized that the forces in front of him were much larger than he had thought. The whole main body of the Prussian army – 58,000 men, 10,000 of them cavalry – commanded by Duke Wilhelm Ferdinand was approaching from the direction of Auerstedt. Almost simultaneously, Napoléon clashed on October 14th with the forces of Rüchel and Hohenlohe at Jena.

In the early morning mist, Davout's divisions, formed in battalion squares, turned back attack after attack of the Prussian cavalry. Not even the elite cuirassier regiments, the 3rd Leibkürassiers, 10th Gendarmes and 13th Gardes du Corps, could break the resistance of the French infantry of the line, which had learned in the Revolutionary Wars how to use every advantage the terrain gave it to defend itself from the cavalry. This, and the wounding of Wilhelm Ferdinand, which disrupted the whole chain of command, decided the outcome of the battle.

The battle at Jena began in much the same way. As they arrived, the French corps joined in the action. The cavalry reserve came last, just in time to push back Rüchel, also freshly arrived. The bulk of the Prussian cavalry was at Auerstedt. Only three cuirassier, four dragoon, three hussar and several Saxon regiments could put down Jena in their regimental histories.

After Jena, Murat undertook an energetic pursuit of the shattered Prussian army, covering nearly 500 miles in the course of 24 days. He was in Jena on October 14th, Magdeburg on the 20th, in Berlin on the 24th, in Stettin, on the Baltic coast, on the 29th, in Lubeck on November 5th, and on the 7th he forced Blücher to surrender at Ratekau. L'Estocq's corps retreated toward the Russians.

This defeat on the battlefield brought with it a complete breakdown of morale, and catastrophe for the state. Napoléon sent back to France 120,000 prisoners and 250 flags, and his army acquired a large number of good horses.

The Prussian Cavalry

At the beginning of the century, the Prussian cavalry had 13 cuirassier and 14 dragoon regiments, with 5 squadrons each. Only the Garde du Corps cuirassiers had 3, and the Königin and Auer dragoons 10. There were 10 hussar regiments, all with 10 squadrons but one, which had only 5. The Towarbzys made up the light cavalry together with the hussars; they were armed with spears, like the uhlans, and formed into a corps of 15 squadrons, each of which had more than 150 men. It is interesting that each squadron had about ten men armed with carbines. Today, we would call them snipers: they were excellent shots, and their task was to go in front of their lines, and disturb and weaken the enemy before the charge with their fire, or to protect the withdrawal of their squadron.

In its heyday, the Prussian cavalry had very high standards of equipment, training and mounts. It had excellent horses of the Holstein, Oldenburg and Ostfriese breeds. Only the French horses of the Norman breed could compare with them. Regimental officers were fined if equipment or horses were in bad shape, so quality was generally well looked after. The tactics of the lower units and discipline had remained unchanged since the Seven Years War. The Prussian cavalry had high fighting spirit and morale, as in the time of Friedrich II, and could have been a hard nut for the French to crack. Napoléon expressly warned of this possibility in a special bulletin issued before the start of the Jena campaign in 1806. The main

Right: Polish lancer of the line in the French Army, 1810.

weaknesses of the Prussian cavalry were an old officer cadre, most of whom had once fought with Zieten and Seydlitz, and the scattering of units among the infantry divisions, which usually included two regiments of the line and several squadrons of hussars. At Jena and Auerstedt, the regiments shattered against the French infantry squares in numerous individual and uncoordinated attacks.

Toward the end of the 18th century, the Prussian and Russian cuirassiers discarded their armor in order to decrease weight and gain in maneuverability. The Austrians kept theirs, and the French, who had previously had only one armored regiment, now fitted out all their heavy cavalry with back- and breastplates. Where cuirassiers were formed as a massed reserve, they kept or were given armor; where they were dispersed in infantry units, armor was rejected as unnecessary. Later, when large divisions were formed again, the cuirassiers got their armor back.

The Eylau Campaign of 1807

After defeating the Prussian army, Napoléon turned to the Russians, who had a force in Poland that numbered 112,000 men, organized into two corps, plus the Prussian forces that escaped captivity and joined the Russians. In December, the main body of the Grande Armée gathered in Warsaw. Napoléon decided that he had to push the Russians back from Pultusk if he wanted to spend

the winter there. This led to several clashes on the right bank of the river Vistula, after which General Bennigsen, the Russian commander, retreated to Biala Piska. With this, Napoléon considered the campaign over, and sent his troops to winter quarters. However, Marshal Ney, pursuing L'Estocq, threatened Königsberg, which induced Bennigsen to move to the north. Hearing of this, Napoléon made for Königsberg; this led, at the beginning of 1807, to the extremely bloody battle of Eylau.

At one point, an extremely violent clash between the French and Russian infantry developed. Both sides suffered heavy losses, and Napoléon's center was threatened, so he ordered Murat to attack the Russian lines with his cavalry reserve. Through a snowstorm, Murat led the charge of 80 squadrons formed in a brigade column. The brunt of the attack fell on the 2nd Division of General Ostermann-Tolstoi and the 8th Division of General Essen. The latter's two brigades, one made up of the Emperor's Guard Cuirassiers and the Kargopolsky dragoons, the other of the St. Petersburg and Livonsky dragoons, were unable to stop the French cuirassiers from bursting through the two lines of their defenses. The Grenadiers à Cheval, who also took part in the attack, at one point found themselves behind Russian lines. Colonel Lepic stopped his regiment, re-formed it, and charged back out the way he had come in.

Only an intervention of the Russian reserves from the rear stopped the French cavalry's advance. Davout's corps had meanwhile rounded the Russian left wing, and threatened its lines of retreat. The arrival of L'Estocq's Prussian corps stopped Davout, and enabled the Russians to get away.

Napoléon considered everything that was not a clear-cut victory like Austerlitz or Jena nearly equal to a defeat. After the battle, both sides proclaimed that they had won, and retreated to winter quarters.

L'Estocq's Prussian corps did not take part in the battle at Eylau in its entirety, but with its 14 battalions, 50 squadrons and 40 guns, it represented a serious fighting force. L'Estocq had at his disposal the 5th Prittwitz hussars, the Auer, 13th Rouquette, 8th Esebeck and 7th Baczko dragoons, and 15 squadrons of Towarczys. Later on, he was joined by the 13th Garde du Corps and 4th Wagenfeld cuirassiers and 6th Zieten dragoons. From the remnants of broken units, the Prussians managed to put together about 40 more squadrons, bringing their total to 90; together with the Russian 208 regular and over 100 Cossack squadrons, this represented a sizable cavalry force.

Eylau turned out to be the Russians' Austerlitz: they realized that with the existing organization of cavalry as part of the infantry formations they would not be able to stand up to the French massed cavalry. Preparing for the next campaign, they conducted a thorough reorganization of cavalry. All cavalry regiments were detached from infantry divisions and grouped into brigades. A cuirassier brigade under General Kogin was formed, consisting of the Emperor's Guard Cuirassiers, Military Order and Little Russia regiments, as well as several dragoon brigades of similar strength, and two even larger formations, one under General Uvarov, with 45 squadrons, another, under Prince Galitzin, with 50, which consisted of dragoons, hussars and uhlans. Ataman Platov headed a Cossack corps, with 17 regiments, consisting of 85 squadrons. On the other side, Napoléon included in his Grande Armée several units from the Confederation of the Rhine, among them the excellent König Kürassiere from Saxony, Chevau-légers from Bavaria and the Württemberg and Polish cavalry of General Sokolnicky.

The East Prussian campaign began in May 1807. Bennigsen was informed that Marshal Lannes's corps, which was in front of him, had strayed too far from the main body. In June, he crossed the river Alle at Friedland and attacked Lannes, who managed to hang on until Napoléon arrived with the main force. In the narrow space between the river and the French lines, the 1st dragoon division of General Latour-Maubourg succeeded in beating back the attack of

30 squadrons under General Kologrivov, who had previously repulsed Ney's attack. Bennigsen sent the guards cavalry into the attack, but they, too, were thrown back. Under pressure from superior forces, the retreat of the Russian units across the bridges on the Alle turned into flight. The Russians lost 16,000 men, the French 7,000. A peace treaty was soon signed, and the Russians returned home.

When Napoléon marched into Warsaw before the battle of Friedland, his guard of honor included Polish noblemen who so impressed the French Emperor with their mounts and their bearing, that he decided to form them into the 1st (Polonais) Chevau-légers Lanciers. This regiment of 968 horsemen in four squadrons formed a part of Napoléon's Guard. Although they were called Lanciers, they were not armed with lances until 1809. The Blue Lanciers, so called because of the color of their Polish-modeled uniforms, were one of the most distinguished regiments in the Napoléonic Wars. In 1808, during operations in Spain, a squadron of 150 men charged and captured fortified Spanish positions at Somosierra, flying in the face of opinion declaring such a thing impossible. The enemy fled, leaving behind four batteries. The squadron lost all its officers and 83 troopers.

By the Treaties of Tilsit in 1807, Napoléon formed the Grand Duchy of Warsaw from Polish territories formerly under Prussian occupation. This entity had self-rule, and an army of 24,000 foot soldiers and six regiments of horse, each with three squadrons. The Duchy of Warsaw provided the most numerous, and probably best, contingent of troops that fought alongside the French army. In 1812, Poland raised 74,000 infantrymen and 23,000 horsemen. In proportion to its 2.5 million inhabitants, this gave Poland the highest percentage of population participation in the armed forces at that time.

Napoléon and Great Britain: The Peninsular War

After defeating Austria, Prussia and Russia, and owing to the favorable terms of the Peace of Tilsit, France had a free rein in relations with Great Britain. Finding it impossible to defeat the British fleet, Napoléon decided to blockade the Continental ports, thus disrupting trade, and damaging Britain economically. This was the reason why French troops marched into Portugal in 1807. A column passing through Spain captured Madrid by surprise in 1808. Using deceit, Napoléon placed his brother Joseph Bonaparte on the throne of Spain, which caused a popular revolt. Britain could still recognize an opportunity when one appeared, and in 1809 sent an expeditionary force under the command of Sir Arthur Wellesley to the Iberian peninsula. It landed north of Lisbon. This was the beginning of a war on Spanish and Portuguese territory that was to last until Napoléon's downfall.

Wellesley, later known as the Duke of Wellington, landed with 13,500 men — 13 battalions 394, light dragoons with 180 horses, and three batteries without a single horse to pull them. His force included several Commissaries, whose

157

Opposite: English dragoon of the Guard. In the Battle of Salamanca they beat the French infantry, 1811.

Right: Arthur Wellesley, Duke of Wellington (1769 – 1852), English commander most successful in combat against Napoléon.

task was to buy from the civilian populace everything needed for the supply and equipping of the army. This system of supply worked well enough in the Low Countries, but the situation in Portugal was something else. It took eight days for the army to get off the beaches, mainly using 500 mules and 300 oxen that had been bought. In that time, the Commissaries had succeeded in buying only 60 horses for the dragoons. Even so, Wellesley had to leave one battery and a significant quantity of supplies behind. Although Britain had two regiments of Life Guards, a regiment of Royal Horse Guards, 7 regiments of Dragoon Guards and 25 regiments of Dragoons and Light Dragoons on its army list at the beginning of the century, Wellesley was chronically short of cavalry in Spain.

Marshal Junot had gathered a force of 11,000 infantry and 2,000 cavalry, with 20 cannon, in order to attack Wellesley at Vimeiro, where he had taken up position to defend the landing of two brigades, with 4,500 men. The French attacks were repulsed three times, with great loss of life. Junot retreated, and suggested to Wellesley to allow him to leave Portugal without hindrance. Wellesley, himself in an unenviable situation, agreed. For this, he was recalled to England and temporarily relieved of command until 1809.

At the end of the year, Sir John Moor, Wellesley's successor, had at his disposal 26,000 infantry, 2,000 cavalry and 60 cannon, approximately 10 times fewer men than the French occupation forces. Napoléon expected the British

army to embark and retreat when it received news of the disintegration of the Spanish army. Moor did the exact opposite. In December 1808, with snow on the ground, he attacked the French communication lines, perilously stretched out, expecting to be able to retreat before the intervention of a larger enemy force. Upon first receiving news of clashes with British troops, Napoléon divined Moor's intentions, and set out to meet him with a force of 70,000 foot soldiers, 10,000 cavalrymen and 200 cannon.

Moor had no option but to withdraw, and so the race toward the sea started. On December 22nd, Napoléon was in Madrid, and on the 28th already in Villalpando, 265 km (159 mi) farther. Moor evaded him successfully, and covered his retreat.

The crossing of the British baggage train over the river Esla was protected by two squadrons of the 18th Light Dragoons, which had recently been turned into a hussar regiment, together with the 7th, 10th and 15th. Suddenly, about 500 Chasseurs à Cheval and Mameloukes of the Garde Impériale, under the personal command of General Lefebvre, appeared at a crossing upriver, with the obvious intention of attacking the British rearguard. Colonel Otway gathered 130 of his 18th Hussars, and charged the French, who had not yet formed for combat, and, surprised, stopped. After a short clash, Otway retreated, only to meet the 3rd Dragoons of the King's German Legion. Together, they charged the Chasseurs again, but this time they were ready, and formed in two lines. Otway hardly got away. However, now the 10th Hussars under Lord Paget, heretofore hidden from sight by the houses of Benavente, charged the French with 450 men. Meanwhile, General Stewart, the brigade commander, stopped the 18th Hussars and 3rd KGL Dragoons, rallied them, and brought them back into the battle. This proved to be too much for the Chasseurs, who retreated at a run. General Lefebvre and 70 troopers were captured. All in all, the unit lost 200 troopers on that day.

At Mayorga, on December 28th, Paget, with his two squadrons of 10th Hussars, was watching the column of Marshal Soult, and did not notice that he was cut off from his main force. Two squadrons of French dragoons formed up on the hill behind him. The only way out was to charge through the French cavalry. He

English hussar, 1811. Contemporary etching.

Austrians, Prussians, or Russians. The English horsemen, compared with the French, showed a new quality: individuality. Wellesley said "I did not like to see four British squadrons opposed to four French," thinking of the Frenchmen's better training. English troopers were, in essence, fox hunters, riders with an excellent knowledge of the equestrian skills, as in hunting, but with one significant flaw: they tended to get carried away by the hunt, thus exposing themselves to the danger of being encircled and destroyed by the enemy.

We have the testimony of the cornet of the 14th Light Dragoons on how the English riders compared with the French. They "had evidently the advantage as individuals. Their boardswords, ably wielded, flashed over the Frenchmen's heads, and obliged them to cower over their saddlebows. The alarm was indeed greater than the hurt, for their cloaks were so well rolled across their left shoulders that it was no easy matter to give a mortal stroke with the broad edge of a sabre, whereas their swords being strait and pointed, though their effect on the eyes was less formidable, were capable of inflicting a much severer wound. Many, however, turned their horses, and our men shouted in the pursuit."

For the protection of communications from Spanish guerrillas, just like several months earlier at Austerlitz, Napoléon detached numerous dragoon squadrons. Of the 30 dragoon regiments, only the 1st, 23rd, 28th, 29th and 30th did not go to Spain, as they belonged to the Army of Italy. Heavy cavalry was represented

formed the 10th Hussars in two lines, and charged. The dragoons were thrown back, leaving behind over 100 prisoners.

When Moor finally made it to the shore at Corunna, he ordered, to the dismay of his riders, that all horses that could not be embarked be slaughtered. The 15th Hussars, for example, brought home only 31 horses, out of 400 they had taken to Spain. While the pursuit was on, Napoléon got news that Austria was preparing for war. He left Soult to attack Moor, and hurried to Paris. At Corunna, Moor won the battle, but lost his life. The English boarded their ships and returned to their island.

The battles at Vimeiro and Corunna, as well as the cavalry skirmishes during Moor's retreat, showed that different rules were in effect when fighting the English then when fighting the in Spain by the newly formed 13th Cuirassiers and the 1st squadron of the 5th Cuirassiers. The French cavalry forces in Spain consisted predominantly of dragoons and chasseurs.

War in Austria (1809)

In the period after Ulm and Austerlitz, Archduke Charles reorganized the Austrian army. In 1809, it had 223,000 foot soldiers, 36,000 horsemen and 760 cannon. Cavalry was organized into divisions according to the French model. The cuirassiers, whose number of squadrons was decreased by two, were organized into two divisions of four regiments each, and the dragoons and other cavalry into brigades of two regiments each.

In April 1809, Archduke Charles, believing that Napoléon would not be able to mass his armies in Germany because of the Peninsular campaign, seized the opportunity to declare war on France. But Napoléon, informed of Austrian preparations for war, issued march orders in time for his troops to arrive at the possible theatre of operations along the Austrian border.

The Battle of Eggmühl

It was the Austrians' intention to attack Davout's isolated 3rd Corps in Bavaria before reinforcements could arrive. At the head of about 110,000 men, Charles struck on April 22nd at Davout on a front stretching between Eggmühl and the Danube. Napoléon, who was at

Landeshut, arrived at the scene of the battle by noon, and ordered a general charge. The Austrian 4th Corps was attacked from three sides by the oncoming Frenchmen. Charles ordered his cavalry reserve to attack, in order to enable the 4th Corps to pull out. Napoléon counterattacked with his reserve of eight cuirassier and two carabiniers regiments, and a large-scale cavalry battle ensued, with the Austrian Kaiser, Erzherzog Franz and Hohenzollern cuirassier regiments taking part on the other side. The Baron de Marbot wrote about this battle in his memoirs. While stressing that the individual qualities of the opposing soldiers were equal, he pointed out that the difference in equipment put the Austrians at a disadvantage. Namely, the French had both a breastplate and a backplate, while the Austrians had only a front cuirass. Thus the French could engage in a melee without fear of being wounded from behind, while in a position to so wound their enemies. After a short fight, the Austrians withdrew, but, as Marbot points out, soon discovered that the lack of a back cuirass was an even greater flaw in retreat. To quote him: "The fight became a butchery, as our cuirassiers pursued the enemy, and for the space of half a league the ground was piled with killed and wounded cuirassiers ..."

Of course, it was not only the lack of a backplate that caused the resounding defeat of the Austrian cuirassiers and their enormous losses, several times greater then the French. After the defeat in the war of 1805, the multinational Austrian army did not have the fighting spirit to stand up to an enemy who had

already defeated the largest armies in Europe. The high morale present at the time of the Seven Years War had been lost. On the other hand, Napoléon's soldiers had lost their revolutionary fervor but had retained an élan, and several dynamic incentives such as a democratic feeling stemming from equality of prospects, the possiblity of promotion for everyone, hatred toward the aristocracy, a sense of soldier's honor, bravery in the face of the enemy, the feeling of being a member of a victorious army marching through conquered Europe, and the like. At the end of the day, the French cavalry re-formed, and attacked the retreating Austrians. The fighting went on well into the night.

After the defeat at Eggmühl, the Austrians retreated to the left bank of the Danube, while Napoléon marched into Vienna along the right one. Napoléon's attempt at crossing ended in failure at the battle of Aspern-Essling. Subsequently, the French fortified the island of Lobau, and built a great number of pontoon bridges in secrecy. Archduke Charles, faced with a huge concentration of Napoléon's forces, and unable to face his cavalry in the open, retreated to the heights behind Wagram. He had at his disposal 15,000 horsemen, and the French 27,000. When Napoléon started the crossing, the Austrian forces were too far away to attack them before they had developed into battle formation. That was the decisive point. After a dogged Austrian defense, Napoléon brought 102 artillery pieces into the center. A fierce cannonade created a breach in the center, and Napoléon sent in his cavalry reserve and

guard. Charles had to withdraw. The Austrians lost 42,000 men out of 155,000, 20,000 of them captured, while the French lost 32,000 out of 150,000. Several days later, an armistice was signed.

The Continuing War in Spain

In Spain, Napoléon left about 200,000 good troops to continue the Peninsular War under the command of seasoned officers. He also left behind a completely undefined chain of command. The commanders would not listen to King Joseph, and, out of vanity, would not cooperate among themselves, or subordinate to one of their number, even if it meant defying Napoléon's orders.

The theater of war in Spain was much harsher than any the French had encountered before in Europe. Mountainous terrain, climatic extremes, lack of roads and scarcity of food for men and horses combined to weaken the troops. But the worst of the "Spanish affair," as Napoléon called that bloody war (1808 – 1819), was the guerrilla activity. Thousands of guerrillas constantly attacked convoys, couriers and isolated strongholds, forcing the French to detach valuable troops for the protection of communications. The British command finally gave in to the insistent Wellesley, who had meanwhile been rehabilitated, and who stubbornly maintained the he could hold Portugal with 30,000 men. Nevertheless, he was issued instructions that he should withdraw if faced with French pressure, rather than to wait until it was too late.

Austrian hussar, 1809. Contemporary etching.

Antoine C. L. de Lasalle (1775 – 1809), French light cavalry commander killed at the Battle of Wagram.

All of Britain's landing power was concentrated on the Iberian peninsula. Wellington made Portugal into a British base. He also organized the Portuguese army, which numbered 25,000 men at the end of 1809. The cavalry consisted of 12 regiments of Portuguese Dragoons. They were supposed to have 594 men in four squadrons at full complement, but in practice, that number rarely surpassed 500. At the same time, two light cavalry regiments of the Portuguese Legion fought on the French side in the battle at Wagram.

After defeating the Austrians, Napoléon sent an additional 140,000 troops to Spain, in order to suppress guerilla activity and push the British out of Portugal. Wellington resisted the French attacks successfully. As time passed, his strength increased. He scored victories at Talavera in 1809, Busaco in 1810 and Fuentes de Onoro in 1811, and captured Ciudad Rodrigo in 1812.

The Battle of Salamanca

After taking Badajoz, too, Wellington set out for Salamanca on July 22nd, 1812. He had been informed of the imminent arrival of the French Army of Portugal and wanted to avoid a battle at all costs, but he also needed to protect Salamanca and the road to Ciudad Rodrigo, to keep open his line of retreat.

The French, under Marmont, had 42,000 infantry, 3,400 cavalry and 78 cannon, and expected the arrival of two more cavalry brigades. This time around, Wellington had more infantry then the French, which had not been the case in the previous battles, and about a thousand more cavalrymen, which was a rarity indeed in the war on the Peninsula. The British had five brigades of cavalry, under the command of General Sir Stapleton Cotton: Le Marchant's Brigade (5th Dragoon Guards, 3rd and 4th Dragoons), Anson's Brigade (11th, 12th and 16th Light Dragoons), Von Alten's Brigade (14th Light Dragoons, 1st KGL Hussars), Bock's Brigade (1st and 2nd KGL Dragoons), and D'Urban's Brigade (1st and 11th Portuguese Dragoons).

Marmont saw a large dust cloud behind Wellington's positions. It was being made by the baggage train of the Allied army, escorted by a regiment of Portuguese Dragoons, but Marmont took it to be the British main force in retreat. Convinced that he faced only a strong rearguard, Marmont sent out the Thomières infantry division to outflank the right wing of the Allied position, while the Maucune division remained facing the enemy. When Wellington noticed that the Thomières division was separating from the French main body, he ordered General Pakenham to attack the unwary opponent with his 3rd infantry division and the Von Alten and D'Urban brigades.

D'Urban struck first with his 1st Portuguese dragoons. Thomières was advancing in battalion columns, without too much in the way of precautions. He was supported by the dragoon division of General Curto, riding behind him. D'Urban's dragoons broke the first battalion in the column, while the others formed into squares and repulsed the Portuguese attacks. Then Pakenham's division opened fire from about one thousand paces away. After several volleys, the Anglo-Portuguese infantry charged with bayonets. On the beginning of the battle of Salamanca, they were attacked by Curto's dragoons, who were thrown back by the 45th infantry regiment, but not before they succeeded in pushing the 5th infantry regiment back by about a hundred paces. Von Alten's Light Dragoons and Hussars then charged the French dragoons and pushed them back. This signalled the end of organized resistance by Thomières's division.

Cavalry pursued the French infantry up to the positions of Maucune's division. Thomières lost half of his 4,500 men. The appearance of cavalry on his flank forced Maucune to form his division into regimental squares. The attack of the 5th Allied division under General Leith soon followed. Leith's line formation was superior to the French, as it enabled more men to open fire on the enemy. This was crucial. Maucune's first two regiments could not withstand the fire, and withdrew toward their reserve brigade. At that point, Wellington ordered Le Marchant to charge with his heavy cavalry. With the 5th Dragoon Guards and 4th Dragoons in the first line, and the 3rd Dragoons in the second, Le Marchant completely broke Maucune's division.

Leaving the French infantry for General Leith to finish off, he ordered a charge on the 3rd French division of General Brennier, which had also formed up into

Austrian cavalry standard, 1806 – 1816.

165

squares. The first regiment in the British line of advance waited for the attack with great discipline. At twenty paces, it fired a deadly volley. Le Marchant was killed, as well as nearly a third of his dragoons. The remaining men retained control of their mounts, and rode into the square, which disintegrated. The men sought refuge in the other squares. The dragoons also withdrew.

Next day, the retreat of the vanquished Marmont was covered by the infantry division of General Foy. At Garcia Hernandez, he was attacked by British cavalry. General Boyer's French cavalry was pushed back by the 11th and 16th Light Dragoons, and the infantry remained defenseless. The French formed up in squares *en échiquiers,* and waited for the cavalry charge. Bock's heavy brigade prepared for the attack. The 1st KGL Dragoons regiment attacked first. The disciplined Frenchmen waited until the Hanoverians were at ten paces, then fired a volley. Those who survived it were stopped by a wall of bayonets. Unable to come any closer, the dragoons began to circle the square. At that moment, a dead horse fell on the French soldiers, and a small breach in the square opened. Several dragoons took advantage of this opportunity, and, sabers flashing, fought their way into the square. More followed, and soon 500 Frenchmen had surrendered. Heartened by this success, the 2nd Dragoons attacked the next square. Not wishing to suffer the fate of the first battalion, the French soon surrendered. The third square repulsed the British attack. The Dragoons lost 127 troopers.

All in all, Marmont lost 15,000 men, 8,000 of them captured. The Allies lost 6,000 soldiers at Salamanca.

There were but a handful of cases in the Napoléonic Wars when cavalry managed to break down a well-positioned infantry square manned by experienced soldiers of high morale. The British success at Salamanca was due largely to the French soldiers' inferior training and lack of fighting spirit. France had over 700,000 men under arms. After 1809, the quality of their training and their morale began to fall off. Four weeks' training was all that the recruits got before being sent to their regiments.

Davout's corps at Auerstedt presented an altogether different picture: it was well officered, its complement consisted of veterans, and it belonged to a victorious army. None of this was true of the French forces in Spain. During intervals between assaults of the Prussian cavalry, Davout went from square to square, animating his troops. At one point, Blücher led 30 squadrons to the attack on Davout's vanguard, but he, too, was beaten back. Nevertheless, the opponents were no slouches, either.

At Jena, the Prinz August Prussian grenadier battalion staved off the assault of three dragoon regiments. The Saxon Winkel grenadier battalion, surrounded by fleeing and surrendering allied units, retreated to the sound of drums in a hollow square formation, repulsing numerous attacks.

Faced with the danger of a cavalry attack, infantry units formed into

Following double-spread: Austrian uhlan of the 3rd Erzherzog Carl Ludwig Regiment. Napoléon patterned his lancers after the Austrian uhlans, 1809.

Opposite: French cavalry attacking a square. Painting by A. Safonov.

Left: French hussar uniform, overalls and sash.

battalion, regimental or even divisional squares, depending on the situation. Infantry training conditioned soldiers to take up the square formation practically instinctively at the very sight of cavalry. Squares were positioned in such a way as to cover each other with their fire. Usually, the first two lines of soldiers would kneel, with the next two to four lines standing behind them, all with their rifles at ready. When the enemy riders approached to between 20 and 10 paces, the order to fire would be given. A battalion of 600 men could bring at least 100 rifles to bear in any one direction, and nearly twice as much if the attack was directed at the corner of the square, although they would be shouting from different distances in that case.

A test of the accuracy and effectiveness of an infantry battalion's firepower was conducted in Prussia near the end of the 18th century. From a distance of 85 paces, in near-ideal conditions, musket-fire was directed at a target measuring 1.8 × 100 meters about 6 × 328 feet. About 70 percent of rounds ended up where they were supposed to. What the effect was at only 20, or ten, paces, can be imagined. The horsemen who remained unhurt were impaled on bayonets.

Of course, cavalry commanders devoted a lot of their time to finding a way to break the square. Prussian and Russian rules of engagement envisaged a charge in two waves. The first consisted of light horsemen simulating an attack — the Cossacks were particularly good at this — and trying to draw the infantry's fire early. Then they moved aside, making space for the charge of the heavy cavalry

of the second wave. Taking into account that well-trained infantrymen could get off three shots a minute, we see, that such a maneuver had to be well coordinated, not to give time to the attacked to reload.

Another possibility was an attack in echelons. A squadron would form in line, four troops, one alongside the other. As they approached the square, the second and fourth troop would fall behind by some 50 paces. The first and third troops would draw the infantry's fire, creating an opportunity for the other two to attack.

A different approach was to detach the best sharpshooters in a squadron to harass the infantry in a square from the flanks, provoking them to fire early. In uhlan or lancer regiments, a part of the men were not armed with spears precisely in order to give fire support to their unit in an attack. In 1811, Napoléon changed six dragoon regiments into the 1st to 6th Chevau-légers Lanciers, and in 1812 the men of the first line in Russian hussar regiments were armed with spears. The reason for this was that a spear, rather longer than a musket with armed bayonet, was much more adequate for breaking into a square then a sword or saber.

The success of cavalry attacking a square also depended on training, skill and morale. The first move was left to the infantry. From the resulting mess of fallen men and horses, the others had to go on. It is very difficult to make a horse run into a man or another animal; it will try to avoid the obstacle at all costs.

*Opposite: French hussar officer of the 7th
Regiment in his elaborate hussar uniform,
1812.*

*Below: Bavarian cavalry regiment on the
march, 1812. Contemporary etching.*

Therefore it was not only a matter of
weaving a course through the mass of
felled animals and their riders, but also
of retaining control over one's horse,
and making it charge the human wall of
the square. Breaking a square was a
much greater accomplishment for
cavalry then defending itself was for
infantry.

War with Russia

Peace with Napoléon put Russia at war
with Great Britain, on paper, and with
Austria, symbolically. Emperor
Alexander's main problem was the
continental blockade to which he had
had to agree after the defeat in 1807.
The blockade was a heavy burden for

Russia. It had to renounce the British export market, and what it needed it had to buy in France, at higher, monopolistic prices. Alexander I began to allow British goods to be imported on ships under neutral flags, and restricted the import of French goods. Of course, the continental blockade of Great Britain could succeed only with Russian cooperation. Both sides were faced with dilemmas. Napoléon's was whether to acknowledge the failure of his system of continental blockade without a fight, or to try to force Russia into submission by arms. Alexander's was whether to give up the independence of his country, or to defend it by force. Both rulers opted for war in 1812. Napoléon's uncontrolled politics brought him into fatal conflict with the last independent power of continental Europe.

In 1812, the Russian army had 232,000 foot soldiers, 45,000 horsemen and 1,200 cannon. In case of need, the emperor could also call on 100,000 Cossacks from the Don, Ukraine, Bug, Black Sea, Siberia and other areas.

The Russian regular cavalry at this time had 12 cuirassier, 37 dragoon, 12 hussar, six uhlan and five Cossack regiments. The Leib-gvarda had six regiments – the cuirassier Chevalier-Garde, the Horse Guards, Guard Dragoons, Guard Hussars, Guard Uhlans and Guard Cossacks. Hussar and uhlan regiments had ten squadrons, cuirassier and dragoon five each. All the regiments of the Guard had five squadrons, except for the Cossacks who had only three. A squadron's full complement was about 140 troopers.

With staff officers, this came to 1,500 men for a ten-squadron regiment.

In 1811, Russian cuirassiers were given breast- and backplates, and organized into two divisions. The rest of the cavalry was organized in Cavalry Corps, which consisted of one light and two dragoon brigades. Each brigade had two or three regiments. The 1st Brigade of the 1st Cuirassier Division was made up of the Chevalier-Garde and the Horse Guards, the 1st Brigade of the 1st Cavalry Corps of the Guard Dragoons and Guard Uhlans, and the 2nd Brigade of the same Corps of the Guard Hussars and Guard Cossacks. After that, the brigades were given serial numbers; e. g., the 14th Brigade of the 4th Cavalry Corps consisted of the Akhtirski Hussars and Litovski Uhlans. Cavalrymen were no longer armed with carabines, save for the 16 best shots in each squadron, who were named flankers. It was not until 1814 that all cavalrymen were issued carabines again.

Opposite: Charge of the Russian cuirassiers of the Guard against French heavy artillery. In the background a counterattack by French cuirassiers, 1812.

Left: Officer of the Saxon cuirassiers of the Guard, 1812.

General Latour-Maubourg, commander of the 4th Cavalry Corps, 1812.

In attack, the Russian cavalry used a formation of line in two rows, or column of platoons. The attack was started at a walk, changed to a trot, and then to full gallop at about 100 paces from the enemy.

Having learned from previous experience, the Russians had adopted the French model of cavalry, so the two forces were very similar in type, organization and tactics of higher and lower units, as well as in quality. The only difference was that the Russian horses were smaller, and, as time showed, hardier.

In 1812, Napoléon started concentrating his force of several hundred thousand men. When French troops started crossing the Prussian border, Prussia signed a treaty of alliance with France, pledging to put at Napoléon's disposal 20,000 men in 24 combined squadrons of hussars, dragoons and uhlans.

Austria followed suit, pledging 34,000 men in 46 squadrons of dragoons and hussars. When spring came, the French army started toward Russia in perfect order. The first line consisted of 446,000 men and 1,146 cannon. Two corps and auxiliary units were in the rear. With forces left behind as reserve, the total came to over 700,000 men, 611,000 of whom crossed into Russian territory. It was the largest army the world had seen, but its quality was far below Napoléon's earlier forces. A large part of the troops were conscripts. The Grande Armée arrived at the Russian border already tired out from long marches.

Nevertheless, 82,000 horsemen in 440 squadrons were under a single command. Lined up in a column of four abreast, they would take up a road for 100 kilometers (60 miles). The head of the column would be three days' march from the rear. This enormous number of horses — not counting an even larger number needed for hauling carts and cannon — consumed 500 tons of oats a day, and a equal quantity of straw or grass. Together with the Russian forces, over 150,000 horsemen cruised the space between Moscow and the rivers Niemen and Berezin.

Napoléon's force consisted of 11 infantry and four cavalry corps. Following earlier practice, each infantry corps had its light cavalry, but its strength had now been increased to two brigades of two or three regiments. Independent cavalry corps of between 8,000 and 12,000 men, with four or five batteries of horse artillery, made their first appearance. The first three cavalry corps — the 1st of General Nansouty, the 2nd of General Montbrun and the 3rd of General Grouchy — had one division of light cavalry and two divisions of heavy cavalry. The light divisions had three brigades of two light regiments each. All the cavalry in the corps was French, except for the third light brigade, which had Polish, Prussian, Bavarian and Saxon light cavalry. Each regiment consisted of four squadrons. The heavy divisions had three regiments of cuirassiers or carabiniers (who had been fitted out with armor in 1810), each of four squadrons, and one regiment of chevau-légers lanciers, with three squadrons, for reconnaissance and protection against Cossack raids.

General Nansouty, commander of the 1st Cavalry Corps, 1812.

The 4th Cavalry Corps of General Latour-Maubourg consisted of the 4th Polish Light Cavalry Division under General Rozniecki, with the 2nd, 7th, 11th, 3rd, 15th and 16th Lancers, with three squadrons each, and the 7th Heavy Cavalry Division under General Lorge, with the Saxon Garde du Corps and Kürassier-Regimente von Zastrow, the 14th Polish Cuirassiers and the 1st and 2nd Westphalian Cuirassiers. Napoléon himself was accompanied only by four complete dragoon regiments — the 7th, 23rd, 28th and 30th — of General Lahoussaye's 6th Heavy Cavalry Division. The other regiments were in Spain and Italy.

The countries of the Confederation of the Rhine met their obligations toward Napoléon with varying degrees of enthusiasm, nevertheless sending their contingents to the Grande Armée. Bavaria, for example, gave 23,000 foot soldiers and 2,800 horsemen. At the beginning of the century, Bavaria had a regiment of Guard Dragoons, two regiments of cuirassiers and four regiments of chevau-légers.

The Guard Dragoons were soon thereafter disbanded, and the cuirassiers reformed, first as dragoons, then as chevau-légers. The units joining the Grande Armée were thus chevau-légers regiments 1 through 6. Although their full complement was six squadrons, with over 1,000 men, they marched off to the campaign with four squadrons each. Württemberg gave 14,000 infantry and the 1. Prinz Adam, 2. Leib-Chevau-léger and 3. and 4. Berittene Jägers regiments.

Westphalia sent 27,000 men organized and uniformed according to the French model. One regiment of chevau-légers was in Spain, and one regiment of chevau-légers lanciers, two regiments of hussars and two regiments of cuirassiers marched off to Russia. Every regiment had 670 men in four squadrons at full complement. Napoléon's younger brother Jérôme, King of Westphalia and commander of the 8th Corps, was accompanied by a company of 120 men of the Garde du Corps.

The Saxon contingent of 20,000 men distinguished itself by its high quality and excellent morale. The Saxon cavalry consisted of the Garde du Corps and Kürassier-Regimente von Zastrow heavy regiments, the Prinz Albrecht, Prinz Johann and von Polenz Chevau-légers light regiments, the Prinz Clemens Uhlans and a regiment of hussars. The full complement of these regiments was also 670 men in four squadrons.

Part of the 9th Corps of Marshal Victor was made up of 15,000 men of the contingents from Berg, Baden and Hesse-Darmstadt. One of the best corps cavalry forces were the brigades of Generals Delâtre and Fournier. The former had the 2. Chevau-légers Lancier de Berg and Hesse-Darmstadt Chevau-légers regiments, each with three squadrons, the latter the Saxon Prinz Johann regiment and the Baden Husaren, with four squadrons each — all in all, 1,900 riders.

When Murat became Grand Duke of Berg in 1807, he formed the Chevau-légers de Berg regiment. In 1809, these

became the Chevau-légers Lancier de Berg, and marched off to Spain with Joseph Bonaparte. In 1812, Murat formed a second regiment of the same name, whose three squadrons joined the Grande Armée.

The Grand Duchy of Warsaw contributed 16 fine Polish cavalry regiments – the 1st, 3rd and 5th Chasseurs, 10th and 13th Hussars, 14th Cuirassiers and eight regiments of lancers. Every regiment had 140 troopers in each of its three squadrons.

Poles fighting in the French army and in French uniforms, known as the Vistula Legion, served as the basis for the formation of the 7th and 8th Chevau-légers Lanciers in 1811. The first six regiments had dark green uniforms and brass helmets, the 7th and 8th dark blue Polish uniforms and caps. The 9th was formed from the old Hanoverian Legion, and made up mainly of Germans.

In 1805, Eugène de Beauharnais, Empress Josephine's son from her first marriage, was named Viceroy to Napoléon and King of Italy. Italian troops were dressed and organized according to French regulations, except that the basic color was green instead of dark blue. The cavalry of Eugène's 4th Corps was made up of Italian troopers in the Garde d'Honneur, two squadrons of the Garde Dragoons, and one regiment of dragoons and two of chasseurs, with four squadrons each. The Garde d'Honneur consisted of five companies, the complements of which were made up of members of Italian aristocratic families. The 1st had been raised in Milan, the 2nd in Bologna, the 3rd in Brescia, the 4th in Rome and the 5th in Venice.

Attached to the Garde Imperiale were three squadrons of Portuguese Chasseurs. Together with the 2nd Régiment de Chevau-légers Lanciers, formed from Dutch Hussars in 1810,

French lancers of the line scouting in advance the front of cuirassiers on the march, 1812.

Napoléon was escorted by 26 squadrons of the Garde Impériale.

The Russian plan of operations envisaged a defense in the border belt centered on the fortified camp of Drissa. Barclay de Tolly's 1st West Arma, 120,000 men strong, was behind the river Niemen, and covered Napoléon's northern forces. Prince Bagration's 2nd West Army, with 60,000 men, was in the center, while the 3rd West Army of General Tormasov, with 45,000 men, covered the south flank. Barclay de Tolly's army was supposed to retreat into the big fortified camp, from where it was to attack the French from the sides, in case they made for Moscow or St. Petersburg. Bagration's task was to disrupt French communications.

In the north, Napoléon had the Franco-Prussian army under Marshal Macdonald, with three armies in the center, one under his personal command, one under his brother Jérôme, and the third under Eugène de Beauharnais. His right flank was protected by the Austrian army of Prince Schwartzenberg.

Napoléon was hoping to decide the war with one or two battles, and had no plan for the eventuality of a Russian withdrawal into the vast interior of the country.

On June 24th, 1812, just before dawn, Napoléon started to cross the Niemen at Kaunas, and met with no resistance. He made for Vilno, hoping to force the 1st Russian army into a battle, but it retreated to Drissa. Contrary to the war plan, Bagration, too, was ordered to withdraw. At Drissa, the Russian command came to the conclusion that the plan of operations was impracticable, and that the 1st Army would be trapped there. Therefore, it was ordered to positions outside Vitebsk, where it was to wait for the 2nd Army, and then take up the battle.

Right: Aide-de-camp at headquarters of Russian cavalry division, 1812.

Napoléon arrived at Vilno on June 28th, but the main body was far behind. The heat was oppressive, and the men choked on the dust. Drums had to be played in the front of a marching battalion so that the men at the rear could know where the head was. Many men and units lagged behind, and the cavalry lost 8,000 horses without ever once entering into a clash. When Napoléon found out that the 2nd Army had started upriver, he followed it with his central and left group, while ordering Davout to take the right group and cut off the 2nd Army's way. Bagration was now in danger of being encircled.

On June 26th, Davout's advance units, headed by the 1st and 3rd Chasseurs, entered Minsk, practically on Bagration's heels; he had only gotten as far as Nesviz. Jérôme was advancing on

Bagration's right flank, his forces headed by General Latour-Maubourg's 4th Cavalry Corps. Bagration's situation was unenviable: if he were to fight Jérôme, Davout would have enough time to encircle him and cut off his retreat. Therefore, he had to withdraw as swiftly as possible. Bagration called Hetman Platov, and ordered him to stop Latour-Maubourg with his Don Cossacks at any cost. In the meantime, a messenger arrived to inform Jérôme of Napoléon's decision that Davout was to take over command of operations on the French right flank. Angered, Jérôme left his army without orders, and returned to Westphalia, escorted by his Garde du Corps.

Platov had at his immediate disposal only 300 men of the Sisoev Cossack regiment, still untested in combat. On June 27th, he prepared to meet the French advance forces at Mir. He placed

French lancer of the line, 1812.

Standard of the Russian cuirassiers of the Guard.

100 Cossacks on either side of the road, and sent the remaining 100 toward the French, with the task of leading them into the ambush.

The French advance forces consisted of the 16th Polish Lancers, from the light brigade of General Turno. Catching sight of the Cossacks, the Lancers galloped at them. The Cossacks retreated, but at such a speed that the Lancers should have caught up with them soon. At a prearranged signal, the Cossacks stopped in their tracks, turned around, and charged with lowered spears. Simultaneously, the other two groups charged from the sides. Surprised, and under attack from three sides, the Lancers were quickly broken, and had to withdraw. General Turno met his 16th Lancers, and sent the 3rd and 15th into a counterattack that rolled back the Cossacks. Bagration sent in the 12th infantry division of General Vasilickov, with 16 squadrons of

Aktirski hussars and Litovski Uhlans in the front. The hussars and uhlans came upon the retreating Cossacks, and, hot on their heels, the Lancers. When General Turno saw on the 27th of June 1812 a Russian reinforcement of 2,000 horsemen facing his 700, he dispatched a messenger with a request for assistance. General Dziewanowski's brigade, with the 2nd, 7th, 11th and re-formed 16th Lancers soon arrived. A cavalry battle lasting four hours then ensued, with the two sides charging by turns. Latour-Maubourg's light cavalry was forced back only by the arrival of General Kuteinikov's brigade of regular Don Cossacks. While the chain of command was reestablished after Jérôme's departure, Bagration got away.

The Russian light cavalry forces to the north had similar defensive engagements. General Kulnev died at the head of the Grodno hussars, defending the crossing at Drissa. On the previous day, he had beaten back an attack by the 11th and 12th Chasseurs under General St. Geniez, from the 2nd Light Cavalry Division of General Sebastiani.

Davout did not succeed in cutting off Bagration's line of retreat, but he did succeed, in the battle at Mohilew, in preventing his link-up with the 1st Army. Also in July 1812 at Stari Bihov, just like at Mir, the French advance troops clashed with the Russian Cossacks and the men of the 4th Cavalry Corps of General Sievers. When Barclay de Tolly heard of Bagration's retreat toward Smolensk, he gave up on the idea of fighting Napoléon, and continued his withdrawal. On July 25th,

Right: Clash between Cossacks and Polish lancers at the Battle at Mira, 1812. Painting by V. Mazurowski.

his rearguard held Napoléon up for two days at Ostrowno. During the night, General Ostermann-Tolstoi's tired 4th Corps was relieved at the Ostrowno positions by the 1st Cavalry Corps of General Uvarov and the 3rd Division of General Konovnitsyn.

In the morning, Napoléon attacked with three corps a position defended by three Russian divisions and 20 squadrons of cavalry. Murat sent the heavy cavalry of General Nansouty's 1st Cavalry Corps to support the 13th Division of General Delzons. The 2nd and 9th French Cuirassiers clashed with the Russian dragoons and the light cavalry of the Guard. It was not until Murat sent General Piré's brigade, with the 8th Hussars and 16th Chasseurs, freshly arrived from Mohilew, on a flanking move across the Dvina, that the Russians retreated in the direction of Smolensk. These two days had enabled the Russians to join forces at Smolensk.

Napoléon's troops were already exhausted. Supply from the rear had practically stopped, and there was less to be found along the way, the deeper into Russia they went. The populace went off to the woods, taking the cattle along, and burnt down the crops and houses. From Niemen to Vitebsk, without any serious combat to speak of, Napoléon lost 150,000 men to exhaustion, illness and desertion. Outside Smolensk he gathered 225,000 men. Everyone in his army, from private to marshal, hoped that he would stop there. Napoléon was undecided. He obviously couldn't stay there indefinitely, but to return would mean failure. The Russian 1st and 2nd

Armies had linked up in Smolensk on August 3rd, and battle had to be joined. This was also the general demand in the Russian army. Bagration wanted a battle, too. Even though he was senior in rank to Barclay de Tolly, he subordinated himself voluntarily. De Tolly, however, broke off the engagement at Smolensk, August 16th – 19th, and continued with the retreat.

After taking Smolensk on the 19th of August, Napoléon's forces crossed the Dnieper, and threatened the Russian army's line of retreat. Barclay de Tolly ordered General Tuchkov and his 3rd Corps to take up position at Valutina Gora and cover the Russian pullback. Tuchkov sent three hussar regiments

under General Konovnitsyn and the Cossack regiments of Karpov and Orlov-Denisov to the crossroads at Lubin. These forces clashed with the van of Marshal Ney's 3rd Corps, the Württemberg light cavalry and General Berumann's brigade, with the 4th and 28th Chasseurs. Tuchkov sent three infantry regiments to their assistance, and succeeded in keeping the crossroads in Russian hands. In the meantime (also on the 19th of August), Murat's cavalry and Marshal Junot's 8th Corps started to arrive in massed columns. The Russians had 15,000 men to their opponents' 35,000, so Tuchkov had to retreat to positions behind the Stragana, a nearby small river. By 5 P.M., the Russians had managed to rebuff two attacks by the infantry of Davout's 1st Corps, which had arrived meanwhile, but had to retreat because of the threat posed by General Nansouty's cavalry. Tuchkov was now reinforced by 8,000 men, among them a cuirassier brigade, and he decided to use these to cover his retreat. Around 7 P.M., at the head of the Ekaterinoslavski cuirassiers, Tuchkov rode out against the third assault of Davout's and Junot's infantry. After the intervention of Nansouty's cavalry, the Russian cuirassiers were pushed back. Nevertheless, Tuchkov had succeeded in slowing down the enemy attack and coordinating his forces. After dark, the Russians retreated unhindered by the French. Both sides lost about 6,000 men.

Matvey Platov (1751 – 1818), general and Cossack ataman. Painting by D. Doj.

Right: Russian General Uvarov, commander of the 1st Cavalry Corps, 1812. Painting by C. Vasiler.

The advance of the Grande Armée through the vast spaces of Russia brought it face to face with some new problems. One of the main characteristics of the French armies, their mobility, hinged on diminished dependence on the plodding supply columns. The rich fields of central Europe provided enough to feed men and horses, at least until the arrival of their supply units.

In Russia, Napoléon wanted to keep up the same tempo of marching as in his previous campaigns. In these earlier undertakings, however, he had not had such an enormous force on the move, had not depended so massively on his own supplies, and had not had such chaos in his rear lines. Before, he had used the principle of exploiting the land as if nothing could be sent from the rear, and sending from the rear as if nothing could be taken from the land. This did not work in Russia. Napoléon could advance much faster than the pace at which the Russian armies retreated. The Russians made up for lost time by fighting constant delaying actions. Advancing practically at a run for two days, sleeping on their feet, then fighting the whole next day, was a pace that no army could withstand for long. It had cost the Grande Armée 20,000 horses by the time it reached Smolensk. The carcasses of dead horses littered the roadside, together with animals too tired or hurt to be of any further use. The best horses of Europe were left lying in the dust. Some of the surviving animals were taken in by Russian peasants, who used them to improve local breeds.

Before the campaign, Napoléon had been cautioned about the characteristics of his future theater of operations by the Poles, who knew Russia well. They had also warned of the mobility of the Cossacks, who always led a spare fresh horse. At the Poles' suggestion, the number of reserve horses in regiments was increased, and every cavalry corps was followed by a herd of free horses. Whenever time allowed, regiments would send their tired and wounded horses to the rear, in exchange for healthy and fresh mounts.

With the enemy always in hot pursuit, the Russians were also on a practically continuous forced march. However, they had one significant advantage: they were approaching their resources, while the Grande Armée was getting farther away from its own.

The light cavalry was busiest on both sides. The Grande Armée was spearheaded by the cavalry corps. General Grouchy's 3rd in the north, General Nansouty's 1st and General Montbrun's 2nd with Napoléon in the center, and General Latour-Maubourg's 4th in the south, facing Bagration. Each corps detached its light division as an advance force, one or two days' march ahead. Each division, in turn, sent out one or two brigades in front, up to a day's march. The brigades detached several squadrons, which fanned out a half day's march in front of their main body. If enemy light cavalry was

Attack led by General Uvarov at the Battle of Borodino, 1812. Painting by C. Vasilev.

encountered, the reserve brigade would intervene if needed.

The infantry corps moved behind the cavalry. Their light horsemen were used to secure the flanks and rear of the corps. If an infantry corps marched independently, then the light horsemen would be detached in front.

Hussars, chasseurs, lancers, uhlans and cossacks cruised through the no-man's-land. Every village, wood, bridge or crossroads was a probable site for a troop of enemy cavalry. Every unit that stopped to rest sent out patrols, guards and outposts, but even so surprises were always possible.

In Smolensk, Napoléon had to come to a decision about future operations. His commanders advised him to go no farther. For a while he wavered, but then opted for pushing on, in the belief that the Russians would not abandon Moscow without a fight, and even if they did, that he would find abundant supplies and quarters in that great city, and force Alexander I into a peace settlement. In any case, he could not winter in the burnt-out remains of Smolensk.

After leaving Smolensk, Barclay de Tolly's position became untenable. He was seen as the sole culprit for the abandonment of such enormous expanses of territory. The emperor was forced to replace him as commander of all Russian armies with General Kutusov, who had gained widespread popularity with his recent successes against the Turks. As a reinforcement, Kutusov was given 25,000 men. Under popular pressure not to give up Moscow without a fight, he decided to take up battle at Borodino.

Borodino

His chosen positions closed both roads from Smolensk to Moscow, and were protected from the front by the river Kolocha. In order to gain time to prepare his position, Kutusov ordered General Gorchakov to take up position at Shevardino, 2 kilometers (1 1/4 miles) in front of Borodino, with 8,000 infantrymen, 4,000 horsemen and 36 cannon. Gorchakov had three days in which to build an earthen redoubt in a good position at Shevardino.

On September 5th, General Konovnitsyn rode in at full gallop, at the head of his Litovski uhlans and six squadrons of Aktirski hussars, with the news that Napoléon was coming. Left and right of the redoubt Gorchakov had emplaced his artillery. Eight battalions of infantry were in the second line behind the redoubt, and in the third the 2nd Cuirassier Division of General Duka, with the Ordenski, Ekaterinoslavski, Glukovski, Malorossyski and Novgorodski regiments. His flanks were protected by the forest. To the left, he detached General Emanuel's brigade, with the Kievski and Novorossyski dragoons and two squadrons of Aktirski hussars; to the right, General Panchulidzev's brigade with the Chernigovski and Kharkovski Dragoons.

About 2 P.M., the Russians could see the French cavalry approach through the thin woods, then stop. Informed of the disposition of the Russian forces, Napoléon decided to reconnoiter the situation himself. He decided that three infantry divisions of Davout's corps — Morand's, Friant's and Compans's — were to attack, with the support of the 1st and 2nd Cavalry Corps. They were

also to be helped by the Polish 5th Corps of Prince Poniatowski, which was coming up on Gorchakov's left side.

The Russians had a well-protected position, which made attacks by the enemy cavalry very difficult, but enabled their own mounted forces to execute forays and then return to safety. Napoléon sent 30,000 infantry, 10,000 cavalry and 186 cannon against the redoubt at Shevardino.

Poniatowski attacked first, but was twice repulsed by General Emanuel's dragoons. Two hussar squadrons protected an outposted battery that was retreating beneath the onslaught of Polish infantry.

Around 4 P.M., Napoléon decided to attack from three directions. Poniatowski struck again at the Russian left wing, Compans's division at the center, by way of the village of Doronino, and Friant's and Morand's divisions at the right wing. Murat's cavalry attacked between the divisions of Compans and Morand.

After an unsuccessful attack on the head of Friant's division, Panchulidzev's dragoons retreated behind the Russian cuirassiers. Morand captured the village of Shevardino, while Compans succeeded in taking the redoubt only in the second attempt, and with strong artillery support. When the Russian infantry counterattacked, Compans had to withdraw. In the meantime, night fell. Compans attacked again at the same time as Morand did from the direction of the village of Shevardino.

Gorchakov sent the Glukovski cuirassiers against one attacking column and the Halorossyski cuirassiers against the other. In the dark, the Russian riders surprised the French, and pushed them back before Nansouty's cuirassiers could come to their assistance. Compans retreated to Doronino, and called in the 111th Infantry Regiment from his reserve, from the direction of the village of Fomkino. Sievers had sent the Chernigovski and Kharkovski dragoons in pursuit of Compans. These, together with the cuirassiers, surprised the 111th in the dark before it could form a square. This cost the French about 300 dead.

As Gorchakov later wrote in his report, he decided to withdraw when he heard the sound of many hoofs. The confusing battle in the dark went on until midnight, when both sides decided to retreat.

Davout brought to Napoléon's attention the weakness of the position of the Russian left wing at Borodino. The emperor, nevertheless, opted for a direct assault over the Russian earthworks. On September 7th, the Grande Armée attacked, with 105,000 infantry, 30,000 cavalry and 587 cannon. Kutusov had at his disposal 101,000 infantry, 17,000 cavalry, 640 cannon and 7,000 Cossacks.

Infantry attacks and counterattacks went on all morning, accompanied by concentrated artillery fire and occasional cavalry forays. About 1 P.M., the Russians decided to retreat to their fallback positions around the village of Semenovskaya, behind the stream of the same name. Their first positions fell into enemy hands. Napoléon now changed his tactics, and proceeded to attack with two cavalry corps.

The village of Semenovskaya was defended by two infantry divisions. On the Russian left wing, six battalions of the Ismailovski and Litovski Grenadiers Guard regiments were formed in squares *en échiquier,* with the 1st and 2nd Cuirassier Divisions behind them. On the right wing, parts of two division were formed in 10 battalion squares beside earthen fortifications (flèches). Behind Semenovskaya was the reserve, consisting of General Sievers's 4th Cavalry Corps and the Alexandrinski hussars and Smolenski dragoons of the 3rd Corps.

Facing the flèches and the Russian right wing, Napoléon placed Latour-Maubourg's 4th Cavalry Corps, with General Wollwarth at the head of the French and Württemberg light cavalry, from Ney's corps, behind him. Friant's and Compans's infantry divisions, and the corps light cavalry — General Girandin's Chasseurs — were in the center, with the task of attacking Semenovskaya. Nansouty's cuirassiers were designated to take on the Russian Guard grenadiers. At about 600 meters (660 yards), the artillery opened up. Napoléon counted on the infantry being so weakened and demoralized by the

Left: General Duka, commander of the Russian 2nd Cuirassier Division, 1812. Painting by D. Doj.

Russian horseman of the Malorossisky Cuirassiers, 1812. Contemporary etching.

bombardment that it would fall apart under the cavalry's charges, and run away. Exactly the opposite happened. Nansouty's 2nd, 3rd, 6th, 9th, 11th and 12th Cuirassiers were rebuffed twice by the grenadier squares. During the third charge, when the Litovski grenadiers saw General Duka's 2nd Cuirassier Division coming to their assistance, they mouned bayonets and charged.

Infantry charging cavalry — this was a case without precedent in the Napoléonic Wars! Attacked by the grenadiers, and under pressure from the Russian cuirassiers, Nansouty had to withdraw.

At the same time as these goings-on on the Russian left wing, Latour-Maubourg's cuirassiers attacked on the right wing, headed by the Saxon Garde du Corps, and followed by the von Zastrow Kürassiers, 1st and 2nd Westphalian and 14th Polish cuirassiers. Twelve squadrons of Polish Lancers from Rozniecki's division charged on their left flank. The Russian infantry could not withstand this tremendous charge, and began retreating. In the confusion, the Saxons managed to take the flèches. The infantry was saved from annihilation by the counterattack of cuirassiers from General Deperadovich's 1st division — two Guards regiments, supported by a brigade of the 3rd Cavalry Corps. Fresh Polish and Westphalian forces threatened the flank of the Russian cuirassiers, and General Sievers's 4th Cavalry Corps had to come to their aid. After a pitched cavalry battle lasting nearly two hours, the Russians had to retreat. Following a dogged defense, the infantry from Semenovskaya also retreated. Because of high losses, Nansouty had to withdraw, but Latour-Maubourg's cuirassiers clashed with Duka's 2nd Cuirassier Division once more before the day was over.

The battle went on until late at night. In the end, the Russians withdrew, leaving Moscow to Napoléon. Both sides lost about 45,000 men. On September 14th, Napoléon entered Moscow. Once there, he sent Alexander I both implicit and explicit calls to peace negotiations, thus revealing the gravity of his situation.

Realizing that the Russians were not about to accept negotiations, on October 19th Napoléon ordered a pullout from Russia. Harsh winter conditions and incessant Cossack attacks turned the withdrawal into a catastrophe. At Studianka, the Baden Hussars and Hesse-Darmstadt Chevau-légers covered the retreat of the rest of the Grande Armée. In their hopeless final charge, they were destroyed by the Russian cuirassiers. Hardly a hundred troopers from both regiments returned. Napoléon lost over 300,000 men in Russia; he would never recover.

The War of Liberation

In spring of 1813, Napoléon was in Germany, with a new army of 133,000 infantry, only 4,000 cavalry and 280 cannon. Prussia had already declared war on France, Great Britain had sent reinforcements to Spain, and Austria was getting its army ready. In Germany, the Allied forces numbered 70,000 Prussians and 80,000 Russians. In a manner reminiscent of his old glory, in May 1813 Napoléon won two battles, at Lützen and Bautzen, but could not fully exploit them due to lack of cavalry. A consolidation of forces was needed before the final conflict, so both sides agreed to a truce that lasted until autumn.

Great Britain no longer felt threatened, and bolstered its forces in Spain. Among other units it sent there were three excellent horse brigades: General Hill's Household Brigade (1st and 2nd Life Guards and Royal House Guards), General Fane's Brigade (3rd Dragoon Guards and 1st Royal Dragoons) and General Grant's Hussar Brigade (10th, 15th and 18th Hussars). General Ponsonby replaced the late Le Marchant at the head of the Dragoon Brigade, and

General Long was sent over with his 13th Light Dragoons. Apart from these new units, the Duke of Wellington could count on 12 regiments of Portuguese dragoons and the cooperation of the Spanish army, which had 24 regiments of cavalry. Each of these consisted of five squadrons, and numbered 600 men with a full complement.

Under the command of the Prince Hessen-Homburg, the Austrians formed a powerful cavalry reserve of three divisions: 1st Cavalry Division Nostiz (Erzherzog Franz, Kronprinz Ferdinand, Sommariva and Hohenzollern Cuirassiers, with 4 squadrons each), 2nd Cavalry Division Lederer (Katzer Cuirassiers with 4 squadrons, Erzherzog Johann, Levenehr and Reich Dragoons, each with six squadrons) and 3rd Cavalry Division Schneller (Hohenzollern and O'Reilly Chevau-légers,

Cornet of the Novgorodski Cuirassiers, 1812. Contemporary etching.

Above: Joachim Murat (1767 – 1815), French marshal and King of Naples, commander of the French cavalry reserve to the Grande Armée, 1812. Etching by Forestier Suly.

Right: French general Grouchy, commander of the 3rd Cavalry Corps, 1812. Etching by Forestier Suly.

Hessen-Homburg and Kienmayer Hussars, with 5 squadrons each. In all, 58 squadrons and 7,899 men. At the head of the main and reserve armies were light combined divisions: 1st Light Division Moritz Liechtenstein (Kaiser and Vincent Chevau-légers, with six squadrons and 1,544 men each, four battalions of light infantry and two batteries of horse), 2nd Light Division Buhna (Liechtenstein, Kaiser and Blankenstein Hussars, each with six squadrons and 2,303 men, three battalions and two batteries of horse) and 1st Reserve Light Division Mesto (Erzherzog Ferdinand and Palatinal Hussars, with six squadrons and 1,598 men each). In addition, there was the Mohr reserve division, comprising the Lothringen and Nassau-Usingen Cuirassiers, with four squadrons and 1,061 men each. The total forces at the disposal of Field-Marshal Schwartzenberg, commander of the Austrian army in 1813, were 139,076 infantrymen, 16,342 horsemen and 368 cannon.

The Russians changed part of their dragoon regiments into eight regiments of Mounted Jägers and Uhlans, so that in 1813 they had 12 regiments of uhlans.

After the defeat of 1807, by the Treaties of Tilsit it was forbidden to Prussia to have standing army of more then 32,000 foot soldiers and 8,000 horsemen in its army. A fundamental reorganization of the army was begun in these conditions, under the command of Generals Scharnhorst, Gneisenau and Clausewitz. In order to create a reserve for the standing army, Scharnhorst discharged three to five men a month from each company,

replacing them with conscripts. This method was called the Krümpersystem, after the name given to surplus artillery horses. In keeping with the idea of a national army, humiliating punishment and aristocratic privileges were abolished. The General Staff was given a significant position in the revamped military administration, and military education was improved. In the fall operations, Prussia succeeded in fielding 270,000 men, 30,000 of them in cavalry units.

Subsequent to their victory over Prussia in 1806, the French had disarmed the Prussian units and left the cavalry without horses. Some of the Prussian cavalry regiments, isolated squadrons or units from depots succeeded in retreating to East Prussia or Poland, where the Russian forces were. When Russia was defeated at Friedland, Prussia managed to avoid the disarming

198

Cossacks charging against French rearguard positions, 1813. Painting by S. Zelohman.

of its remaining troops by signing a separate peace. These units were the nucleus of the future army. In 1808, the Prussian army list had four regiments of cuirassiers, six regiments of dragoons, seven regiments of hussars and two newly formed regiments of uhlans. The number of squadrons in a regiment was decreased to four, except in the Gardes du Corps, which had five, and the Prittwitz Hussars of L'Estocq's corps, where it was decreased to eight. The No. 1 Westpreussisches and No. 2 Schlesisches Uhlans were formed from the 15 squadrons of *Towarczys,* and also had four squadrons each. The strength of a squadron was usually about 150 troopers.

The disaster of the Grande Armée in Russia caused great excitement in conquered Europe. Allies suddenly became enemies. In Prussia, there was a sudden resurgence of patriotism. In 1813, the people were called to arms. Numerous squadrons of National and

Militia Cavalry *(Landwehrkavallerie)* were formed, and grouped into regiments according to their territorial affiliation. Besides serial numbers, regiments were also given the name of their district — Pommersches, Brandenburgisches, Neumärkisches, Kurmärkisches, Schlesisches, Ostpreussisches, Westpreussisches, Rheinisches, Westfälisches and Elbisches.

National and Militia Cavalry consisted mainly of hussars and uhlans. A Light Cavalry Guard Regiments was formed from the Guard Uhlans and the newly raised Guard Cossack Squadron. In 1813, the Prussian cavalry had a total of 13,000 troopers in regular regiments, 13,000 more in National and Militia units, and 4,000 in depots.

Count von Luetzow was given permission to establish the *Freikorps.* Beside infantry, he formed a regiment of Black Chasseurs, so called because of their black uniforms. These chasseurs had a red and gold sash tied around their waists. Together with their black uniforms, this was the inspiration for the flag of the State of West Germany. For his regiment von Luetzow recruited poets, painters, writers, students and other educated adventurers. They were renowned for their parties in towns in which they stayed. Precisely because they easily achieved rapport with the local populace, they were entrusted with the gathering of various information. Patrols of this regiment often left messages in verse or drawing on the walls of houses for their main body. Several well-known writers, artists and musicians died as soldiers of the Black Chasseurs.

Prussian regulations and drill instructions clearly showed that Prussia had no intention of facing the French cavalry in the open by forming cuirassier and dragoon divisions. There were two main reasons for this: one was the still-vived experience of 1806, the other purely economical. The fitting out of a least 10,000 heavy cavalrymen was a costly and protracted process, so Prussia opted for a model in which part of the cavalry was equipped by the state, the other part by rich volunteers. Only a few heavy regiments remained in the army; all the rest were light cavalry. Regulations required close cooperation among infantry, artillery and cavalry, and the basic formation consisted of 8 – 10 battalions, 8 – 12 squadrons and 2 or 3 batteries, one of them of Horse.

Although this combined model was a retrogression for cavalry, it was the only possible solution at that time. It was in some aspects similar to the British model.

The largest tactical formation was the brigade, consisting of 1 – 2 regular regiments and 1 – 2 National or Militia regiments. The sole exception were three cuirassier regiments that constituted an independent brigade. The Prussian cavalry was traditionally well mounted and highly trained.

Cossack of the Reserve Regiment, 1813. Contemporary Watercolor.

Hostilities were resumed in the second half of August 1813. Napoléon had 450,000 infantry and 40,000 cavalry, organized in 14 and 5 corps, respectively. The Allies had 800,000 men under arms. Their operative army stood at 450,000 men in three armies, the rest were reserve and garrison troops. The Russians had 45,000, the Prussians 30,000 and the Austrians 25,000 cavalrymen.

The Battle of Dresden

As Friedrich II had once done, Napoléon decided to outwit his opponents by maneuvering, and defeat their armies one by one. Schwartzenberg, however, threatened Dresden with the 170,000 men of the Army of Bohemia. As this city was the hub of the French supply system, it had to be defended. The Allies were defeated in the resulting battle, with the loss of 35,000 men. On the left wing, separated from the center by the swollen Weisseritz River, two Austrian infantry divisions under General Weissenwolf — 24 battalions, but no cavalry — faced Victor's 2nd Corps and two of Murat's cavalry corps. Weissenwolf was expecting Klenau's corps, 21,000 men strong, to come to his assistance from the rear. Because of bad roads, Klenau was late, arriving just in time to witness the dissolution of the Austrian position, with Schwartzenberg helplessly looking on. A cavalry charge, in which the newly formed Jung von Zastrow Cuirassiers also took part, broke the resistance of the Austrian infantry. Nearly 18,000 men were captured, and Schwartzenberg had no option but to withdraw.

The Army of Bohemia was saved by an ineptly organized pursuit. This enabled Schwartzenberg to destroy Vandamme's isolated corps at Kulm. After the defeats of Oudinot at Gross Beren, Macdonald at the Katzbach River and Ney at Denewitz, Napoléon had to take up position at Leipzig if he was not to be cut off from his line of retreat to France.

Opposite: Prussian hussar of the Brandenburg Regiment, famous for its victory at Liebertwolkwitz, 1812.

Swedish Vastgota Dragoon in Prussia, 1813.

203

Charge of the Austrian dragoons at Kulm, 1813. Contemporary painting.

Right: Austrian cuirassier in winter coat, 1813. Drawing by R. von Ottenfeld.

Opposite: Austrian hussar of the 4th Hesse Homburg Regiment. Austrian hussars lost much of their fame acquired in the Seven Years War, 1813.

Liebertwolkwitz

Napoléon had at his disposal 160,000 infantrymen, 24,000 horsemen and 700 cannon, while the Allies had 260,000 foot soldiers, 65,000 cavalrymen and 1,330 artillery pieces. Such a massive concentration of troops in a single place had not yet been recorded in the history of Europe.

While his forces were assembling around Leipzig, Napoléon sent Murat and his cavalry to watch the southern approaches to the city, in order to prevent the reconnoitering and potential encirclement of the French positions. Earlier, General Wittgenstein had sent three formations of Cossacks — about 1,500 men — behind French lines, and they had done quite a lot of damage. General Bennigsen was now approaching, and his army included a Cossack corps, consisting of nine regiments of Ural Cossacks and Bashkirs — a total of 3,500 riders capable of seriously threatening the French rear.

To cover the French troops concentrating around Leipzig, at Liebertwolkwitz, Murat gathered the cavalry of the Guard, the 5th Cavalry Corps, Milhaud's dragoon division of Spanish War veterans, and one of Berkheim's light divisions. The total came to 8,000 men, who, just a year before, would have hardly filled a cavalry corps of the

Russian hussars gather information on the field, 1812. Painting by A. Sifonov.

Grande Armée. In 1813, the corps had been reduced to six regiments in one light and two heavy brigades, with 18 – 20 squadrons.

On the morning of October 14th, the Allied advance forces came up to Murat's position. General Phalen had four Cossack regiments, the Grodno, Loubni, Sumski and Oliviopolski hussar regiments and the Tchougouievski Uhlans, with the Prussian No. 2 Ostpreussische Cuirassiers, No. 6 Neumark Dragoons and No. 2 Schlesische Uhlans in the rear − a total of 4,000 sabers. Seeing that the enemy cavalry was superior, Phalen sent for reinforcements. General Röder was to the left of him, on the road to Cröber, with the No. 4 Brandenburgische and

No. 1 Schlesische Cuirassiers and two batteries of Horse. To the right was Klenau, who sent his Kaiser Cuirassiers, Erzherzog Ferdinand Hussars, O'Reilly and Hohenzollern Chevau-légers and a battery of Horse.

Murat sent one division to the attack, in echelons two squadrons wide. Although the French pushed back the Russian hussars and Cossacks, they were stopped by a frontal attack by the No. 2 Cuirassiers and No. 6 Dragoons, who rolled the first echelon back onto the second. A strike by the No. 2 Uhlans on the side of the French echelons finally disrupted Murat's attack, and his horsemen were forced to retreat, covered by two light regiments from the reserve.

Murat's second attack consisted of Milhaud's division formed in a column in several echelons. The first echelon was made up of the 22nd and 25th Dragoons riding abreast, each with a front of two squadrons. The next echelons consisted of one regiment each, also with fronts two squadrons wide. They rode in the following order: 20th, 21st, 19th and finally 18th Dragoons, 3,000 men in all. L'Heritier's 5th Corps moved behind Milhaud, also with regiments in echelon formation.

Fortunately for Phalen, Röder arrived at the scene of the battle with his cuirassiers and artillery. Three Prussian cuirassier regiments riding abreast clashed with the head of the French column. Owing to the greater width of

their front, several squadrons of the No. 4 Cuirassiers attacked Milhaud's column from the side, falling upon the 22nd Dragoons. They were joined in this by the Russian hussars, so the whole enemy column first stopped, and then began to retreat. The Prussian cuirassiers chased it up to the French lines, where they succeeded in cutting down several gun crews. However, they had gotten carried away by the pursuit and gone too far, so they did not notice that Murat had encircled them with two light divisions from the reserve. They were saved from destruction by the timely intervention of the No. 6 Dragoons and the No. 2 Uhlans, but not without heavy losses on both sides.

Charge of the French cavalry of the Guard near Mormant, 1814. Painting by Woiceck Kossak.

207

Murat re-formed Milhaud's dragoons, and organized a third attack, putting into it all the cavalry he had at his disposal. Milhaud's division, advancing in regimental echelon column, was at the head, followed by L'Heritière's Corps and Surbervie's and Berkheim's divisions. Murat decided to lead the attack personally.

The French columns, pounded by artillery, then came upon the first Allied line – Oliviopolski and Sumski Hussars, No. 4 Brandenburgische Cuirassiers and No. 2 Schlesische Uhlans.

The Russian hussars' greater width of front enabled them to attack the French from the side again, this time the right. From the left, they were attacked by the fresh, newly arrived Austrian cuirassiers, hussars and chevau-légers. This was too much for the French, who retreated toward their lines in complete confusion. It was at this point that general Duka arrived with his Russian cuirassier division, but all he could do was to congratulate the victors.

The battle at Liebertwolkwitz is of interest for several reasons. It was not part of a larger battle at Leipzig, nor was it decisive in any respect. The cavalry clash took place in the space between the French lines and the oncoming Allied columns. The main battle, which was to last for two days, did not begin until two days later, which shows that Liebertwolkwitz was not part of any wider operations. There were not positions, supplies or anything else to defend behind the Allied cavalry, so the battle took place practically in the open.

Right: French trooper of the 3rd Cuirassier Regiment, 1813. Contemporary painting.

Napoléon had replaced the cavalry he had lost in Russia with inexperienced, ill-trained and unmotivated recruits. This is why two of Murat's attacks were led by troops from Spain. Also, in situations like this, the use of deeply echeloned columns is proof that the troops are not well trained, the purpose of this simple formation being the easier control of several thousand men during the attack.

On the other side, the excellent coordination between the Allies was a surprise, as they had had no opportunity to fight together before. It is even more of a surprise when we remember that

At the Prussians' insistence, operations were continued in the winter of 1814, on French soil. In a series of lesser engagements, Napoléon was progressively pushed toward Paris. In a manner reminiscent of their former glory, Milhaud and Kellermann took their revenge on Phalen at Mormant, even though they commanded only the remnants of three dragoon and one light division. In a series of charges, they first shook up, then completely broke the Russian corps, consisting of one infantry, one cavalry and one Cossack division. The French captured several of Phalen's battalions, nearly all his artillery and his supplies. But that was just a drop in the ocean. Napoléon was beaten; he abdicated his throne and accepted exile on the island of Elba.

The Bourbon Restoration was met with widespread displeasure in France. Former revolutionaries, republicans and liberals were united in disgust. News of popular sentiment reached even the island of Elba, and Napoléon decided to return. On March 1st, 1815, he landed at Antibes, with 1,200 men, among them a squadron of the Chevau-légers Lanciers Polonais de la Garde. On March 20th, he entered Paris triumphally. The 100 days of his second rule ended at Waterloo, in the battle against the Anglo-Dutch army under Wellington and the Prussian army under Blücher.

Left: French officer of the 5th Cuirassier Regiment, 1813. Contemporary painting.

there was also the problem of a lack of common language to overcome. Usually, the Prussian cuirassiers took it on themselves to lead the attack, leaving to the Allies and to their own light troops the possibility of striking at the enemy from the sides. Another significant factor was the high motivation of the Prussian units and their excellent officer cadre. In any case, this was the last large-scale charge that Murat led.

Three days later, Napoléon was defeated at Leipzig, and had to withdraw to France. Less than 60,000 men crossed the border, nearly a third of them sick.

Below: Prussian cavalry saves General Blücher, who has his horse shot from under him. Campaign in Belgium, 1815.

Waterloo

Napoléon had assembled a force of 49,000 infantry, 16,000 cavalry and 256 cannon. Facing him were Wellington with 50,000 infantry, 12,000 cavalry and 156 cannon, and Blücher with 80,000 infantry, 10,000 cavalry and 250 cannon. Only Napoléon's Guard cavalry shone with their old splendor: Grenadiers à Cheval had 1,042 troopers, Dragoons 935 troopers, Chasseurs 1,267 troopers, Lanciers 964 troopers and Gendarmes 102 troopers.

The rest of the cavalry was organized in four cavalry corps, with about 2,500 men each, and as corps cavalry in combined units, with 1 – 2,000 light horsemen.

Wellington had seven cavalry brigades, among them the elite Lord Somerset Household Brigade, with the 1st and 2nd Life Guards, Royal Horse Guards and 1st King's Dragoon Guards, 1,220 men in all, and Ponsonby's brigade, with the 1st Royal Dragoons, 6th Inniskilling Dragoons and 2nd Royal

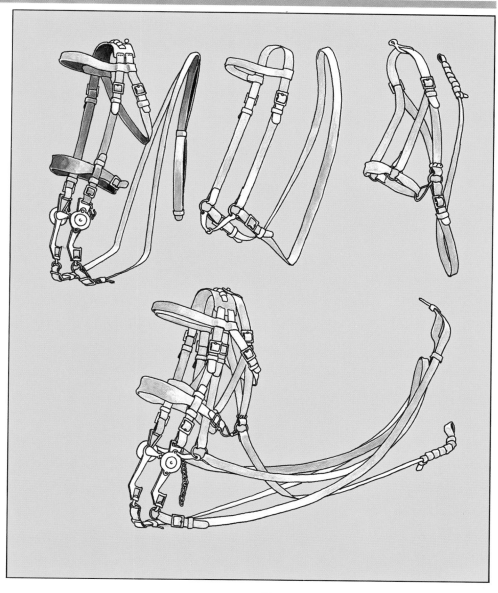

Heavy cavalry reins of the French cavalry; beginning of 19th century.

North British Dragoons, known as Royal Scots Greys, a total of 1,186 men. He also had four Allied brigades, the best known of which was general Trip's 1st Dutch Heavy Brigade, with the 1st and 3rd Dutch Carabiniers and 2nd Belgium Carabiniers, with 1,237 men.

The main features of the battle were the artillery bombardment and the attempts of the French infantry to break Wellington's line. Around 2 P.M. on June 18th, 1815, Napoléon sent General d'Erlon's three infantry divisions into the attack, supported by Travers's 7th and 12th Cuirassiers, Farine's 6th and 9th Cuirassiers and General Jaquinot's 1st Cavalry Division, with the 7th Hussars, 3rd Chasseurs and 3rd and 4th Lanciers. When the French infantry approached the enemy lines, it was met by a murderous volley. After that came a charge that has become emblematic of cavalry charges in the Napoléonic Wars. Ponsonby went to the attack with his dragoons, headed at full gallop by the 2nd Dragoons on their gray horses. They broke the first French regiments, captured three standards, and, instead of stopping, charged on toward the French artillery, in true fox hunter style. This unwise move was punished by Jaquinot. Ponsonby was killed, and his brigade lost over 600 troopers. Travers broke a German battalion that was trying to reinforce the defense of the grange of La Haie Sainte before d'Erlon's attack. Lord Somerset intervened, charging into the French cuirassiers. Travers was saved from destruction by Farine's counterattack. The Household Brigade lost over 500 men.

Around 4 P.M., Ney led the charge of 10,000 cavalrymen, but their attacks broke against the British squares, with great losses. Then the Prussians appeared on Napoléon's flank, and the battle was over. Napoléon fled to Paris. He had lost 41,000 men, the battle, the war and the throne. The Allies had about 22,000 casualties.

Left: General Ponsonby, commander of the Dragoon Brigade, 1815.

The Creation of Larger Cavalry Formations

The Russian campaign, and its finale on the field at Borodino, signaled the advent of large cavalry formations of permanent make up. Their creation was

Below: Charge of the Scottish cavalry at Waterloo, 1815. Drawing by Jean Augé.

Above: Charge of the French cuirassiers against British infantry squares at Waterloo, 1815. Contemporary painting.

Saddle of the English light cavalry, made after the Hungarian saddle; beginning of 19th century.

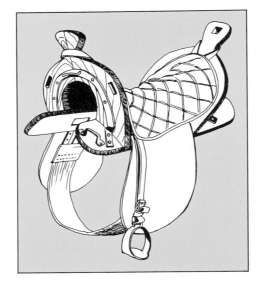

Opposite: English light dragoon of the 13th Regiment with campaign equipment, 1815.

the result of a need to control effectively great masses of horsemen, so that a powerful blow could be struck at a chosen spot in the enemy's formation at a precise moment. Heavy cavalry divisions, 15 to 20 squadrons strong, were unified in make up, and now consisted of cuirassiers and dragoons. Light cavalry divisions were of a much more heterogenous composition, owing to their various functions. At Borodino,

Latour-Maubourg's corps and Duka's division attacked three times, and regrouped in squadrons in a different position every time, rallying around their flags and cornets, just like Seydlitz had done with his cavalry more than 50 years ago at Rossbach. Repeated charges were frequent, but usually from the same starting position, and against a stationary enemy. To re-form 2 or 3,000 horsemen in a place chosen at will demanded high-quality training and an effective system of command.

Regiments in a division could be given tactical tasks, as advance or reserve units, etc., or individual targets, like the Russian cuirassiers were at Shevardino. In Europe, the Austrians were the only ones to accept this Franco-Russian model. England and Prussia adhered to their combined brigade formations, at the divisional and corps cavalry levels, as well as at the level of independent reserves.

Bavarian Cavalry Regiment, 1804

STAFF:

Owner (Inhaber)	1
Colonel	1
Lieutenant Colonel	1
Major	1
Quartermaster	1
Adjutant	1
Standard-bearers	2
Surgeons	5
Smith	1
Trumpeter	1
Provost	1

COMPANY:

Captain	1
1st Lieutenant	1
2nd Lieutenants	2
1st Sergeant	1
2nd Sergeant	1
Corporals	6
Trumpeters	2
Smith	1
Saddlemaker	1
Troopers	132

The regiment has 6 squadrons.

Chapter Five: The new Age

1815 – 1865

After the War of Independence, the American economy developed rapidly, with farming and industry predominant in the North, and a more plantation orientated economy in the South. The Constitution of 1787 marked the creation of the United States of America, with Congress as the main legislative body. At that time, the United States had approximately four million inhabitants; about 500,000 of them were black and a further 400,000 were native Indians, living in several hundred tribal communities throughout America. Economic expansion and a great influx of immigrants forced the United States to expand toward the south and west, thus displacing and destroying the Indian tribes, which put up a stiff resistance. The first steps in this direction were the purchases of Louisiana, from Napoléon, in 1803, for the sum of 15 million dollars, and Florida, from Spain, in 1819. With these acquisitions, the territory of the USA stretched from the Atlantic Ocean to the Mississippi, and from Canada to the Gulf of Mexico. Canada, to the north, belonged to Great Britain, and harbored refugees from the losing side in the War of Independence; Mexico, to the south, considered Texas, New Mexico, and all territories west of the Rocky Mountains its own.

The War of 1812

Napoléon's accession to power and related events on the other side of the Atlantic did not leave America unaffected. In 1807, Great Britain placed an embargo on American trade with European countries that Napoléon had occupied; the same year, the U.S. government responded by closing its ports to foreign shipping. British support of the Indians, who fought against the USA under the leadership of Chief Tecumseh, worsened the situation. In 1812, war broke out; for the most part, it took place at sea and along the Canadian border. Congress voted to increase the standing army to 35,000 men, and empowered the president to raise a further 30,000 volunteers and 100,000 men in the state militias. In practice, however, the regular army never numbered more than 10,000 men during the whole war, while the militia was undisciplined and unreliable. On the other hand, because of the European wars, Great Britain could never afford to have more than 6,000 regular soldiers and 2,000 militiamen in America.

In an act dating back to 1799, Congress had allowed for the mobilization of 24 infantry and three cavalry regiments in case of war. Equipment for 3,000 horsemen was bought and stored in war reserves for such a contingency. When relations with Great Britain deteriorated, one regiment was brought up to full complement and another one raised. Thus, in 1808, the U.S. Cavalry consisted ot the 1st and 2nd Regiment of U.S. Light Dragoons. Each regiment had eight companies, with 400 men at full complement. Following the precedent set during the War of Independence, the blue-uniformed dragoons were divided into smaller

U.S. cavalry officer with the regimental guidon in the American Civil War. Painting by Detsy Ross, 1870.

formations that took part in the expeditions into British territory.

In 1813, Col. Richard M. Johnson, a popular congressman, was granted permission by the Secretary of War to raise two battalions of Mounted Volunteers for four months' service. The force numbered 1,200 men in 14 companies. For several months Johnson's Volunteers patrolled and carried out reconnaissance along the border. During pauses Johnson trained his men to charge in line, and in order to accustom them and their horses to the sound of gunfire, he would dismount part of the troops and have them play the enemy by firing blanks. These exercises also served to help the men conquer their fear of charging the British infantry.

In autumn of 1813, 800 Redcoats of the British 45th Foot clashed with Johnson's Volunteers by the river Thames, about 90 miles east of Detroit. The British, accustomed to the accurate fire of enemy light infantry, took up an extended order in two lines, so as to present a smaller target. Johnson saw his opportunity in this, ordered his men to develop in line, and commanded the first battalion to charge. Five hundred riders armed with tomahawks, hunting rifles and knives could not be stopped by two volleys. They rode through the British lines at full gallop, swinging away with their tomahawks, stopped, dismounted, and opened fire. The Brisith, under fire from the back, and faced with the charge of 500 more horsemen from the front, surrendered immediately.

At the beginning of 1814, Congress disbanded one of the dragoon regiments in order to cut expenses. At the end of the year, the war ended after several inconclusive battles. The Peace of Ghent restored the status quo ante. The remaining dragoons were discharged at the end of 1815, with the explanation that they were too expensive.

American Indian Wars

As more traders and settlers moved west, the east bank of the Mississipi became a constant battleground between whites and Indians. This was why Congress adopted the Removal Act in 1830, which envisaged moving all Indian tribes to the west bank of the river. In order to protect the settlers, keep open the caravan trail to Santa Fe, and guard against an attempt by the Indians to come back, in 1832 Congress approved the creation of the U.S. Mounted Ranger Battalion, made up of volunteers organized in six companies, with 100 privates each. Each volunteer, together with his own horse and equipment, enlisted for a year, and was paid 1 dollar a day.

The Rangers faced Indian warriors in the open and wild country between the river and Great Plains. The Comanche, whose equestrian skills and knowledge of horses rivaled that of the Mongols and Tartars, were the best-known of them. After the Spanish conquerors arrived in Mexico, the Indians quickly realized the value of horses, and started providing themselves with them, either by capture in war, or by simple theft.

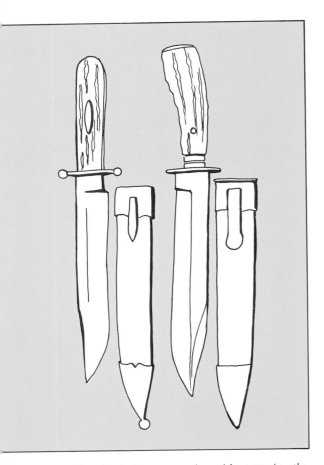

Bowie knives were in wide use in the American West.

The combination of brave warriors and horses descended from the excellent Spanish breeds resulted in hard mounted fighters. Even though the Rangers did not lag behind the Indians in fighting qualities, they lacked reliability, good organization and discipline. That was why Congress decided, in 1833, to form a regular unit, the U.S. Regiment of Dragoons, which consisted of ten companies, marked with the letters, A – J, and with a total complement of 750 men.

In Florida, which America had acquired from Spain, the government took (from 1821) a similar policy towards the Seminole Indians as towards those on the east banks of the Mississippi. In 1835, Osceola, chief of the Seminoles, led his tribe into war against the white settlers. As the militia and volunteer units could not stand up effectively to the Indians, Congress decided in 1836 to approve the creation of the 2nd U.S. Regiment of Dragoons.

The dragoons were armed with a saber, two pistols and a carbine. Fifty new Colt six-shot revolving rifles were distributed to the best shots in the regiment in 1838. Their uniform was dark blue, except those of the units stationed in the subtropical climate of Florida, which were light-colored and made of cotton. Every company had a red-and-white guidon with the regiment's mark and the letter of the company.

Below: Field uniform of the U.S. Dragoons, 1848.

The U.S.-Mexican War (1846 – 1848)

The constant skirmishes with the Great Plains Indians, the war with the Seminoles, which would last for nearly seven years, and the Texas declaration of independence from Mexican rule in 1836 complicated the situation of America's southern border. As Mexico still considered Texas a part of its territory, America's annexation of Texas in 1845 was taken as a declaration of war.

On April 24th, 1846, 1,600 Mexican horsemen crossed the border at the Rio Grande, and surprised two companies of the 2nd Dragoons. Eleven Americans were killed, and the remaining 52 captured. Taylor informed the president that war had begun, and moved toward the Mexicans. At Palo Alto, 800 Mexican lancers attempted to attack Taylor from the right flank, but they were stopped by the sudden assault of a company of Texas Rangers, armed with one or two Colt revolvers. When two companies of the 2nd Dragoons arrived, also armed with Colts, the Mexicans retreated in panic. They lost 257 men, Taylor only 55. The cavalry clash at Palo Alto demonstrated a new dimension of mounted warfare. The 120 American soldiers taking part could fire about 800 shots from their revolvers without reloading. The results of this impressive firepower were five times greater Mexican losses. From this time on, firearms supplanted swords and lances as the principal weapons in hand-to-hand combat.

Mexican General Santa Anna with his cavalry, 1848. Contemporary etching.

For the war with Mexico, Congress allowed the raising of 50,000 volunteers, the forming of the 3rd U.S. Regiment of Dragoons, the U.S. Regiment of Mounted Rifles, and seven regiments of Mounted Volunteers from Kentucky, Tennessee, Missouri, Arkansas and Texas. The structure of both regular and irregular regiments remained the same – 10 companies designated by letters. Some of the volunteer regiments, though, numbered over 1,000 men.

The Mexican army had 15 infantry regiments, four artillery brigades, 15 regiments of regular cavalry and five regiments of militia cavalry. The basic horseman of the Mexican army was armed with a lance, saber and carbine, and rode a lighter horse than the

dragoons. The Mexicans were fighting against what probably was the best cavalry of the time. Armed with rapid-fire revolvers, with officers educated at the U.S. Military Academy at West Point, privileged in the choice and quality of equipment and horses, and with ten years of experience in the war with the Indians, the U.S. Dragoons were a formidable troop of the highest quality. Also, among the immigrants from Europe there were German cuirassiers, Prussian uhlans and English dragoons and hussars, who volunteered for the U.S. Dragoons.

In February 1847, at Buena Vista, Taylor waged a defensive battle against the vastly superior forces of General Santa Anna. General Torrejon's Lancer Brigade threatened the Americans' rear, but in a near-replay of Palo Alto, 100 troopers of the 1st Dragoons attacked and broke the Mexicans. Santa Anna had to retreat. Both sides suffered heavy losses.

Meanwhile, Frémont, with his mounted frontiersmen and immigrants, and with the help of the Fleet, captured California, and Colonel Kearny took New Mexico. After landing at Vera Cruz, General Scott, with the regular Mounted Rifles, made his way to Mexico City and captured it. At the beginning of 1848, Mexico was forced into a peace settlement, and had to cede the territories of California, New Mexico, Texas, Utah and Nevada. With these gains, the USA stretched from the Atlantic to the Pacific, and south to the Rio Grande.

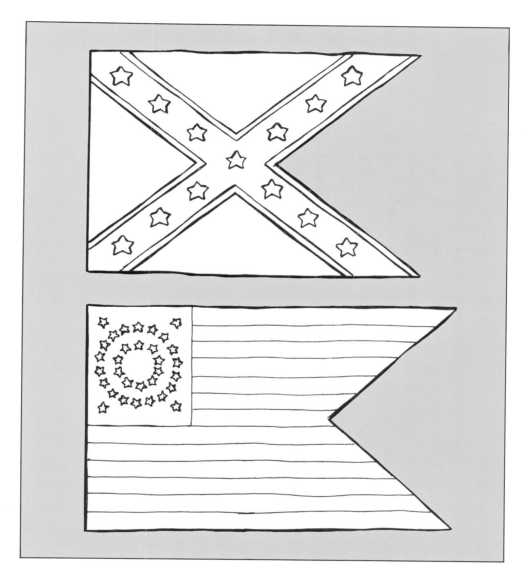

Top: Confederate Cavalry guidon, 1861.

Below: U.S. Cavalry guidon, 1863.

Right: J. E. B. Stuart (1833 – 1864), the most famous cavalry commander of the South.

U.S. Cavalryman wearing an overcoat.

Opposite: Confederate cavalryman of the 1st Virginia Regiment, known for its fight at Bull Run and very much respected by both sides, 1861.

Progress was always important to America, and Americans were quick to take up on new developments. America was the second country in the world (after Great Britain) to open a railway line, in 1830. The pace of expansion of the railroad network was so fast that at mid-century there were already 15,000 kilometers (9,000 miles) of track. Following the first public demonstration of the telegraph in 1837, the nation was soon covered with telegraph poles and wires. A breech-loading rifle built according to Von Dreys's construction was produced in 1854; it increased firing speed twice, and extended the useful range to 600 paces. The practical uses of mass production of steel opened the way for higher quality in weapons production. In 1860, Williams presented the first machine gun, and Spencer and Winchester the fast-firing rifle. All these advances would lead to changes in the way war was waged, and a different role for cavalry.

The American Civil War (1861 – 1865)

The growth of the American economy led to increased differences between the North and the South. From the mid-19th century, the abolitionist movement in the North gathered steam. Significant moments in the fight against slavery were the armed conflict between farmers and slave owners in Kansas, and John Brown's uprising. The influence of the Republican Party, founded in 1854, and opposed to slavery, increased. Abraham Lincoln, a Republican, was elected president in 1860. The 11 states of the South — South Carolina, North

Carolina, Mississippi, Florida, Alabama, Georgia, Louisiana, Texas, Virginia, Arkansas and Tennessee — whose ruling circles had decided to preserve slavery at any cost, seceded from the Union and formed the Confederate States of America. Richmond was chosen as the capital of the Confederacy, and Jefferson Davis elected president. The attempts by the North to preserve the Union without bloodshed became hopeless when Confederate forces took Fort Sumter, near Charleston, on April 14th, 1861. War between the 22 states of the North, with 23 million inhabitants, and the 11 states of the South, with 9 million inhabitants, including 3.5 million Negro slaves, become inevitable.

At the middle of the 19th century, the U.S. Army was mainly involved in combat with the Indians. Nearly four-fifths of its forces were in the border areas. At the end of 1855, the U.S. Army had 15,752 men. That same year, Congress decided to raise two more regiments, simply called the 1st and 2nd U.S. Cavalry, whose structure was the same as the Dragoons'.

The day after the fall of Fort Sumter, President Lincoln called up 75,000 volunteers for a period of three months, and immediately after that, 42,000 more for the regular army and navy, for a

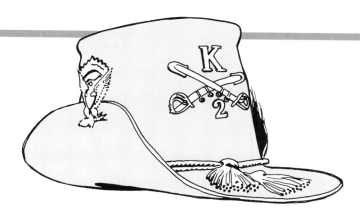

Left: Jeff Davis's hat that was worn by the U.S. Cavalry during and after the Civil War.

period of three years. As part of these measures, the 3rd Cavalry was formed, as well as two regiments of Mounted Volunteers. The general opinion was that the war would soon be over, and that no more cavalry would need to be raised and trained.

General Lee gathered two rebel armies — 20,000 men under General Beauregard at Manassas, and 11,000 men under General Johnston at Harper's Ferry. Before the beginning of operations, the Union assembled 30,000 men under General McDowell on the Potomac, near Washington, and 25,000 men under General Patterson at the mouth of the Shenandoah River. McDowell, at the head of his still unprepared army, headed for Manassas on July 16th, but was defeated at Bull Run. The defeated Yankees were pursued by the gray-uniformed 1st Virginia Cavalry of Col. James Ewell Brown Stuart (better known as J.E.B. Stuart) and other rebel cavalry units.

After the battle of Bull Run, Congress empowered Lincoln to call up 500,000 more volunteers. A similar mobilization of industrial and human resources would be repeated in the First and Second World Wars. The country would demonstrate the ability to quickly organize large and effective armies, the standards of which would be accepted by many armies with longer traditions and more experience. Lincon switched on what was later to be called the U.S. war machine.

The six existing regiments were renamed, the 1st Dragoons becoming the 1st U.S.

Cavalry, the 2nd Dragoons the 2nd U.S. Cavalry, and so on by seniority. Twenty-eight new regiments were formed, and named after the places were they were recruited, e.g., 7th New York Cavalry, 5th Pennsylvania Cavalry, etc. The number of companies in a regiment was increased to 12, and they were renamed troops, with about 100 troopers each. Theoretically, each regiment should have numbered 1,200 men, but in practice they rarely exceeded half that number. The 6th U.S. Lancers were formed in Pennsylvania, and they carried lances until 1863.

Views on the role of cavalry had not changed much after the Napoléonic

Opposite: Union cavalryman of the 6th Pennsylvania Regiment, the only horse regiment that was armed with lances, in the European tradition, 1862.

Cavalry boots, second half of 19th century.

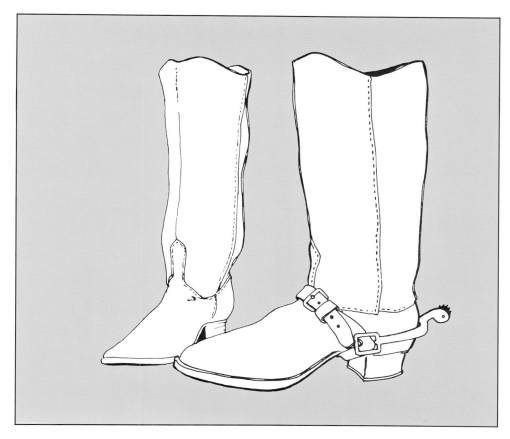

227

Union bugler.

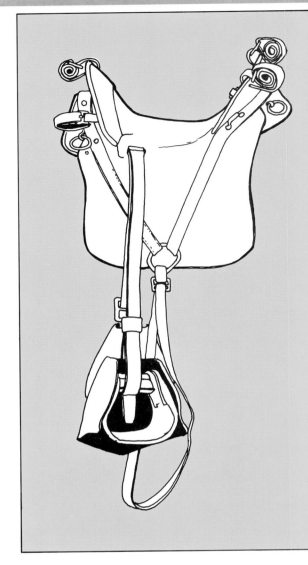

McClellan saddle made for the U.S. Cavalry after the Prussian saddle, second half of 19th century.

Wars. Military authors still held to the belief — the development of firearms notwithstanding — that cavalry was the branch of the army most useful in decisive operations, especially on large battlefields. It could play an important part in the preparation of the battle, in its conclusion, in covering a retreat, or in pursuing the enemy. The introduction of rifled guns and breech-loading rifles increased the infantry's firepower, but the cavalry's as well; horsemen therefore had to learn to fight as well on foot as on horseback. That is why nearly all the cavalry in the Civil War was of dragoon type, armed with single-shot rifles or carbines, revolvers and a heavy saber.

The Union was faced with many problems in realizing its ambitious plan of raising and equipping an army of half a million men. Over 100,000 horses with equipment had to be procured immediately. The old acquisition system did not work any more, so the first depots for buying and equipping horses were formed. With the forming of the Cavalry Bureau on the 28th July 1863 under General Stoneman the new system began to function properly. The Bureau oversaw six large depots — in Giesboro, District of Columbia, Greenville, Louisiana, St. Louis, Missouri, Nashville, Tennessee, Harrisburg, Pennsylvania and Wilmington, Delaware. Each of these could hold 5 – 10,000 horses in specially constructed stables and stockyards. These depots also served for the treatment of sick, wounded and exhausted horses. Soldiers were trained in camps that were just as well organized. The federal war machine succeeded in increasing the cavalry

forces from 5,000 to 60,000 battle-ready troopers inside of two years.

The South, chronically short of war equipment and armaments, had a numerous class of landed gentry and farmers, whose way of life was linked with horses, and who represented a source of excellent riders and high-quality horses. Regiments were organized territorially, and consisted of ten squadrons, with 60 to 80 men each. At first, every man brought his own horse, and armed himself with what he could find. At Bull Run, Stuart's Virginians had hunting rifles, shotguns, pistols, revolvers, and a few sabers of obscure origin. Regiments were named after their place of recruitment — 6th Texas Cavalry or 10th Virginia Cavalry, and so on. As the officers of both sides were schooled at West Point, the cavalry drill was similar. Cavalry maneuvered in a column of four, and changes were executed in a double line. A double line was also foreseen for attack, but this practice was abandoned in 1863 in favor of the single line. For dismounted action, one man in four was detached as a horse holder.

The events of the beginning of the war demonstrated the importance of the training and discipline of the troops. Large and quick operations could not be executed with untrained troops, which at first constituted the majority on both sides. Unprepared commanders, especially in the North, and lack of organization in the higher staffs were further obstacles in the carrying out of planned operations.

The Civil War demonstrated that frontal attacks on strong enemy positions seldom succeeded. Maneuvering became paramount in importance, and this was an opportunity for cavalry. The difficulties of supply and movement over great distances, which had frustrated Napoléon in Russia, were lessened by the use of rail transport. Railroads became vital communication links. Many complex operations depended on the proper running of the railway system for their success, so the rail network was a permanent target for the enemy. The success and effectiveness of cavalry it not apparent in the well-known battles of the Civil War but in the raids and expeditions into the opponent's rear, executed by forces ranging in size from a single troop to several thousand men, and equipped with batteries of horse.

Alfred Pleasanton, Union general and commander of the 1st Cavalry Corps, 1863.

229

Right: John Hunt Morgan, Confederate general who led one of the most successful raids against Union troops in 1862.

One of the most successful cavalry raids was undertaken by Confederate forces under J.E.B. Stuart (now a general) between June 12th and 15th, 1862, and is known as "ride around McClellan."

Of his 1,200 men, Stuart lost only one. He circled the whole Army of the Potomac, gathered important information, which would influence the outcome of future operations to the advantage of the rebels, and took 165 prisoners. On the night of August 23rd, Stuart and his riders burned down the transport trains in Catlett's Station, on

the Orange & Alexandria Railroad, capturing 300 Yankees and 220 horses, and all the personal baggage of General Pope and his staff. Two days later, he was joined by General Thomas Jonathan (Stonewall) Jackson and 1,200 men in a raid on the Orange & Alexandria Railroad, and on August 26th he destroyed a Union supply dump at Manassas Junction, demolished the bridge across the Broad Run and destroyed two trains.

General Bragg, the Confederate commander in Tennessee, sent General Forrest with 3,000 troopers and General Morgan with 3,900 men and seven cannon behind Grant's army, with the task of destroying railroads and trains. Morgan's assignment was to demolish the networks in Nashville and Louisville. Among his men he had 400 unarmed, whom he was hoping to equip with captured weapons. They started out on December 22nd 1862 and arrived in Glasgow, Kentucky on the 24th, also a 144 kilometer (90 mile) march; on the 25th, the van clashed with a smaller formation of Union infantry. On the 26th, the road was cut at Upton, and a

Left: Union cavalrymen of the 3rd Pennsylvania Cavalry, Company D, 1864.

Union patrol captured; Elizabethtown was taken on the 27th with the help of cannon, and the 650 men of its garrison made prisoners. Muldraugh's Hill was taken on the 28th, two small forts destroyed with cannon, and 700 men captured, as well as two big bridges on the track to Nashville and Louisville demolished.

The expedition clashed with the forces of Colonel Harlan on the 29th, crossed the Rolling Fork at Lebanon on the 31st, and returned on January 2nd. It had achieved the destruction of the tracks at several points, the capture of 2,000 men, and a plentiful bounty in horses and weapons, with losses of 66 dead and disappeared and 24 wounded.

After two years of effort, the North succeeded in putting a formidable cavalry arm in the field in 1863, with the creation of the Cavalry Corps of the Army of the Potomac, under the command of General George Stoneman. It consisted of three cavalry divisions — 1st, commanded by General Budford, 2nd, commanded by General Kilpatrick and 3rd, headed by Colonel Gregg — totaling 9,000 men. Divisions consisted of two or three brigades, each with three or four cavalry regiments, and two batteries of horse. General Alfred Pleasonton was soon appointed to command the Cavalry Corps. With well-armed, well-equipped, well-dressed and well-mounted Yankee riders, he was ready to tackle the hitherto invincible men of J.E.B. Stuart.

The first two years of the war brought advantage to neither side. But as the Union's strength grew, the South's position deteriorated. Fewer ships from Europe were making it through the Union blockade, the Confederacy's financial resources were running out, and Grant had come down the Mississippi and in June 1863 laid siege to Vicksburg, the key position on the Confederacy's west flank. Bragg's Army of the South was in Tennessee, facing the forces of General Rosecrans, and Lee's 89,000 men in Virginia faced Hooker's 130,000 troops. Lee, one of the greatest generals in modern history, after the victory at Chancellorsville, near Fredericksburg on May 3, 1863, had several options: stay on the defensive, and protect Richmond from behind fortified positions, send some of his forces to help Bragg in Tennessee, or, characteristically, attack, and try to decide the war with one great battle. Lee decided on attack. The site of the historic battle was Gettysburg.

On June 2nd, Lee headed from Virginia toward Pennsylvania with an army of 76,000 men, with 272 cannon. Hearing that Lee was moving north, Hooker prepared to defend Washington and Baltimore with 115,000 men and 362 cannon. Stuart, whose riders had been the eyes and ears of the Southern armies in previous campaigns, was ordered to take his 8,000 veteran horsemen and prevent the enemy from reconnoitering Lee's movements, while gathering information about their intentions at the same time. Pleasonton was given an equal assignment on the other side — find out Lee's intentions at any cost, and stop Stuart from spying on the Union army. These were tasks akin

to those Murat had given his chasseurs and other light cavalry.

In order to protect Lee's troop concentration at Culpeper County, Stuart guarded the crossings over the Rappahannock with his five brigades and artillery. Hooker, informed of the arrival of Lee's forces, ordered Pleasonton to cross the river at Brandy Station with his Cavalry Corps, and, by aggressive reconnaissance, find out the possible concentration and intentions of the rebels. Pleasonton sent Budford's division across Beverley's Crossing, to the north, with the support of an infantry brigade and three batteries of horse. The divisions commanded by Duffee (who had replaced the wounded Kilpatrick) and Gregg crossed 10 km (6 mi) to the south, also backed by an infantry brigade, and two batteries of horse.

On the morning of June 9th, the 8th New York Cavalry, in the van of Budford's division, crossed the river, and encountered a company of the 6th Virginia Cavalry guarding the crossing. The defensive action of the Virginians gave enough time to the rest of the regiment to arrive, together with the 7th Virginia Cavalry. The two regiments held Budford back for an hour, and enabled Stuart to concentrate his four brigades and artillery at St. James's Church. Stuart thus achieved a nearly 2-to-1 superiority, which he decided to take advantage of. Budford put up a stubborn resistance, particularly the 6th Pennsylvania Cavalry, half of whom died in a frontal charge on a rebel horse battery.

About noon Stuart received word from Robertson, the commander of his fifth brigade, positioned to the south, that a mass of Yankee horsemen had crossed the river at Kelly's Crossing, threatening the flank and rear of the Southern position. At first, Stuart did not take this information seriously. Only an artillery bombardment at Brandy Station, behind his back, forced him to intervene. He sent two brigades, which clashed with Gregg's division in successive charges. Gregg's 1st New Jersey Cavalry beat back the 12th Virginia Cavalry, which headed the arriving Confederate forces. Charges succeeded one another as the regiments arrived, until exhaustion prevailed on both sides. The Union troops withdrew, together with Duffee's division, which was securing the direction to Stevens-burg.

Stuart had narrowly escaped defeat, even though he had lost 450 men to the Yankees' 850.

Fifteen thousand men had taken part the Battle at Brandy Station, the largest cavalry clash of the Civil War. The battle was the introduction for a whole series of conflicts in the next month, while Lee's operation lasted: Alide, Middleburg, Upperville and Paris. At Fairfield, the 6th U.S. Cavalry shattered the 7th Virginia Cavalry, but suffered heavy losses itself from freshly arrived rebel reinforcements. Two Union brigades of horse dismounted and held back with their fire a whole division of Southern infantry for several hours, in order to enable the development of their units. On July 3rd, at the height of Lee's

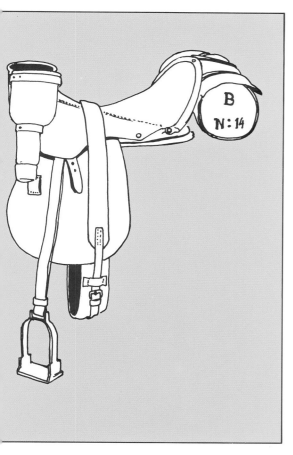

English heavy cavalry saddle; second half of 19th century.

efforts to break the Union's defensive lines at Gettysburg, Stuart started out with four brigades and three batteries of horse — about 6,000 riders, in all — to penetrate the enemy's rear, prevent the arrival of supplies, and gather information. Receiving information of Stuart's intentions, Gregg, with three brigades, blocked the road at Spangler's Springs. Two brigades attacked the rebels from the sides, and one from the front. After a pitched cavalry battle lasting for over two hours, Stuart had to withdraw.

The Union cavalry, which had prevented diversions in its rear and stopped Stuart from gathering key information that could have changed the course of the battle, was one of the main factors of Lee's failure at Gettysburg. Soon, Lee would receive news that he had lost Vicksburg on July 4th, 1863. The defeat of the South was now only a matter of time.

In May of 1864, Grant gave Gen. Philip Sheridan the opportunity to raid Richmond with 10,000 riders and accompanying artillery. On the 11th of the same month, Stuart was killed at Yellow Tavern while trying to stop Sheridan with twice weaker forces. In a raid lasting a month, the Yankees, some of them already armed with seven-shot Spencer carbines, wrought chaos and destruction in the South's rear lines, with the loss of some 600 men. The South had increasing trouble in replacing losses in men, weapons and horses. From the second half of 1864 to May of 1865, when the war ended, the blue cavalry dominated the battlefields

Charge of the Heavy Brigade at Balaclava against Russian Cossacks. Scots Greys, famous since Waterloo, headed the attack, 1854. Contemporary painting.

and was one of the key elements in
military operations of the North.

The Union fielded three million soldiers
during the Civil War the Confederate
States one million. Americans were to
remember the Civil War as the bloodiest
in their history: over 500,000 people
died. Some elements of future conflicts
were foreshadowed in this war: the use
of railroads and the telegraph,
destruction of enemy rear lines and
construction of field fortifications for
economy of forces.

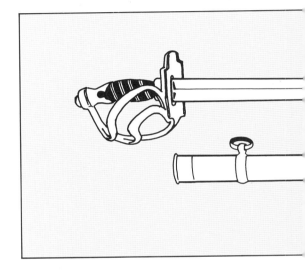

Europe:
The Crimean War
(1853 – 1854)

Another war, considered to be the first
positional war in history, with
immobilized and entrenched opposing
armies, is ironically better known for the
charge of the English Light Cavalry
Brigade than for the 349-days-long siege
of Sevastopol, in which 400,000
Russians and 300,000 Allies (British,
French, Turks and Sardinians) were
killed or died of various diseases.

The Allies decided to resolve
disagreements over control of the
Dardanelles and Bosphorus straits and
influence in the Middle East by landing
an expeditionary corps in the Crimea. In
September of 1854, 300 ships landed,
27,000 British, 23,000 French and 7,000
Turkish soldiers, who pushed back the
35,000 Russian troops there and laid
siege to Sevastopol. The defenders

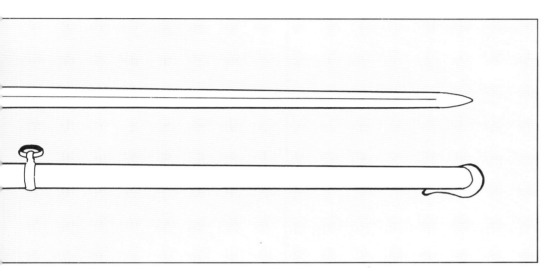

stubbornly held on, both sides brought in reinforcements, and soon each army had over 200,000 men. The Britain chose as their base the port of Balaclava, some 7 miles from Sevastopol. Through there they funneled supplies and reinforcements. Realizing the importance of this port, Russian General Liprandi attempted to take it and destroy it in a diversion with a force of 20,000 infantry, 3,400 cavalry and 78 cannon. Marshal Lord Raglan had at his disposal several battalions of Turkish infantry, 550 foot soldiers of the 93rd Highlanders, Lord Lucan's cavalry division and the French cavalry regiment, 4th Chasseurs d'Afrique, to defend Balaclava.

On October 25th, informed of the Russians' approach, Raglan placed the Highlanders on the road to Balaclava, and the cavalry division beside it. In this way, the enemy would have to pass in front of the cavalry, exposing his flank. The two brigades making up Lord Lucan's division were separated by a hill, which the Britain called Causeway Heights, and could not see each other. Soon, a column of 3,000 horsemen appeared in front of General Scarlett's Heavy Brigade.

Scarlett ordered his brigade forward. The Heavy Brigade moved in two parallel columns. The one nearer the enemy consisted of a squadron of 6th Dragoons, Inniskilling and two squadrons of the 2nd Dragoons, Scots Greys, the other one of a squadron of Inniskillings and two squadrons of the 5th Dragoon Guards, with the 1st Royal Dragoons and 4th Dragoon Guards behind them. Scarlett ordered both columns to turn left in line, thus achieving a battle formation in two lines, with 300 men in the first and 500 in the second one. Then he ordered the charge. It was so violent that the Russians were forced to flee toward their lines in just a few minutes. Scarlett did not pursue them. The mass of fleeing Russian horsemen crossed the front of Lord Cardigan's Light Brigade;

Lord Cardigan, following instructions, did nothing. The Russians retreated to the end of the valley, and took refuge behind their artillery. Meanwhile, Raglan was informed of Russias attempts to remove two British cannon from the Causeway Heights, which they had captured that morning. He sent orders to Cardigan to prevent that, and to bring the cannon back. By a twist of fate, these orders were misinterpreted, and Cardigan, instead of taking his men to Causeway Heights, started a charge against 30 Russian cannon emplaced at the other end of the valley, two kilometers away (1.2 miles).

According to mid-19th century training manuals, light artillery, when defending itself from cavalry, had to open fire at 1,600 yards. By the time the enemy was at 710 yards, each piece should have fired seven spherical case shots (hollow iron spheres containing a number of bullets, charge and fuse to cause them to burst at the correct point, usually several meters above ground). When the riders were at 380 yards, two round shots had had to be gotten off, and two more case shots in the remaining time. This whole bombardment had to take place in six minutes, which was the approximate duration of a cavalry charge. The cavalry was supposed to cover the first 780 yards at a trot, the next 430 yards at a gallop, and the final 430 yards in full charge.

Cardigan led his men in to the charge. It was like charging down an artillery testing ground. The flower of the British cavalry were destroyed there, the most expensive and best mounted regiments in the world. The 17th Lancers and 13th Light Dragoons were in the first line, the 11th Hussars in the second, and the 8th Hussars and 4th Light Dragoons in the third one, 673 men in all. Regardless of appalling losses, the Light Brigade rode right through the artillery positions and cut down the gun crews. When the Russian cavalry came up from the rear, the British retreated, covered by the Heavy Brigade and the Chasseurs d'Afrique. In the twenty minutes of the clash, the Light Brigade lost 250 men, dead and wounded, and over 500 horses. Fewer than 50 men from the first line survived.

During the reign of George IV, and later William IV, the uniforms of the light regiments achieved unsurpassed heights of adornment and quality. Hussar uniforms and saddles were especially ornate, trimmed with gold, silver and mother-of-pearl. The money spent on the equipping of the Light Brigade would have been enough to outfit an infantry division of 5,000 men, complete with weaponry. In any case, the British reorganized their cavalry immediately after the Crimean War.

The cavalry charge at Balaclava was the last one reminiscent of the period of the Napoléonic Wars. The American Civil War had heralded the onset of a new age.

Charge of the Union cavalry at Cedar Creek, 1864. Contemporary painting.

British Cavalry Regiment, 1850

STAFF:

Colonel	1
Major	1
Captain	1
Adjutants	2
Paymaster-Quartermaster	1
Sergeant	1
Veterinary Sergeant	1
Aides	2
Trumpeter	1
Tailor	1
Saddlemaker	1
Armorer	1

COMPANY:

Captain	1
Lieutenant	1
Second Lieutenant	1
Sergeant Major	1
Sergeants	4
Corporals	8
Trumpeter	1
Smith	1
Troopers	72

The regiment has four squadrons.

Chapter Six: The Apocalypse

1863 – 1939

During the Napoléonic Wars, the corps was established as the largest organizational from for cavalry units, especially in large-scale battles. Reconnaissance and pursuing of enemy units could be effected without the need to form great cavalry masses; the reason that corps were formed lies in the need to dispose of a large number of horsemen who could be the decisive factor in the defense of one's own position, or in an attack on the opponents.

In the American Civil War, cavalry was rarely seen on the field during great battles. The explanation lies in the fact that the infantry's and artillery's firepower had greatly increased, and that the erection of fortifications and obstacles on the battlefield had become a matter of course, enabling units to shelter themselves from cavalry charges.

The cavalry corps remained the highest organizational form, but with an added quality: it had become an army unto itself, capable of independently carrying out a whole series of tasks. As we have seen, 10,000 horsemen could set out an a month-long raid, during which they covered 670 miles without resupplying from their rear lines. Such a corps took care itself of the protection of its supply train and wounded men, of the prisoners it had taken, of its artillery, and even of the timber needed to build improvised bridges over swollen streams. General Morgan even used several telegraph machines during his raid, creating great confusion.

In the second half of the 18th century, infantry and artillery became the dominant branches of the military. The horse was increasingly just a means of transport, and cavalry the "mechanized" units. From the forming of the first regular regiments until the end of the American Civil War, the individual successes of cavalry units in battle were just examples of a general rule. As the end of the 19th century neared, cavalry exploits and charges became episodes to remember. In Europe, events demonstrated that cavalry regiments were no longer of much battle value, and owed their existence largely to prestige and wrong military doctrine. These factors were responsible for the large number of cavalry divisions at the beginning of the 20th cavalry; Germany and Austria-Hungary each had 11, Russia 36, France 10, Turkey 2 and Britain, Belgium and Servia one each. These units were the crown of an age that had belonged to cavalry, or, as one historian put it, the great finale that came long after the show was over.

The second half of the 19th century was marked by the colonial expansion of Great Britain, and the struggle of the 35 German states to unite in a Greater Germany, which was bitterly opposed by Austria and France.

The Austro-Prussian War (1866)

In the Austro-Prussian War of 1866, the Prussians, who defeated the Austrians in an attempt to break Austria's dominance of the German states, did not have an

British trooper and his horse protected against mortal gas during the First World War.

independent cavalry. Infantry divisions had cavalry regiments, corps a regiment or a brigade, and armies a division or a corps.

Austrian corps had one cavalry regiment, but the Austrian army also had an independent cavalry arm, with two light and three heavy divisions. The lessons of the American Civil War had not been learned. It was still considered that European cavalry should act according to old rules of engagement — attacking with cold steel. This, together with inept use of cavalry units, ensured that there were hardly any results worth mentioning.

In the Bohemian theater of operations, cavalry masses moved behind the troops. The Austrians detached only one light cavalry division for reconnaissance. In the Prussian army, this task was carried out by the divisional cavalry. Cavalry did not intervene in the critical moments in battles, as it was stationed behind the front. Only at the battle at Königgätz, when the Austrian army was forced to retreat, did the Prussians send their cavalry in pursuit. However, three Austrian cavalry divisions from the reserve routed the Prussian horsemen at Strezetice, enabling their main force to disengage. The Austrian cavalry was more successful in the Italian theater of operations. It created an impenetrable shield for its army, and did not hesitate to charge the enemy infantry. At Custoza, two brigades of horse charged the squares of two Italian infantry divisions, losing nearly half their men in the process; nevertheless, the Italian divisions were tied down all day long.

Prussian General von Bredow, commander of the 12th Cavalry Brigade, 1871.

The Franco-Prussian War (1870 – 71)

Napoléon III, fearing that Prussian attempts to place a Hohenzollern prince on the throne of Spain in 1870 would present a possible two-front threat to France, declared war on Prussia.

The Prussian cavalry was organized along lines similar to those in 1866. The French independent cavalry had three divisions. The Prussian cavalry carried out intensive reconnaissance with a wide network of patrols, but often did not go out far enough. For example, two

cavalry divisions of the 2nd Army were four days' march ahead; when they made contact with the enemy, they were only 3 miles in front of their main body, and on the day of the Battle of Vert they were deep behind their own lines, and thus unable to pursue the defeated enemy.

The French cavalry was badly commanded, moved only in divisional masses, and was saved for use in battle, as in the times of Napoléon. It carried out only close reconnaissance, and as a result, the French were nearly always surprised by the appearance of the Prussians. At points of crisis in battles, the cavalry charged the infantry and artillery, with great loss of life, but without much success. At Reichshoffen, the French cuirassier regiments were massacred in two attempts to attack the flank of the Prussian infantry. At Mars-la-Tour on August 16, 1870, the cuirassiers of the Guard lost half their men trying to charge the Prussian 10th Infantry Brigade. After that, the French infantry turned back an attack by the reinforced 6th Prussian Cavalry Division, inflicting great losses, and completely destroying it in a repeated charge at 8 P.M., even though the Prussians succeeded in breaking through the first line of defense. The only partial success was achieved in a valiant charge of General Bredow's 12th Cavalry Brigade, which also resulted in a great number of casualties. This attack of the 7th Magdeburgisches Kürassierregiment and 16th Uhlanen, called the Todesritt, stopped the French infantry, and the artillery was forced to take up a new position, which allowed the 10th

Infantry Division to pull out. On the same day, a violent clash between French and Prussian cuirassiers took place; the French riders were pratically annihilated.

The practice of forming cavalry divisions only in case of war proved unsatisfactory, as the commanders were insufficiently acquainted with the units, and these were not trained to operate in divisional formation. France introduced standing divisions in 1873. Besides training, these units were also meant for border protection. Other armies soon followed suit. Divisions consisted of two or three brigades, with two to four regiments each. Engineering, telegraph (or telephone) and medical units became part of the divisions. The British threw in a pontoon bridge, too. Gradually, all the cavalry was trained to fight like infantry, and became dragoon-type, even though the units kept their old names − cuirassiers, hussars, uhlans, etc. − all the more an anachronism as

there were no differences in equipment or armaments among them.

In 1870 − 71, cavalry suffered great losses from firearms, and achieved little. Even so, it was still believed that an adaptation of tactics of the new conditions of war and a more rational disposition of resources would again give cavalry an important role in war. French cavalry regulations of 1876 envisaged the use of cavalry divisions for frontal or flank attacks, as well as in the role of reserves. The prescribed battle order for division was in three lines, by brigades. The back lines were supposed to support the front ones, increasing the impact of the attack or executing flanking operations. French instructions of the same year foresaw a three-line formation for reconnaissance cavalry; the first one was to make contact with the enemy, breaking his protective screen; the second was to support the second one; and the third waited in reserve. In most countries, in

Charge of the 2nd Regiment of the Prussian Dragoons of the Guard at Mars-la-Tour. Painting by K. Beder, 1871.

case of war the independent cavalry was to be made up of cavalry divisions.

At the end of the 19th century, cavalry weapons began to change. High-precision carbines with a longer range were introduced. The use of breastplates by cuirassiers was discontinued in Austria-Hungary in 1881; they became purely ceremonial in Germany from 1888. The Russians had discarded them already in 1859, and the French in 1880, although they reintroduced them in 1883. Bicycle units were formed as part of cavalry divisions, as well as infantry hunter battalions in some countries, so their firepower was increased, and they could now operate independently. There were no corresponding changes in tactics. German rules of 1886 still considered the charge the principal way of attack by cavalry, and prescribed a three-line formation. Even though recent wars had clearly demonstrated that the time of big cavalry charges was over, and that cavalry had to fight mainly on foot, European armies still clung to the notion that mounted combat was the most effective.

The Colonial Wars of France

While the situation on European battle-fields gave ample reason to doubt the future of cavalry, it was still indispensable in Britain's and France's colonial wars, and in the American West, until the beginning of the 20th century.

Opposite: French Chasseurs d'Afrique one of the rare regiments that fought on three continents: North Africa, North America and Europe; around 1900.

Winchester rifle and Cheyenne bow and arrow; around 1870.

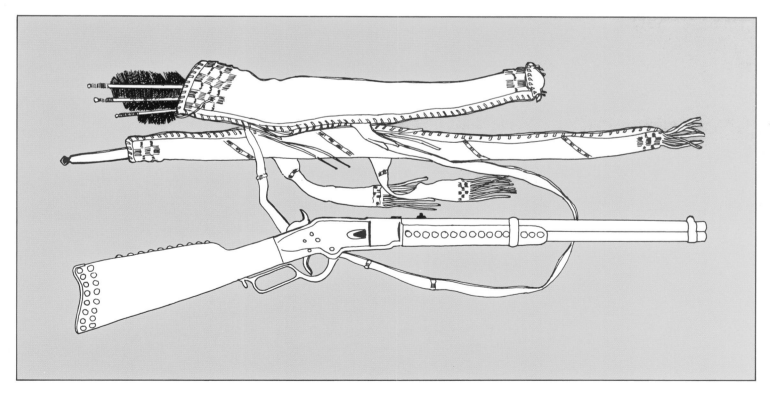

General George Armstrong Custer, commander of the 7th U.S. Cavalry Regiment, 1876.

Red Cloud, Chief of the Oglala Sioux tribe, some of whose members fought at Little Big Horn, 1876.

Following double-spread: Equipment of the 7th U.S. Cavalry Regiment.
U.S. Cavalrymen trained their horses to lie down so that they would be a smaller target for the enemy and so that they could hide behind them, 1876.

After the end of its unsuccessful attempt to expand in Europe, marked by the fall of Napoléon, the French bourgeoisie began to turn its sights upon North Africa. In 1830, General Bourmont's corps, assisted by the fleet, landed at Algiers and captured the city. When the French tried to take the rest of the country, they met with the stiff resistance of Algerian tribes led by Abd-el-Kader. In 1835, at the head of 8,000 light desert horsemen, he destroyed General Trezel's column of 2,500 men and six cannon. Abd-el-Kader's successful guerrilla operations in the vast, semi-desert expanses forced France to increase its occupation force to 100,000 men.

The desert tribesmen were excellent riders, and in hundreds of years of breeding they had produced that incomparable mount, the Arabian stallion. One of the ways in which the French attempted to stand up to this formidable enemy was by recruiting Turkish regular horsemen − the sipahis. Their regiments had been disbanded after the arrival of the French in Algiers, which had hitherto belonged to Turkey. The sipahis were organized in regiments with French officers, and outfitted with Arab costumes and various weapons. They became known by their cloaks − red on the outside and white on the inside. Fighting alongside the sipahis were the Chasseurs d'Afrique units, French cavalry mounted on light Arabian horses, and equipped for that particular theater of war. At the beginning of the 20th century, the French army list had four regiments of sipahis and six regiments of chasseurs.

With the pretext of collection of unpaid debts, France landed an expeditionary corps of 30,000 men in Mexico in 1862. This force was commanded by General Forey. In 1864, Napoléon III made Archduke Maximilian the Emperor of Mexico. The new emperor set up a dictatorship, with the backing of strong invasion forces − 25,000 French soldiers, 6,500 Austrian volunteers, 1,500 Belgians, and 8,000 men of the Légion Étrangère (Foreign Legion) − and the local bourgeoise. The French contingent included seven squadrons of the 1st, 2nd and 3rd Chasseurs d'Afrique. Used to the climate of North Africa and the conditions of guerrilla warfare, they proved a remarkably efficient troop in Mexico. Particularly noteworthy were their Arabian horses, which could trot for hours on end without the least sign of weariness. With 1,000 of the Austrians Maximilian formed a hussar regiment named the Red Hussars. The rest of the army was organized and armed following the French model. After the United States demanded that all foreign forces leave Mexico, and under pressure from the people's army of Juárez and Díaz, the French withdrew. Maximilian was soon captured and executed (1867).

Wars in the American West (1850 – 1900)

On the other side of the Mexican border stretched an expanse of deserts, mountains, steppes and forests known as the Wild West. In it lived the original inhabitants of America, mistakenly named "Indians." These peoples were mainly warriors and hunters. Unlike the Indian tribes of South and Central America, the North American Indian lived in numerous smaller tribal groups. Only a few tribes were united in tribal communities, the federation of which encompassed 50 related tribes. Armed with bows and arrows, tomahawks, spears and clubs, the Indians made their livelihood mainly by hunting and fishing. Most of the several hundred tribes were perpetually at war with each other, most often over the problems of rights to hunting grounds. Disunited, and spread out over an enormous space, they were in no position to put up an effective and organized resistance to the European colonizers. Starting in the 17th century, the European settlers pushed back and exterminated the Indians in the process of expanding their colonies. The Indians resisted as best they could.

Trying to stop the invasion of the white settlers, Tecumseh, chief of the Shawnees, worked for 16 years on the federation of all Indian tribes in the territory now covered by Ohio, Indiana and Illinois, and the creation of a united Indian state. However, after the defeat he suffered at the hands of General Harrison in 1811 at the Tippecanoe

River, he had to flee to Canada. There the British gave him the rank of general, and made him commander of the Indian army in the war with the United States.

From 1865 to 1891, U.S. troops undertook 13 expeditions against the Indian tribes, the best known of which were the Cheyenne, Sioux, Navajo, Apache, Comanche, Cherokee, Kiowa, Pawnee and Delaware.

In order to pacify the Wild West, protect the colonists from Indian attacks, and introduce law and order among them, after the end of the Civil War the U.S. government formed three more regiments, the 7th, 8th and 9th U.S. Cavalry. In 1876, after destroying several camps of the Cheyenne, Arapaho, Kiowa and Sioux Indians in previous campaigns with the 7th Cavalry, Gen. George Armstrong Custer was defeated by a combined force of several thousand Indians in the battle at Little Bighorn. He was killed and scalped, together with 210 of his men. The 7th Cavalry's total casualties on that day were 263 dead and 53 wounded.

In the 16th century, Spaniards brought the first horses to America. In time, the Indians, too, came into possession of horses. Spanish horses had a lot of Arab blood, and most of the properties bred into horses during hundreds of years in the arid climate of North Africa. Such a horse, called a pony by the Indians, gained a new quality in America — the ability to survive in even the harshest conditions. The ponies were out in the open all the time, day or night, rain or shine, and they could withstand all of

Opposite: English colonial cavalryman in uniform adapted to the hot climate of Africa and Asia, end of 19th century.

Following double-spread: Austrian uhlan, First World War. The Austrian cavalry was to good put use on the wide Russian front.

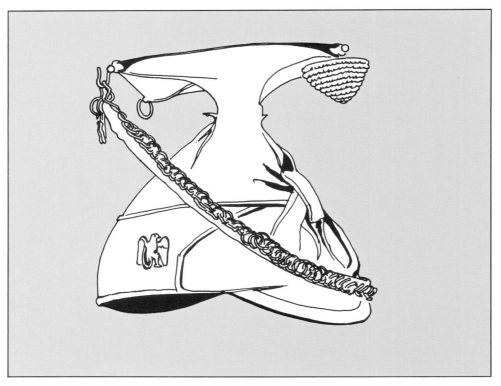

Chapka of the French Guard Lancers, 1856.

nearly until the end of the century. The British colonial empire, enlarged by the choisest possessions of its rivals, spread out over all the continents, and had over 120 million inhabitants. Only the native peoples stood in the way of its colonial undertakings.

After the death of Rnjit Singh, the ruler who had managed to unite all Sikhs in the powerful state of Punjab, the British succeeded in defeating the Sikh army in the war of 1845 – 49, subsequently annexing the last free territory in India.

The development of the Indian army under the British followed the course of British territorial expansion and policy. The first Indian troops were organized by the East India Company immediately after its arrival in India, in the middle of the 18th century. These were hired natives, whose task was to protect the trading centers. After seven years of war, three armies were formed – those of Madras, Bombay and Bengal. In 1784, the Madras army had eight regiments of Indian cavalry, one European cavalry regiment, and 25 regiments of Indian infantry; the Bengal army had five regiments of Indian cavalry, one European cavalry regiment, and 30 regiments of Indian infantry; the army of Bombay had only ten regiments of Indian infantry. Low pay, novelties which offended the religious feelings and centenary traditions of the Indians, and especially social and economic changes brought on by British rule were the causes of frequent mutinies. The largest of these, in 1857, brought about the demise of the East India Company and the introduction of dual rule.

nature's caprices. It was no coincidence that Americans chose ponies for the mail line from California to the East. Also, the Indians mastered the skill of riding bareback, which required considerable dexterity. Only a well organized and equipped cavalry, employing the services of scouts from friendly tribes, could effectively oppose the Indians and their hit-and-run tactics.

The British in India and Africa

On the other side of the Atlantic, Great Britain had emerged from the Napoléonic Wars as the leading world power. It would keep its naval, trade, financial and industrial monopoly

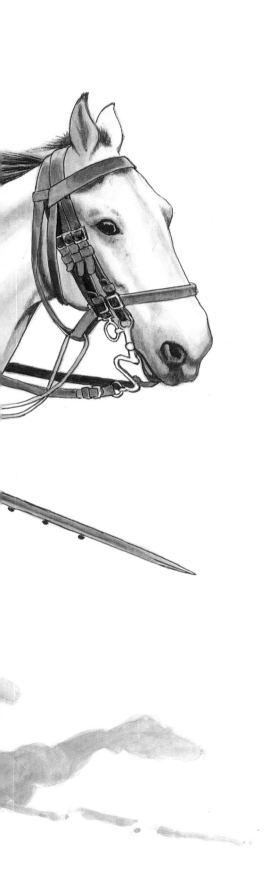

The 20th Century

The advent of the machine gun and fast-firing artillery at the end of the 19th century restricted the usefulness of cavalry even further. In the Boer War (1899 – 1902), British brigades of horse had to fight on foot. The Boers, riding excellent horses, mounted a very successful guerrilla campaign. In the Russo-Japanese War of 1904 – 05, increased firepower completely prevented the use of cavalry. The numerous Russian mounted troops had little success in reconnaissance, too, bringing back only scanty reports of the enemy's position and his intentions. Due to bad officering, General Miscenko's raids met with a similar fate, his cavalry withdrawing as soon as it met with any serious resistance. The Japanese cavalry, though reinforced with machine guns and artillery, was small in number, and did not dare stray far from its troops, carrying out close-range reconnoitering.

During World War I, cavalry corps of temporary and unequal composition were formed from divisions in France, Germany, Austria-Hungary and Russia. Divisions had artillery, ranging in force from one battery to a regiment, and some machine guns, distributed among their component brigades. The mounted charge was still considered to be the basic type of cavalry action, with only the German cavalry paying more attention to dismounted combat. At the beginning of the war, cavalry was used to protect troop concentrations, and later for reconnaissance and covering the front. On the Western Front it was

French dragoons securing railroad pass on the Western front; First World War.

Provinces under the direct administration of the Crown were known as British India, while the 560 provinces known as the Indian States were ruled by vassal princes.

In 1861, the Anglo-Indian army was reorganized. A fourth army was formed in Punjab. Nearly half of all Indian cavalry was in the Bengal Lancer regiments, numbered 1 through 20. The 1st Bengal Lancers, or Skinner's Horse, and 2nd Bengal Lancers, or Gardner's Horse, were named after cavalry commanders in the Indian wars of the beginning of the 19th century. Indian cavalry regiments were organized according to the British model. The Sikhs, Pathans, Punjabis, Dogras, Rajputs and other peoples serving in them gained a reputation as good soldiers. The Indian Lancers took part in many of the British colonial wars — in Abyssinia, Afghanistan, Egypt, Sudan and even in World War I, in France!

placed in cordon formation. German cavalry successfully masked and covered the movement of troops through Belgium. It had less success in reconnaissance, because it did not move far enough from its infantry. In the first stages of the war it executed its only charge, against the excellent Belgian cavalry, and suffered very heavy losses. From then on, it fought mainly on foot.

The French cavalry repeatedly tried to drive away the German cavalry by a full-scale engagement, and thus create favorable conditions for reconnoitering. This never came about, as organized fire easily kept cavalry away. Only occasionally would small units execute mounted charges. In attempts to penetrate the German cavalry screen, the French cavalry was sent to various sections of the front, but had hardly anything to show for its pains. In the battle on the Marne, on September 12th, 1914, the 1st and 2nd German Cavalry Corps defended the breach between their 1st and 2nd Armies, but were not able to stop the British Expeditionary Force and the left wing of the French 5th Army. The French cavalry corps of General Conneau and the British cavalry division maintained communication between the French 5th Army and the British, and General l'Espée's corps did the same for the French 9th and 4th Armies, without taking part in active combat. Only when the battle was over did French cavalry succeed in penetrating the Germans' rear lines, but was easily pinned down by infantry fire.

Wishing to strengthen their cavalry on the Eastern Front, the Germans sent the

Below: German uhlans against wire obstacles; First World War.

Below: Chapka of the Prussian Uhlans of the Guard; First World War.

8th Cavalry Corps as a reinforcement to the 9th Army after the battle on the Marne. During Western Front operations known as "the race to the sea", the French cavalry corps of Generals Mittry and Conneau protected the landing of British troops, and covered French forces when they were going into action. The Germans used their mounted troops to extend their wing positions. In this case, they were mounted only in name, as they fought on foot, preparing the terrain in the same way as infantry, thus increasing their staying power.

The greater expanse and smaller concentration of troops on the Eastern Front seemed to create a more favorable environment for cavalry operations. Even so, results were meager. The numerous Russian cavalry, consisting of 12 Guard, 20 dragoon, 20 uhlan, 18 hussar and 11 cossack regiments, was very inactive, and did not succeed in gathering data about the enemy. The German cavalry, consisting of only one division, was much more effective, but could not penetrate the Russian cavalry screen. On the front between Russia and Austria reconnaissance was much more intensive, but no deep sorties were carried out because of high firepower.

In the first days of the war, some cavalry charges were executed. After crossing the border at the river Zbruch the 5th Honved Cavalry Division, supported by its artillery, pushed back four Russian infantry companies from their position, but at en enormous cost in lives. While advancing toward the river Stir, a regiment of the 2nd Cossack Combined

Division charged and cut down the crew of an Austrian battery, and the Don brigade broke up two Hungarian squadrons on protective assignment.

The only large cavalry clash of World War I took place at Jaroslaw, on August 21st, 1914. The 10th Russian Cavalry Division clashed at full gallop with the 4th Austro-Hungarian Division; both units were formed up in two lines. The Russians used lances and sabers, the Austrians only sabers. After heavy fighting, the Austro-Hungarian division was defeated, and its artillery captured.

The Serbian independent cavalry in this war consisted of one cavalry division, which protected the troop concentration in the direction of the Danube. In the

Cer battle, it secured the right wing and rear lines of the Second Army, and also took action against the wing and rear lines of the enemy, pursuing him afterwards, and gaining a rich bounty of war. In the battle of Kolubara, it first protected the retreat of its infantry, with great losses; when the Serbian army took the offensive, it pursued the enemy until Belgrade.

When the fronts were stabilized, there was no longer much of a role for cavalry. In the period of trench warfare, 1915 – 1918, with battlefields covered with wire and other obstacles and strafed with machine-gun and artillery crossfire, significant changes took place. France re-formed four of its cavalry divisions as infantry. Due to

Charge of the Austrian cavalry against the Russians, 1916. Painting by Woiceck Kossak.

lack of horses, the German cavalry also shrank. During the offensive in Galicia in 1917, Germany had only one brigade. In Austria-Hungary, the size of the regiments was decreased to 440 men in 1916, then they were re-formed into one mounted and one infantry squadron, and finally, in 1917, all cavalry was turned into infantry. Russia turned part of its cavalry into infantry, and reinforced the remaining units with machine guns. In 1915, France added a company of machine guns to each cavalry regiment, while cavalry corps were given two companies of armored cars and an infantry regiment.

The British attempt to pierce the German lines with a five-division cavalry corps at Cambrai in 1917 did not succeed, the Germans having closed the breach in time.

On the Eastern Front cavalry was more active. In the counteroffensive in the 9th Army, in summer of 1915, two cavalry corps and two cavalry divisions with about 160 squadrons, pursued Austro-Hungarian units, attacking them from the flanks, and cleared the space between the Dniester and the Prut in a matter of days. While trying to outflank the Russian army at Vilnus, at the end of 1915, the Germans used General Garnier's corps, consisting of five divisions, to cut the railway line to Minsk. As late as 1916, the Russian cavalry did not hesitate to occasionally charge opposing infantry and artillery, even at the cost of terrible losses. On July 11th, at Sniatyn, the Austro-Hungarian infantry repulsed an attack by Russian cavalry. At Dubowyja

Following double-spread: Russian Cossack officers. The officer on foot belongs to the Christian Cossack Army and the officer on horseback to the Islamic Cossack army; First World War.

German cavalryman wearing a gas mask at the Western Front; First World War.

Korczmy, two Russian divisions — 1st Combined and Zaamur — attacked the 48th Austro-Hungarian Infantry Division, which had entered the breach created by the piercing of the front of the 45th Russian Corps. At Kościuchńowka Russian cavalry passed through a breach in the Austrian positions and advanced for 40 kilometers (24 miles), attacking individual batteries and infantry units.

During the third Battle of Flanders, in 1918, the 2nd French Cavalry Corps covered 180 kilometers (108 miles) in 60 hours in order to reinforce the front in the area of Kemmel. At Amiens in 1918, a British cavalry corps made up of three divisions was sent behind German lines when the tanks had reached the end of their range. Divided into squadrons, the corps attacked smaller German infantry units and machine-gun emplacements, using both saber and revolver. The squadrons often passed through the

Red Army Cavalry, 1918.

Opposite: Serbian cavalry officer from the beginning of the First World War. Serbia had only one cavalry division, whose soldiers lead two successful raids against Austro-Hungarian troops in 1914.

spaces between German positions, and attacked the infantry from the rear, causing panic. When German reserves arrived, the corps was withdrawn because of high losses.

During the final operations in World War I, cavalry was successfully used in strategic pursuit. In September of 1918, in Syria, a British cavalry corps with three divisions quickly and energitically pursued the Turkish 7th and 8th Armies toward Damascus. Going behind enemy rear lines for a month, the unit ranged as far as 800 kilometers (480 miles) from the front, cutting communications and thus foiling Turkish plans for retreat. Over 48,000 enemy soldiers were captured along with large quantities of war materials. During the breaching of the front at Thessaly, a French

brigade, consisting of two regiments of sipahis and Chasseurs d'Afrique, and the 2nd Serbian Brigade of Horse chased Bulgarian and German troops for 45 days, covering 600 kilometers (360 miles).

During the civil war in Russia (1918 – 20), use was again made of large cavalry masses. This was due to three factors: vast theaters of operations, large expanses of unoccupied land, and decreased firepower, a direct result of lack of munitions. In 1919, the Red Army formed a cavalry army under the command of General Budenny. It consisted of four divisions and one brigade, two armored trains, a company of armored cars and several airplanes. Each cavalry division had 3,000 men, 12 guns, 72 machine guns and 400 wagons.

This army defeated the cavalry corps of General Mamontov and cavalry formations in the Kuban and north Causasus. In 1920, the Red Army had 17 cavalry divisions and 40 divisional regiments.

The Russo-Polish War of 1920 saw only limited cavalry clashes. Large Russian cavalry units moved in a unique formation: three regiments would form a triangle, sheltering a regiment in battle formation ready to intervene on any of the three sides. The whole formation was surrounded by wagons with machine guns. Russia used nine, and Poland two divisions. These two Polish divisions executed a raid on Kasatin, taking 8,500 prisoners, capturing 28 cannons and 180 machine guns and destroying 120 railway engines, 3,000 boxcars and two armored trains.

In the Greco-Turkish War of 1919 – 22, a Turkish cavalry corps penetrated the Greek rear lines, capturing 35,000 soldiers, 10 airplanes, several hundred cannons, 75,000 rifles and 200 trucks.

As a result of ever-increasing firepower and the rapid development of aviation and mechanized and armored units, cavalry units were gradually disbanded from the 1930s on. Only the USSR still maintained significant mounted forces.

At the beginning of World War II, west of Grudziądz, with heavy losses and no results, Polish lancers charged against German tanks, the cavalry of the new age.

Seventh U.S. Cavalry, 1866

STAFF:

Colonel	1
Lieutenant Colonel	1
Majors	3
Quartermasters	2
Commissaries	2
Veterinary Surgeon	1
Surgeons	2
Saddlemaker	1
Trumpeter	1

COMPANY:

Captain	1
1st Lieutenant	1
2nd Lieutenant	1
1st Sergeant	1
2nd Sergeants	5
Quartermaster	1
Corporals	8
Trumpeters	2
Farriers	2
Smiths	2
Troopers	78

The regiment has 12 companies.

The Cavalry Horses

Light horse of the Arabian breed

In military terminology, the term light cavalry refers to the tactical role of such units, which was characterized by speed and maneuverability. This required horses that could take their riders both far and fast. Such horses, usually of a lively disposition, were called light horses, as they were about 60 inches tall and weighed between 880 and 1,100 pounds. As horses can carry 25 to 30% to their own weight, light horses could carry a rider, saddle and equipment up to a total weight of 220 to 265 pounds. This was approximately the weight of a not-too-tall hussar with his equipment and saddle. Light horses have a more delicate build, thin legs and small hoofs, and their food requirements are modest.

Heavy horse of Holstein breed

Unlike the hussars, chasseurs and other light horsemen, the cuirassiers, who tended to be burly and could weigh over 440 pounds in their armor, needed stronger and therefore larger horses. These mounts could be 65 to 69 inches in height and weigh 1,300 to 1,550 pounds. In heavy cavalry charges, it was essential to preserve the compactness of the battle order and keep control of the horses. Because this could be accomplished only at lower speeds, speed was of less importance than with light cavalry. Heavy horses are of a more docile temperament, a stronger build and a greater need of good and plentiful nourishment. In the illustration we see a heavy horse of the German Holstein breed.

Baroque horse of Lipizzaner breed

Light cavalry had fast horses, heavy cavalry strong ones. And the elite and guard regiments of horse, which took part in court ceremonies and were a matter of prestige among the monarchs of baroque Europe at the end of the 17th and first half of the 18th century, had beautiful horses of noble bearing with a high and elegant walk. Such horses, which had a lot of Arabian and Spanish blood, were as a rule very expensive and needed a lot of care and attention. In time, as military campaigns became longer and wars more expensive, these horses became a needless luxury. Towards the end of the 18th century, breeding and selction resulted in new and better military breeds, which soon displaced baroque horses from the front ranks. In the illustration we see a horse of the Lipizzaner breed, 67 inches tall, and weighing about 1,200 pounds.

Horses from the Asian steppes were 53 to 57 inches tall and weighed about 770 to 880 pounds. Their size and their drab gray or dark brown color indicated the harsh conditions of life that, judging by their appearance, had made them strong and hardy animals, resistant to all of nature's whims. The most important characteristic of these horses, which could not compare with western European mounts in strength or speed, was their ability to cover great distances while staying in good health on minimal feedings of grass or hay. In the illustration we see a Polish horse of the Konik breed.

Eastern horse of Polish Konik breed

Index

Bibliography

H. C. B. Rogers. *Napoléon's Army*. London, 1974.

B. M. Holmquist and B. Gripstad. *Swedish Weaponry Since 1630*. Arlöv, 1982.

The Company of Military Historians: Military Uniforms in America. Volume III. Novato, California, 1982.

P. Newark. *Sabre and Lance. Illustrated History of Cavalry*. New York, 1987.

T. F. Rodenbough. *The Photographic History of the Civil War*. Vol. 2. USA, 1987.

E. L. Reedstrom. *Bugles, Banners and War Bonnets*. New York, 1986.

The Armoury of the Moscow Kremlin: Russian Arms and Armour. Leningrad, 1982.

Z. Zygulsku Jan. *Stara Bron w Polskich Zbiorach*. Warsaw, 1984.

G. J. W. Urwin. *The United States Cavalry*. Pool, 1986.

J. Mollo: *Military Fashion*. London, 1972.

P. MacGregor Noris and N. Lugli. *Horses of the World*. London, 1973.

H. Lachouque. *Waterloo*. Rome, 1975.

P. Young. The Fighting Man. London, 1986.

W. Y. Carman. *Uniforms of the British Army: the Cavalry Regiments*. 1982.

J. B. R. Nicholson. *The British Army of the Crimea*. London, 1974.

J. Hook. *The American Plains Indians*. London, 1985.

R. Wilkinson-Latham. *The Sudan Campaigns 1881 – 1898*. London, 1976.

C. Taylor. *Warriors of the Plains*. London – New York – Sydney – Toronto, 1975.

M. Glover. *Wellington's Peninsular Victories*. London, 1963.

V. Melegari. *The World's Great Regiments*. London, 1969.

R. Müller. *Die Armee Augusts des Starken*. Berlin, 1984.

D. Howarth. *Waterloo*. New York, 1968.

D. Chandler. *The Art of Warfare on Land*. London, 1974.

P. Haythorntwaite: *The Russian Army of the Napoleonic Wars (2) Cavalry 1799 – 1814*. London, 1987.

E. Bukhari. *Napoléon's Guard Cavalry*. London, 1978.

P. Hofschröer. *Prussian Cavalry of the Napoleonic Wars (1) and (2)*. London, 1986.

P. Haythorntwaite. *The Boer War*. Dorset, 1987.

A. Seaton. *The Russian Army of the Napoleonic Wars*. London, 1973.

E. Bukhari. *Napoléon's Cuirassiers and Carabiniers*. London, 1977.

R. D. Pengel and G. R. Hurt. *Austrian Dragoons and Cuirassiers*. Birmingham, 1982. *Austro-Hungarian Hussars 1740 – 1762*. Birmingham, 1983. *French Cavalry and Dragoons 1740 – 1762*. Birmingham, 1981.

R. D. Pengel. *Prussian Hussar Regiments*. Birmingham, 1983.

J. Lawford. *The Cavalry*. New York, 1976.

A. Seaton. *The Austro-Hungarian Army of the Napoléonic Wars*. London, 1973.

Knötel. *Uniformkunde picture album, 1893*.

Military Archive, Vienna.

C. Gazales. *Mémoires de Bennigsen*. 1911.

"Misli." *Borodino 1812*. Moscow, 1987.

Periodicals: *Gazette des Uniformes,* Paris. *Gazette des Armes,* Paris. *Tradition,* London. *Arméemuseum,* Stockholm. *Armi Antiche,* Turin.

Picture Credits